ROCKIN' IN TIME
A Social History
of Rock and Roll

DAVID P. SZATMARY

PRENTICE-HALL, INC., Englewood Cliffs, New Jersey 07632

Library of Congress Cataloging-in-Publication Data

Szatmary, David P.
    Rockin' in time.

    "Selective discography": p. 226
    Bibliography: p. 215
    Includes index.
    1. Rock music—United States—History and criticism.
I. Title.
ML3534.S94   1987   784.5′4′00973   86–9490
ISBN 0-13-782285-5

★★
To My Father and My Mother
★★

Editorial/production supervision and
    interior design: **Patricia V. Amoroso**
Cover design: **Photo Plus Art**
Manufacturing buyer: **Ray Keating**

©1987 by Prentice-Hall, Inc.
A Division of Simon & Schuster
Englewood Cliffs, New Jersey 07632

Printed in the United States of America

10 □ 9 □ 8 □ 7 □ 6 □ 5 □ 4 □ 3 □ 2 □ 1

ISBN 0-13-782285-5   01

PRENTICE-HALL INTERNATIONAL (UK) LIMITED, *London*
PRENTICE-HALL OF AUSTRALIA PTY. LIMITED, *Sydney*
PRENTICE-HALL CANADA INC., *Toronto*
PRENTICE-HALL HISPANOAMERICANA S.A., *Mexico City*
PRENTICE-HALL OF INDIA PRIVATE LIMITED, *New Delhi*
PRENTICE-HALL OF JAPAN, INC., *Tokyo*
PRENTICE-HALL OF SOUTHEAST ASIA PTE. LTD., *Singapore*
EDITORA PRENTICE-HALL DO BRASIL, LTDA., *Rio de Janeiro*

Contents

Preface

This book intends to be a social history of rock and roll. It will guide the reader through American history from roughly 1950–1986, using rock music as a prism through which the many-faceted American experience hopefully will become more apparent.

This book offers a number of main themes. One is the connection between rock and roll and black American culture. Black musicians, singing and playing the blues, laid the foundation for the music that became known as rock and roll. At the beginning of the civil rights movement in the mid-1950s, white teens began to dance to black rock 'n' rollers who belted out an urbanized, electric, crazed version of the blues. Throughout its almost forty-year existence, rock continued to reflect and draw inspiration from black men and women striving for their civil rights: It is especially evident in the Dylan era and the "soul" explosion of 1967.

Besides emphasizing the influence that black Americans had on rock and roll, *Rockin' In Time* explores the impact of technological advances upon rock. Inexpensive transistorized radios broadcast the sound of rock music across the country. From the *Ed Sullivan Show* to *MTV*, television similarly brought rock to the teenaged masses of baby-boomers and created a larger market for the music. The advent of the 33 rpm long-play record and the less costly 45 rpm allowed teens to buy their favorite hit, which they heard on radio and television; the compact disc made that record virtually indestructible. These technological breakthroughs helped to transform rock from the passion of a few fanatics in Chicago to the popular music of four generations.

The economic climate also affected rock and roll. Interest in rock music during the 1950s mushroomed amid a favorable economy. Good economic times later permitted the excesses of hippiedom and the platinum derby of the early 1970s. On the flip side, a poor economy helped spawn the social protest of Bob Dylan and the punk explosion of the late 1970s. Although not deterministically controlled by the economy, rock and roll has reflected the ebb and flow of American and British commerce.

Likewise, American business influenced the course of rock. From the selling of Elvis Presley to the merchandising of the Beatles to the marketing of Duran Duran on MTV, rock and roll has operated as a business enterprise. Over the years it has become a big business that profoundly affects the music and the performers.

This book also deals with the relationship between politics and rock music. At times rock and rollers have channelled their anger, frustration, and rebellion into political activism. The pointed lyrics of Dylan, the more amorphous pontificating of the Haight-Ashbury hippies, and the vehement left-wing rhetoric of punk exemplify rock and roll radicalism. At other times, performers have latched onto more right-wing political doctrines: Rockers in the seventies such as David Bowie and Rush provide good examples. As with the issues of race, technology, and business, the political climate prevalent in the general society from 1950 to the present have been reflected in and influenced by rock and roll.

This book is more interested in understanding rock than in presenting an exhaustive compilation: No attempt has been made to review, photograph, document, or discographize the thousands of well-known and obscure bands that have existed throughout the years. Some of my favorites—the Bonzo Dog Band, Root Boy Slim, Wildman Fischer, and Fred Blassie—have been omitted from these pages because they are sidelights to the main show.

Neither do I claim to be totally impartial. Any writer who disavows bias either deludes his readers or bleaches the passion from his work. I grew up in Milwaukee, Wisconsin, and attended my first rock concert in 1966, a Jimi Hendrix Experience. I subsequently have danced to the likes of Patti Smith, B.B. King, Roy Buchanan, George Thorogood, Richard Hell, Muddy Waters, and the Stray Cats, among others. At times, as Lou Reed sang about so many other children of the fifties and sixties, "my life was saved by rock and roll." Later, as the general manager of a chain of record stores in Seattle, I learned about rock as a business enterprise.

These experiences convinced me that rock and roll, at its best, can be found in the anguished cries of the blues, adopted and ingeniously modified by rebellious American and British youths. Over the thirty years that it has been a dominant part of our culture, rock music has reflected the frustrations, hopes, and concerns of the discontented. The different forms it has assumed, some of them intensely defiant and others tame, have been influenced by and have influenced the changing social climates in the United States and Great Britain.

These pages, then, are a somewhat biased exploration of the American past through rock music. More than anything else, I hope to uncover American history by at least partially capturing the desire, anger, joy, fear, and ambition that defines rock and roll.

Acknowledgments

I have many people to thank for this volume. Jerry Kwiatkowski introduced me to the sub-world of rock and prodded me to listen to everyone from Captain Beefheart to Eric Clapton. Mike Miller helped me explore the summer concert scene in Milwaukee. Ramona Wright, Neil Fligstein, Bruce Mamel, Eileen Mortenson, Gail Fligstein, and Tom Speer did the same for me in Tucson and Seattle. On the East Coast, Dave Sharp fearlessly accompanied me on journeys to the lands of Sid Vicious and Root Boy Slim.

I would like to acknowledge everyone at Second Time Around Records, Roxy Music, and Yesterday and Today Records in Seattle — owners Wes and Barbara Geesman, Gregg Vershay, Dan Johnson, Mike Schwartz, Michael Wellman, Howie Whalen, Jim Rifleman, and Dave Wolters — for adding to my knowledge of rock music and the rock business. At the University of Arizona in Tucson, Donald Weinstein graciously allowed me to teach a class on the social history of rock and roll, the beginnings of this book; Rick Venneri did the same at the University of Washington Extension. Students in those classes added to my knowledge of rock music. Thanks to Dudley Johnson at the University of Washington for putting me in contact with Prentice-Hall.

I owe a special debt to Bob "Wildman" Campbell, who spent many hours with me analyzing the lyrics of Larry Fischer, the nuances of Tibetan Buddhist chants, Bonzo Dog Band album covers, and the hidden meaning behind the grunts of Furious Pig. Besides reading and commenting on this manuscript, he expanded my musical horizons with a series of demented tapes, which twisted this book into shape. Such a debt can never be repaid.

I wish to thank my parents, Peter and Eunice, for instilling in me a love of music and the written word. Thanks go to my mother for commenting on the manuscript and giving suggestions for a title. And most of all I would like to thank my wife, Mary, for her love and companionship, her musical prowess, her editorial comments, and her indulgence of my vinyl addiction.

CREDITS

I wish to thank the following for use of photos and help in finding them: Alligator Records, especially Bruce Iglauer; Peter Asher Management; Roberta Bayley; Bill Graham Presents (BGP) Archives; Capitol Records; Chrysalis Records; Dick Clark Television Productions; Columbia Records; The Daily of the University of Washington with special thanks to Barbara Krohn; Delmark Records and Bob Koester; Alan Douglas and the staff at Are You Experienced?; Elektra Records; the Estate of Elvis Presley, especially Marc Magaliff; Don Everly; Cam Garrett; Richard Hell; Hilly Kristal; the Library of Congress; Living Blues Archival Collection, University of Mississippi Blues Archive; MCA Records; RCA Records, especially Mary Jo Myselow and Marguarite Renz; Rounder Records with special thanks to William Nowlin; the Seattle Times; Sire Records; Specialty Records; Chris Stamp; Arnold Stiefel Management; Sun Records; UPI/Bettmann Newsphotos; Vision Management, especially Shelly Heber; and Warner Brothers Records.

Every effort has been made to locate, identify, and properly credit photographers, songwriters, and song publishers. Any inadvertent omissions or errors will be corrected in future editions.

The Blues, Rock 'n' Roll, and Racism

A smoke-filled club. The Burning Spear in the black ghetto of Chicago, late on a Saturday night in 1953. On a small, dimly lit stage stood an intense, young black man dressed in a bright-yellow suit, white shirt, and a black, six-inch-long bow tie. He gripped an over-sized electric guitar — the revolutionary new instrument born in the postwar, urban environment — caressing, pulling, pushing, and bending the strings until they produced a sorrowful but razor-sharp cry, which cut through his listeners, who hollered and squealed back a carnal, an almost dev- ilish response. With half-closed eyes, the guitarist peered through the smoke at the twenty tables jammed with patrons and littered with half-emptied beer bottles, and whined the lyrics of "Three O'Clock Blues." The rest of his face contorted in a painful expression that told of cotton fields in Mississippi, poverty in Memphis, and the burden of being black in Middle America during the 1950s. The singer's name was B. B. "Blues Boy" King, and he was playing a new, electrified music called rhythm and blues.

   The rhythm and blues of B. B. King and other urban bluesmen like him laid the foundation for Elvis, the Beatles, the Rolling Stones, Led

Zeppelin, the Sex Pistols, and most other rock and roll groups. The musical talent and spirit of black men and women, a subtle blend of African and European traditions and the postwar urban experience, laid the foundation for what eventually became known as rock and roll. But despite their innovating roles, blacks seldom received the recognition or the money that they deserved. Established crooners, disc jockeys, and record company executives, watching their share of the market shrink with the advent of the R & B-inspired rock and roll, torpedoed black rockers by offering toned-down, white copies of black originals, which left most of the black trailblazers penniless and, sometimes, broken.

THE BIRTH OF THE BLUES

The blues, sailing to the United States on the first African slave ships, provided the roots of rock and roll. Although having to bear the inhumanity of the journey from their homes in West Africa and forced into a brutally servile way of life, blacks retained through their music some continuity with their cultural heritage. They pushed and pulled their notes, bending them between the lines of the more rigid European musical scale to create a bluesy sound. To the plantation owners and the overseers, the music seemed to be "rising and falling" and sounded flat to their ears.

It also involved a calculated repetition. In this call-and-response, one worker would call or play a lead part and his fellow slaves would follow suit with the same phrase or an embellishment of it until another took the lead. As one observer wrote in 1845, "our black oarsmen made the woods echo to their song. One of them, taking the lead, first improvised a verse, paying compliments to his master's family, and to a celebrated black beauty of the neighborhood, who was compared to the 'red bird.' The other five then joined in the chorus, always repeating the same words." Some slaves, especially those from the Bantu tribe, whooped or jumped octaves during the call-and-response. This whooping became an important aspect of field hollers.

But probably most important, the slaves, accustomed to dancing and singing to the beat of drums, concentrated on rhythm rather than harmony. In a single song, they clapped, danced, and slapped their bodies to several different rhythms (drums were outlawed by plantation owners, who feared that the instrument would be used to coordinate slave insurrections). One ex-slave, writing in 1853, called the polyrhythmic practice "patting juba." It was performed by "striking the right shoulder with one hand, the left with the other — all the while keeping time with the feeting and singing." In contrast, noted President John Adams, whites "droned out [Protestant hymns]. . . like the braying of asses in one steady beat."

These African musical traits, nurtured by American slaves, carried over into American black religion. One writer in the *Nation* commented about a "praise-meeting" held in 1867: "At regular intervals one

Photo by Dorothea Lange; reproduction from
the collections of the Library of Congress

On the cotton plantation, 1937

hears the elder 'deaconing' a hymn-book hymn, which is sung two lines at a time, and whose wailing cadences, borne on the night air, are indescribably melancholy." The subsequent response from the congregation to the bluesy call of the minister, along with the accompanying instruments, created the rhythmic complexity so common in African music.

Such African-inspired church music, later known as gospel, became the basis of the blues style, which incorporated it and applied it to secular themes. Bluesman Big Bill Broonzy, who recorded some two hundred songs from 1925 to 1952, started as "a preacher — preached in the church. One day I quit and went to music." But Broonzy maintained that "the blues won't die because spirituals won't die. Blues — a steal from spirituals. And rock is a steal from the blues. . . . Blues singers start out singing spirituals."

Listening to the blues. The South, early 1940s

FROM THE RURAL SOUTH
TO THE URBAN NORTH

During and after World War I, many Southern blacks brought the blues
to Northern cities, especially Chicago, where the black population
mushroomed from five thousand in 1910 to eighty thousand in 1926.
Many left to escape the boll weevil, an insect parasite that ravaged the
Mississippi Delta in 1915 and 1916. Some left to break loose from the
crippling racial discrimination in the South. As Delta pianist Eddie
Boyd told *Living Blues,* "I thought of coming to Chicago where I could
get away from some of that racism and where I would have an opportunity to, well, do something with my talent. . . . It wasn't peaches and

cream [in Chicago], man, but it was a hell of a lot better than down there where I was born." Once in Chicago, blacks took jobs in steel mills, foundries, and stockyards that had materialized because of the wartime draft and a sudden cutoff of European immigration. They settled in Chicago's South and West Side neighborhoods.

Among the migrants to the Windy City was the Georgia-bred Speckled Red, who first played his blues to workers in the turpentine, lumber, and sawmill camps of the South. Eurreal Wilford "Little Brother" Montgomery, born in 1907 on the grounds of a Louisiana lumber company, performed around logging camps until he ended up with Speckled Red in Chicago. Big Bill Broonzy, an ex-slave's son who worked as a plowhand in Mississippi and laid railroad track in Arkansas, headed for the same destination in 1916, when drought destroyed the crops on his farm. Tampa Red, coming from Georgia, reached Chicago in 1925; four years later, Roosevelt Sykes, "The Honeydripper," took the same route; and John Lee "Sonny Boy" Williamson (the first Sonny Boy) migrated from Jackson, Tennessee. All told, said George Leaner, who began selling blues discs in Chicago during the 1930s, "the Illinois Central Railroad brought the blues to Chicago. With the thousands of laborers who came to work in the meat-packing plants and the steel mills came Peetie Wheatstraw, Ollie Shepard, Blind Boy Fuller, Washboard Sam, Little Brother Montgomery, Blind Lemon [Jefferson], Memphis Minnie, and Rosetta Howard."

These migrants played a stylistic mixture. At first they delivered straight country blues. The influence of the city, however, seeped into their music, and by the early 1940s they recorded a hybrid of blues, vaudeville styles, and newer swing rhythms, which included the boogie-woogie, rolling-bass piano, a sound that had been widely disseminated by the jump blues band of Louis Jordan. Some dubbed the early Chicago blues the "Bluebird Beat" because many of the acoustic bluesmen recorded for the Bluebird label.

The blues became even more entrenched in Northern urban areas during and after World War II, when thousands of Southerners in search of work streamed into the cities. "World War I started bluesmen up North and No. II made it a mass migration," pointed out Atlantic record executive Jerry Wexler. From 1940 to 1944, estimated *Time* magazine, over fifty thousand blacks from Mississippi alone headed for Chicago. They paid around fifteen dollars for the trip on the Illinois Central Railroad and ended in the Windy City, the home of the *Defender,* the widely read, black-owned newspaper that encouraged Southern share-croppers to migrate to the North. By the end of the 1940s, 154,000 Southern blacks had arrived in Chicago and the black population in the city had increased by 77 percent in just one decade (1940–1950). About half the migrants came from the Mississippi Delta region, which stretched two hundred miles from Memphis to Vicksburg.

Many of the Delta migrants had heard a propulsive, acoustic, personalized style of blues on their plantations when they were growing up. On Saturdays at parties, at picnics, and in juke joints, they listened to the moans, the heavy bass beat, and the bottleneck slide guitar playing of local musicians. Their favorites included Charley Patton, the king of the Delta blues, who played around Will Dockery's plantation during the 1920s and in 1929 recorded his classics "Pony Blues," "Pea Vine Blues," and "Tom Rushen Blues." He played with Eddie "Son" House, a one-time preacher who in the 1930s cut such discs as "Preachin' the Blues." Robert Johnson, one of the most celebrated and legendary of the Delta bluesmen, learned guitar technique from the Patton disciple Willie Brown and picked up Delta stylizings from Son House. During his short recording career, he released such gems as "Dust My Broom," "Sweet Home Chicago," and "Rambling on My Mind."

MUDDY WATERS AND CHICAGO R & B

Muddy Waters (a.k.a. McKinley Morganfield), who grew up in Rolling Fork, Mississippi, listening to Johnson, Patton, and Son House, merged his Delta influences with his new urban environment in Chicago.

Photo by Marion Post Wolcott; reproduction from the collections of the Library of Congress

R & B dancers, Memphis, 1939

Muddy had bought his first guitar when he was thirteen. "The first one I got," he told writer Robert Palmer, "I sold the last horse we had. Made about fifteen dollars for him, gave my grandmother seven dollars and fifty cents, I kept seven-fifty and paid about two-fifty for that guitar. It was a Stella. The peoples ordered them from Sears-Roebuck in Chicago." A young Muddy played locally around his home base, a plantation owned by Colonel William Howard Stovall. In 1940, on a trip to the Mississippi Delta in search of American folk music, musicologists Alan Lomax and John Work discovered Waters, then a tenant farmer, and recorded him for the Library of Congress.

Three years later, Muddy moved to Chicago "with a suitcase, a suit of clothes, and a guitar," hoping to "get into the big record field." "I wanted to get out of Mississippi in the worst way," Waters told a journalist. "They had such as my mother and the older people brain-washed that people can't make it too good in the city. But I figured if anyone else was living in the city, I could make it there, too." Waters worked in a paper container factory and then as a truck driver by day, playing at parties during the evenings.

In 1944 Muddy bought his first electric guitar and two years later formed his first electric combo. Muddy Waters, possibly the archetype of Chicago R & B artists, combined his Delta upbringing with the electrified guitar and amplifier, which blasted forth the tension, volume, and confusion of the big-city streets.

The resulting marriage between city and country, a nitty-gritty, low-down, jumpy sound, reflected the optimism of postwar American blacks, who had at least temporarily escaped during World War II from the seemingly inescapable Southern cotton fields. Urban blacks now hoped for more permanent change, and their music contrasted with the more subdued country blues, born in slavery. Remembered Willie Dixon — a bassist from Vicksburg, Mississippi, and composer of such blues-rock classics as "Hoochie Coochie Man," "I'm a Man," and "Just Want to Make Love to You," — "there was quite a few people around singin' the blues but most of 'em was singing all *sad* blues. Muddy was giving his blues a little pep." The peppy blues of artists such as Waters became known as rhythm and blues.

After four years of perfecting his electric sound in Chicago clubs, Muddy signed with Chess Records, owned by Polish immigrants Leonard and Phil Chess, who operated several South Side bars, including the Macomba. At first, as Muddy told journalist Pete Welding, Leonard Chess "didn't like my style of singing; he wondered who was going to buy that. The lady [Evelyn, his partner] said 'You'd be surprised.' . . . Everybody's records came out before mine, Andrew Tibbs had two records before me. . . . But when they released mine, it hit the ceiling." "I had a hot blues out, man," Muddy remembered about his first disc, "I Can't Be Satisfied," backed with "I Feel Like Going Home." "I'd be driving my truck and whenever I'd see a neon beer sign, I'd stop, go in, look at the jukebox, and see my record on there. . . . Pretty soon I'd hear it walking along the street. I'd hear it *driving* along the street."

The Muddy Waters band, early 1950s. From left to right: Muddy Waters (guitar); unknown; Otis Spann (piano); Henry Strong (harmonica); Elgin Evans (drums); and Jimmy Rogers (guitar)

Buoyed by success, in 1951 Chess released a series of Muddy Waters sides that became hits on the "race" charts: "Louisiana Blues," "Long Distance Call," "Honey Bee," and "She Loves Me." By the mid-1950s he had become a living legend of the urbanized, electric Delta blues, recording "Rolling Stone," "Got My Mojo Working," the Delta standard "Rollin' and Tumblin'," "Mad Love," and "I'm Ready" among many others. His group of the early fifties, which included Otis Spann on piano, Little Walter on harmonica, Jimmy Rogers on guitar, and Leroy "Baby-Face" Foster on drums, stands out as one of the most explosive R & B units ever formed.

THE WOLF

Chester "Howlin' Wolf" Burnett, Waters's musical rival at Chess, also delivered an electric version of the Delta blues. Burnett, a native of the Delta, moved to Will Dockery's plantation in 1926 and, as he told Pete Welding, "Charley Patton started me off playing. He took a liking to me, and I asked him would he learn me, and at night, after I'd get off work, I'd go and hang around." During his teens he listened to the country yodeling of another Mississippian, Jimmie Rodgers, and decided to emulate his hero. But Burnett's harsh, raspy voice never mastered the yodel technique and the bluesman earned a series of nicknames for his distinctive style, which included "Bull Cow," "Foot," and "The Wolf." "I just stuck to Wolf. I could do no yodelin' so I turned to Howlin'," remembered Burnett. To perfect his raspy blues, Howlin' Wolf traveled across the Delta during the next three decades and played with legendary bluesmen of the area such as Robert Johnson and Rice Miller (also known as Sonny Boy Williamson II).

In 1948, at the age of 38, The Wolf plugged his Delta blues into an electric amplifier and in West Memphis formed an electric band, which at times included harp players James Cotton and Little Junior Parker. A few years later he joined the exodus to Chicago and signed with Chess Records, recording such shattering R & B songs as "Moanin' at Midnight," "Killing Ground," "Sitting on Top of the World," originally done by the Mississippi Sheiks and later covered by the rock-blues outfit Cream, "How Many More Years," and "Smokestack Lightin'," later popularized by the Yardbirds.

Wolf's stage performances presaged later rock and roll hysteria. At the end of one performance, he raced toward the wings of the stage, took a flying leap and grabbed onto the stage curtain, still singing into his microphone. As the song built to a climax, The Wolf scaled the curtain and, as the song drew to a close, slid down the drapery. He hit the floor just as the song ended to the screams of the audience. Recalled Sam Phillips, the genius behind Sun Records who recorded a few Howlin' Wolf songs for Chess, "God, what it would be worth on film to see the fervor in that man's face when he sang. His eyes would light up, you'd see the veins come out on his neck and, buddy, there was *nothing* on his mind but that song. He sang with his damn soul."

OTHER CHESS DISCOVERIES

The Chess brothers recorded other hard-driving rhythm and blues performers from the Delta. Born Elias McDaniel in McComb, Mississippi, Bo Diddley moved to the Windy City with his family. "Oh, I played street corners until I was 19 or 20, from about 15 on," he told rock critic and musician Lenny Kaye. "Then I walked the streets around Chicago for about 12 years, before I got somebody to listen to me." Eventually, he landed a job at the 708 Club and in 1955 signed with Chess, where Leonard Chess gave him his stage name, Bo Diddley, "because it meant 'funny storyteller.' " That year Diddley hit the charts with "Bo Diddley" and "I'm a Man" and subsequently with "Mona," "You Can't Judge a Book by Its Cover," and "Say Man." Though sometimes crossing over to rock and roll fans, Diddley stood firmly rooted in the electrified Delta sound. The striking similarity between his "I'm a Man" and Muddy Waters's "Mannish Boy," both recorded in 1955, attests to Bo Diddley's Delta foundation.

Chess also recorded two pioneers of the amplified harmonica. Walter Jacobs, otherwise known as Little Walter, grew up in the cotton

Little Walter Jacobs at the Chess Studios.

fields of the Mississippi Delta. He learned to play the harmonica, the harp as he called it, during his teens, patterning himself after Rice Miller, whom he discovered on the "King Biscuit Hour" radio show. A year or two after World War II, Little Walter left home for Chicago, where he joined the Muddy Waters band. After impressing the Chess Brothers with his talent, Little Walter recorded his own compositions: In 1952 he hit the charts with "Juke," which remained in the R & B top ten for fourteen weeks. The harp player followed with "Sad Hours" and "Blues with a Feeling."

Leonard Chess snagged Rice Miller (Sonny Boy Williamson II), the idol of Little Walter and the undisputed king of the R & B harmonica, when Miller moved to Milwaukee in 1955. His band included the Muddy Waters outfit and, sometimes, Robert Jr. Lockwood, who had learned guitar from Robert Johnson. Though already an established artist when he signed with Chess, Sonny Boy cut a number of now-classic singles for the Chicago label.

THE MODERN "BLUES BOY"

Modern Records and its various subsidiaries, owned by Saul and Jules Bihari of Los Angeles, gave Chess its stiffest competition in the search for R & B talent. During the late forties and early fifties, the Bihari brothers made numerous scouting trips to the Mississippi Delta. They also commissioned as talent scout Ike Turner, who was then the leader of the Rhythm Kings and later gained fame as half of the Ike and Tina Turner duo.

The Biharis's efforts resulted in the signing of one of the most successful rhythm and blues artists: Riley "Blues Boy" King. Born on a cotton plantation near Indianola, Mississippi, the heart of the Delta, King was forced into the fields at the age of nine, working for fifteen dollars a month. As with most R & B performers, he began his musical career in the church. "Singing was the thing I enjoyed doing, and when I started in school, I sang with a group: a quartet singing spirituals," B. B. told *Downbeat*. When he was fifteen, his father bought him an eight-dollar guitar, which became the boy's constant companion. King continued to "sing gospel music, using the guitar to tune up the group I played with," he related. "When I was introduced into the army at the age of 18, I started playing around little towns, just standing on the corner. People asked me to play gospel tunes and complimented me real nicely: 'Son, if you keep it up, you're going to be real good someday.' But the people who asked me to play the blues tunes normally tipped me, many times getting me beer. So that motivated me to play the blues, you might say."

In 1949 King hitchhiked to Memphis, Tennessee, and moved in with a cousin, Booker T. "Bukka" White, himself a renowned Delta blues figure. He found a part-time job singing Pepticon commercials on the black radio station WDIA. Remembered the guitarist: "This Pepticon was supposed to be good for whatever ails you, y'know, like a toothache. Anyway, they put me on from 3:30 to 3:40 and my popularity began to grow. I sang and I played by myself and I later got two men with me . . . Earl Forrest playing drums and Johnny Ace playing piano."

After a year on WDIA, King, by now called "Blues Boy" or just B. B. for short, signed a contract with Modern Records and its subsidiaries, RPM, Kent, and Crown. His music, now almost fully developed, fused his Delta influences with a piercing falsetto vocal style and a jazzy, single-note guitar attack picked up from jazz guitarist Django Reinhardt and Texas bluesman Aaron "T-Bone" Walker, who in turn had electrified the technique he had learned from country bluesman Blind Lemon Jefferson. In a few years King's new synthesis produced dozens of

R & B classics that subsequent rock guitarists have either copied or stolen: "Everyday I Have the Blues," "I Woke Up This Morning," and "You Upset Me Baby."

Elmore James eventually joined B. B. King at Modern Records. Born on a farm near Richland, Mississippi, James taught himself guitar by stringing a broom wire to a wall of his cabin and plunking on it. He

Living Blues Archival Collection, University of Mississippi Blues Archive

B. B. "Blues Boy" King

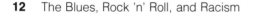

listened to such Delta giants as Robert Johnson and Charley Patton, and by the late 1940s he had become a master of the slide guitar. Lillian McMurray, who set up Trumpet Records in Jackson, Mississippi, first recorded James. In 1952 Trumpet released his gut-wrenching, slashing version of Robert Johnson's "Dust My Broom." The next year, the Bihari brothers lured Elmore to Chicago, and he began to record for the Meteor label, another subsidiary of Modern. His output included a number of now-indispensable R & B tunes — such as "Shake Your Moneymaker," "It Hurts Me Too," "The Sky Is Crying," and "Hawaiian Boogie" — that rocker George Thorogood recently has revived and popularized. As with his fellow transplanted Delta performers, Elmore James captured in his music the pain and anguish of three centuries of slavery and tenant farming. As black producer Bobby Robinson suggested, listen "to the raw-nerved, spine-tingling picking of the guitar and the agonized screams and the soul-stirring of Elmore James. Close your eyes, you'll see the slave ships, the auction blocks, the cotton fields, the bare backs straining, totin' that barge and liftin' that bale. You will smell the sweat, feel the lash, taste the tears and see the blood, and relive 300 years of the Blues."

The Biharis also recorded John Lee Hooker, the Delta-born guitarist who traveled North to Detroit during the postwar era. Hooker learned the guitar from his stepfather, Will Moore, who had played with Charley Patton on Dockery's plantation. He sang with various gospel groups in the Delta, but by the age of fourteen he left home. In 1948 John Lee signed with Modern and recorded "Boogie Chillin," an electric, chantlike, darkly superstitious-sounding stomp that vividly described black Detroit's main thoroughfare, Hastings Street. It sounded a bit more countrified than the songs of R & B artists like Muddy Waters, but the single "caught fire," Hooker told a *Living Blues* interviewer. "It was ringin' all around the country. When it come out, every juke box you went to, everyplace you went to, every drug store you went, everywhere you went, department stores, they were playin' it in there." Hooker followed with such rhythm and blues chart climbers as "Hobo Blues," "Crawling Kingsnake Blues," and "I'm in the Mood."

Vee Jay Records of Chicago, noticing the success that Chess and Modern had achieved with the electrified Delta blues, jumped into the R & B field with Jimmy Reed. Born on a plantation near Dunleith, Mississippi, Reed discovered the guitar with friend and later back-up musician Eddie Taylor, whose style derived from Charley Patton and Robert Johnson. He learned harmonica by "listening to Sonny Boy Williams [Rice Miller]. . . . I'd slip out of the fields and go up to the house to listen to them do the 15 minutes he had to do over the radio show. He was broadcastin' for King Biscuit flour out of Helena, Arkansas." In 1948 Reed headed toward Chicago, where he worked at various steel mills and foundries. During his breaks and lunch hours, he practiced one-chord, Delta guitar shuffles and a laid-back vocal style that masked the biting lyrics of such songs as "Big Boss Man." In 1953, after being rejected by Leonard Chess, who "was too tied up with Little Walter and

Muddy Waters and Wolf and them, till he didn't have no time for me," Reed signed with the newly organized Vee Jay Records, created by black disc jockey Vivian Carter and her husband, Jimmy Bracken. He first topped the R & B charts in 1955 with "You Don't Have to Go" and followed with a series of hits that included "Ain't That Loving You Baby," "Hush-Hush," "Honest I Do," and "Take Out Some Insurance on Me, Baby," the last covered by the Beatles in their early years.

R & B OUTSIDE CHICAGO

Small, independent record companies in cities other than Chicago specialized in different styles of the new R & B sound. Los Angeles had a number of such recording outfits. Aladdin, owned by the Mesner brothers, recorded a postwar Texas sound that included the relaxed vocal stylings of Amos Milburn and Charles Brown. The company also released Shirley and Lee's "Let the Good Times Roll," which became a rallying cry for rock and rollers twenty years later. Lew Chudd established Imperial Records in 1945 and achieved success with the barrelhouse, rolling piano of Antoine "Fats" Domino, who from 1949 to 1962 had forty-three records that made *Billboard's* charts, eighteen gold records, and total sales of thirty million dollars. In addition, Imperial recorded the Southwest blues of the electric guitar innovator T-Bone Walker.

In Cincinnati Syd Nathan set up King Records in an abandoned ice house and recorded the velvety, big-band sound of Ivory Joe Hunter, Lonnie Johnson, and Wynonie "Mr. Blues" Harris. In 1942 Herman Lubinsky incorporated Savoy Records in Newark, New Jersey, and signed R & B shouters Little Esther and Big Maybelle. Black entrepreneur Don Robey established Peacock Records in Houston. In 1952 he bought the Memphis-based Duke Records and scored hits with the smooth-voiced, gospel-influenced Bobby Blue Bland and teen star Johnny Ace, a former member of the B. B. King band, who lost his life in a senseless game of Russian roulette on Christmas Eve, 1954, at the age of twenty-five.

In New York City, the bustling hub of urban America, independent labels such as Herald, Regal, Old Town, and Deluxe delivered a distinctive, heavily gospel-based R & B sound with the "do-wop" vocal group. Ghetto youths, too poor to afford a guitar, banded together on street corners and sang their way through Harlem, using the voice of each member of the group as a different instrument. The names of many of the groups reflected the urban dreams of the youths: the Edsels, the Fiestas, the Impalas, the Imperials, the Cadillacs, the Belvederes, and the Fleetwoods — the automobiles they saw glide down the city streets.

The Ravens led the way for subsequent do-wop groups. Formed in 1946, the four-man choir featured the deep bass tone of Jimmy Ricks. They signed with King Records and released their first hit, "Bye Bye Baby Blues." The song inspired a spate of other R & B singing combinations: the Willows; the Regents; the Heartbeats; the Charts; the Charms, led by Otis Williams; the Jive Five; the Monotones, from nearby New Jersey, who scored a hit with "The Book of Love"; the Jesters, who faced off with another New York do-wop group in the now sought-after album *The Paragons Meet the Jesters;* the Crows, who prompted George Goldner to start Gee Records with their 1954 song of the same name; and Harlem's favorites, the Harptones.

The most well-known New York do-wop combinations centered around Clyde McPhatter and Frankie Lymon. McPhatter first joined the Dominoes, a gospel group ruled by the iron hand of Billy Ward, which appeared on the *Arthur Godfrey Show.* Soon after their television debut, the group began to record blues numbers and in May 1951 released the classic "Sixty Minute Man." Within two years, leader McPhatter bolted from the Dominoes and formed probably the most famous of the R & B vocal groups, the Drifters, settling on that name because the members "drifted" from one group to another. The Drifters signed with Atlantic Records, the company founded in 1947 by Ahmet and Nesuhi Ertegun, sons of the Turkish ambassador to the United States, who were avid jazz and blues record collectors and who auctioned off fifteen thousand of their 78s to start Atlantic with Herb Abramson. In 1953 the Drifters reached the *Billboard* charts with "Money Honey." A string of hits followed ("Such a Night," "Honey Love," and "Bip Bam") before McPhatter left the group in 1955 for the army.

The Teenagers, spearheaded by thirteen-year-old Frankie Lymon, picked up where the Drifters left off. In 1955 this group practiced on street corners, in a junk-filled backyard, or on the top of a Harlem tenement house. One day, Richard Barrett, the lead singer of the Valentines, overheard the Teenagers as he passed by a street corner. Excitedly, he brought the boys, all in their teens, to the offices of his label, Gee Records, and there they sang "Why Do Fools Fall in Love." Company executives George Goldner and Joe Kilsky asked Lymon if he had the sheet music for the song. "Nope," replied Frankie, "We don't know anything about written-down music." The next day, the Teenagers recorded "Why Do Fools Fall in Love" for Gee. It was released in January 1956, and within a few months it became a national hit. Though more pop-oriented and gospel-flavored than the electrified guitar sound of Chicago — "devil's music" in the words of B. B. King — New York do-wop mirrored the cityscape of America in the 1950s and became a popular form of R & B.

FROM R & B TO ROCK 'N' ROLL: LITTLE RICHARD AND CHUCK BERRY

A few young R & B showmen completed the transition from an acoustic, more slow-moving country blues to the jumpy, electric, urban sound that became known as rock and roll. The term *rock and roll,* originally a black euphemism for sexual intercourse, at first generically referred to all R & B artists. At some vague point in time, it began to be applied to the most frenetic, hard-driving version of an already spirited rhythm and blues. As Howlin' Wolf suggested, with "a twelve-bar and a four-bar intro, you're playing the blues. You step the stuff up and you're playing rock and roll."

Little Richard and Chuck Berry stood in the vanguard of the rock and roll pioneers. Little Richard, born Richard Penniman in Macon, Georgia, in late 1932, sang in a Baptist Church choir as a youth and traveled with his family gospel troupe, the Penniman Family. He joined various circuses and traveling shows and in the Broadway Follies met gospel-R & B shouter Billy Wright, who secured a recording contract from Camden Records for the eighteen-year-old Little Richard. In 1951 Richard cut eight sides for Camden, which featured boogie-woogie, urban blues numbers in the style of Billy Wright.

However, the next year a local tough shot and killed Little Richard's father, the owner of the Tip In Inn. To support the family, Richard washed dishes in the Macon Greyhound Bus station by day and at night sang with his group, the Upsetters, at local theaters for fifteen dollars a show. "We were playing some of Roy Brown's tunes, a lot of Fats Domino tunes, some B. B. King tunes and I believe a couple of Little Walter's and a few things by Billy Wright," remembered Little Richard.

After a few years of one-night stands in black Southern nightclubs, Penniman began to change his style. He transformed himself from a traditional R & B singer into a wild-eyed, pompadoured madman who crashed the piano keys and screamed nonsensical lyrics at a breakneck speed. Richard later recalled that, "It was funny. I'd sing the songs I sing now in clubs, but the black audiences just didn't respond. They wanted blues stuff like B. B. King sings. That's what they were used to. I'd sing 'Tutti Frutti' and nothing. Then someone would get up and sing an old blues song and everyone would go wild."

On the advice of rhythm and blues singer Lloyd Price of "Lawdy Miss Clawdy" fame, Richard sent a demo tape of two rather subdued blues tunes to Art Rupe at Specialty Records in Los Angeles, which had recorded Price as well as R & B artists such as Roy Milton and Jimmy Liggins. The tape, according to Specialty's musical director Bumps Blackwell, was "wrapped in a piece of paper looking as though someone had eaten off it." Blackwell opened the wrapper, played the tape, and recommended that Rupe sign Little Richard.

Richard arrived in New Orleans in late 1955 for his first Specialty recording session. Reminisced Little Richard: "I cut some blues songs. During a break in the session, someone heard me playing 'Tutti Frutti' on the piano and asked about the song. We ended up recording it and it sold two hundred thousand copies in a week and a half." And a legend was born. During the next four years, Richard cut a wealth of rock standards, which defined the new music: "Long Tall Sally," "Slippin' and Slidin'," "Rip It Up," "Ready Teddy," "The Girl Can't Help It," "Good Golly Miss Molly," "Jenny, Jenny," "Keep a Knockin'," and "Lucille."

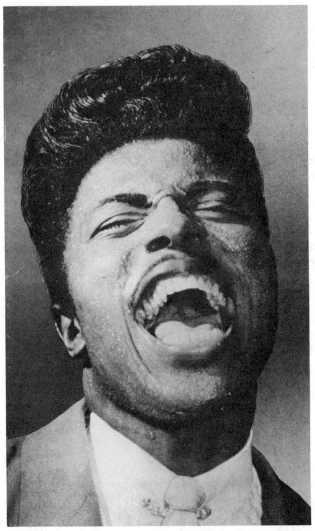

Specialty Records, Inc. (from LP cover Here's Little Richard*)*

The fabulous Little Richard

If anyone besides Little Richard can claim to be the father of rock and roll, it would be Chuck Berry. Berry, unlike almost all other R & B musicians, spent his youth in a sturdy, tree-lined, brick house in the middle-class outskirts of St. Louis. But after a stay in reform school and various odd jobs, which included work as a cosmetologist and an assembler at the General Motors Fisher Body plant, Berry turned to rhythm and blues. He obtained his first guitar from St. Louis R & B performer

Joe Sherman, and in the early fifties he formed a rhythm and blues trio with Johnny Johnson on piano and Ebby Harding on drums that played "backyards, barbeques, and house parties."

In the spring of 1955 Berry traveled to Chicago, then the mecca of urban blues, and asked to sit in during one of Muddy Waters's shows. He so impressed Waters that the veteran bluesman recommended the novice to Leonard Chess. The rest is history. Chess promptly recorded "Maybelline," a country song adapted to a boogie woogie beat, which hinted at the marriage between country and R & B that would reach full fruition with the rockabillies. Within weeks, Berry's upbeat song had received national airplay. The guitarist-songwriter followed with "Roll Over Beethoven (Dig These Rhythm and Blues)," "School Days," "Rock and Roll Music," "Sweet Little Sixteen," "Johnny Be Goode," "Rockin' and Rollin'," and an almost endless list of others, and embarked upon a whirlwind tour of the country: He played 101 engagements in 101 nights, where he perfected antics such as the duckwalk. Berry's music, like that of Little Richard, took the jumpy R & B to an extreme and bridged the short gap between rhythm and blues and what became known as rock and roll. "It used to be called boogie woogie, it used to be called blues, used to be called rhythm and blues. . . . It's called rock now," Berry told a journalist.

THE GROWING LEGION OF ROCKERS

The market for the new sound expanded with the number of blacks who flooded into Northern and Western cities during and after World War II. The migrants, some of them having a little extra cash for the first time, demanded entertainment but faced a number of obstacles. "Harlem folks couldn't go downtown to the Broadway theaters and movie houses," recalled Ahmet Ertegun, co-founder of Atlantic Records. "Downtown clubs had their ropes up when they came to the door. They weren't even welcome on Fifty-Second Street where all the big performers were black. . . . Even radio was white oriented. You couldn't find a black performer on network radio. And when it came to disc jockeys on the big wattage stations, they wouldn't play a black record. We had a real tough time getting our records played — even Ruth Brown, who didn't sound particularly black."

For their leisure, some urban blacks frequented segregated clubs such as the Roosevelt in Pittsburgh, the Lincoln in Los Angeles, the Royal in Baltimore, Chicago's Regal, the Howard in Washington, and the now-famous Apollo Theater in New York City. The owners of Town Hall, the only dance hall for blacks in Philadelphia, claimed that "swollen Negro paychecks at local war plants and shipyards" helped to increase their profits. Other blacks frequented segregated taverns and demanded music by black artists on the jukeboxes. The majority of migrants, however, bound closer to home by their families, found entertainment through the record. As Ahmet Ertegun suggested, most "black people had to find entertainment in their homes — and the record was it." They bought 78 rpm discs by their favorite artists in furniture stores, pharmacies, shoe-shine stands, and anywhere else they were sold.

Most favored the electrified R & B sound. "The black people, particularly the black people I knew, never lived in the country," said Art Rupe, the owner of Specialty Records, recalling the late 1940s. "They looked down on country music. Among themselves, the blacks called country blues 'field nigger' music. They wanted to be citified." And according to Jack Allison, an executive at Modern Records, jazz seldom reached the "average Negroes." They demanded the more popular R & B.

At first only blacks bought R & B discs. Johnny Otis, a white bandleader who grew up in a black section of Berkeley and later helped many black artists rise to stardom, noticed the trend: "As far as black music was concerned we had what was known as race music. Race music was Big Bill Broonzy, Peetie Wheatstraw, and things like that. Now, these things were very much part of the black community but they didn't occur anywhere else and these cats could hardly make a living plying their trade." A successful rhythm and blues recording generally sold only four hundred thousand copies. And according to Jerry Wexler of Atlantic Records, "sales were localized in ghetto markets. There was no white sale, and no white radio play."

But in the early 1950s more and more white teenagers began to become aware of R & B. At first young Southern whites started to buy records by black artists. As Jerry Wexler noticed in the early 1950s, "we became aware that Southern whites were buying our records, white kids in high school and college." In California at the same time, Johnny Otis saw the changing composition of the R & B audiences, which were becoming dotted with white faces. In 1952 the Dolphin Record store in Los Angeles, which specialized in R & B records, reflected the trend, reporting 40 percent of its sales to whites. Eventually white teens in all parts of the country turned to rhythm and blues. In April 1955 Mitch Miller — then head of Columbia Records and later famous for the "sing along" craze that he masterminded — complained that "rhythm and blues songs are riding high." This " 'rock and roll' began among Negro people, was first recorded by Negro performers and had its following among Negroes in the South and also Negro urban areas in the North." But "suddenly," Miller saw that "millions of white teenagers who buy most of the 'pop' records in America have latched on to rhythm and blues."

SOCIAL CHANGE AND ROCK 'N' ROLL

The sudden transformation that Miller observed, and later viciously criticized, came about through a number of social changes. Technologically, television made radio space available to more recording artists. Before the 1950s, network radio shows, many of them broadcast live, dominated the airwaves, and as Johnny Otis argued, "in the thirties and forties, black music was summarily cut off the radio." It "simply was not played, black music of any kind — even a Louis Armstrong was not played on the air." But after television absorbed the network shows, black records started to get some airplay.

Many of the disc jockeys who spun the R & B records became diehard advocates of the music. B. Mitchell Reed, who still broadcasts on the leading Los Angeles rock station, KMET FM, became "enthralled with rock" in the 1950s and convinced the management to switch from a jazz format to rock when he "realized that the roots of the stuff that I was playing — the rock — had come from the jazz and blues I'd been playing before." Even earlier than Reed's conversion to rock, the Los Angeles "dean of the DJs," Al Jarvis, "wanted the black artists to be heard" and introduced them on his show.

Rock and roll's superpromoter was Alan Freed. Freed, a student of classical trombone and music theory, began his broadcasting career in New Castle, Pennsylvania, on the classical station WKST. After a four-year stint in Akron, Ohio, he landed a job in Cleveland in 1951 on the independent station WJW. Although hired to play classical albums, Freed witnessed the reaction of white teenagers to tenor-sax players Red Prysock and Big Al Sears as the music blared in a local record store and "went to the station manager and talked him into permitting me to follow my classical program with a rock 'n' roll party." He picked "Blues for Moondog," a King release by Todd Rhodes, for his theme song and named his show "The Moon Dog Rock 'n' Roll House Party."

Not confining himself to radio, in 1952 and 1953 Freed organized rock and roll concerts in the Cleveland arena that met with enthusiastic responses: In the first, the "Moon Dog Coronation Ball," which included the Orioles, Charles Brown, the Moonglows, and the Dominoes, he sold eighteen thousand tickets for an auditorium that seated nine thousand and was forced to cancel the show. And by 1954, his commercial success propelled him into the key nighttime spot on the influential New York station WINS. While there, the DJ introduced thousands of young whites on the East Coast to black music, consistently befriending black artists on the small independent labels at the expense of the major, "all-white" companies. The movies in which he appeared — "Don't Knock the Rock," "Rock, Rock, Rock," and the now-famous "Rock Around the Clock," which caused riots in the United States and Europe — further familiarized white youths with R & B, now being called rock and roll by Freed.

Young teens listened to disc jockeys such as Freed on a new invention — the portable, transistorized radio. First developed in 1947 at the Bell Laboratory in New Jersey, it reached the public in 1953. Within a decade, the hand-held radio was bought yearly by more than 12 million consumers, many of them teens. It offered an inexpensive means of experiencing the exciting new music called rock and roll.

The car radio served the same purpose as the portable transistor model. Marketed initially in the 1950s, it became standard equipment within a few years. By 1963 music blasted forth from the dashboards of over 50 million automobiles that sped down the highways and back-roads of the country. The car radio introduced rock and roll to many teens who used the automobile in such rites of passage as the school prom and the first date. In 1959 a nervous, clammy-palmed youth, sitting next to his girlfriend and behind the wheel of his father's El Dorado, could hear Chuck Berry detail his exploits with Maybelline that occurred in a similar car. The car radio provided a bridge between rock and roll and a mobile, young, car-crazy generation.

The civil rights movement also helped to make the popularization of black-inspired rock possible. In 1954, the year that the Canadian group the Crewcuts made "Sh-Boom" into rock's first commercial success, the Supreme Court handed down *Brown v. the Board of Education of Topeka*. Convinced by the arguments of Thurgood Marshall, counsel for the NAACP and later a Supreme Court justice himself, the court unanimously banned segregation in public schools and ordered school districts to desegregate. "In the field of public education," Chief Justice Earl Warren contended, "the doctrine of 'separate but equal' has no place. Separate educational facilities are inherently unequal." By overthrowing the "separate but equal" doctrine of the 1896 *Plessy v. Ferguson* case, the court had come out strongly for black rights and had helped to start a civil rights movement that would go hand in hand with the development of rock and roll in the 1950s.

The number of youths who would feel the impact of the Brown decision was growing rapidly. In 1946 over 5.6 million teenagers attended American high schools. Ten years later the number climbed to 6.8 million, and in 1960, to 11.8 million. Observers called it the "war-time baby boom." "No decrease is in sight this century," predicted a Census Bureau official in 1955. "We have come to consider it routine to report new all-time high records."

Many of these teens, living during prosperous times, had money in their pockets to spend on records. Between 1940 and 1954 the United States Gross National Product (GNP) rose from $200 billion to $360 billion, and the average yearly family income increased from about $5,000 to $6,200. Having more leisure time than past generations, most Americans spent much of this extra money on consumer items such as paperback novels, television sets, cameras, and electrical appliances. Teenage sons and daughters, who received the sizable allowances of over $9 billion in 1957 and $10.5 billion in 1963, followed in their parents' footsteps by entering the consumer society. Rather than cameras or electrical gadgets, the youths bought records. In a 1960 survey of 4,500 teenage girls conducted by *Seventeen* magazine, the average teen had "a weekly income of $9.53, gets up at 7:43 A.M., and listens to the radio two hours a day." Craving the songs that they heard, over 70 percent of the girls bought records with their allowances. An affluent society, along with other factors, paved the way for the mass consumption of rock and roll.

By 1954 rock and roll was beginning to achieve a general popularity among white youths. Teens bought discs by Chuck Berry, Little Richard, and Fats Domino. Soon they started to dance to the music. When Ralph Bass, a manager for Chess Records, went on the road with black acts in the late 1940s and early 1950s, "they didn't let whites into the clubs. Then they got 'white spectator tickets' for the worst corner of the joint." But in time, "they had to keep the white kids out," so "they'd have white nights sometimes, or they'd put a rope across the middle of the floor. The blacks on one side, whites on the other digging how the blacks were dancing and copying them. Then, hell, the rope would come down, and they'd all be dancing together." Touring with Fats Domino in 1957 and 1958, Chuck Berry also saw integrated audiences: "Salt and pepper all mixed together, and we'd say, 'Well, look what's happening.' "

RACIST BACKLASH

Such integration of white and black youths elicited a racist response from many white adults. In 1956 as white Southerners lashed out against desegregation and attacked civil rights workers, a spokesman for the White Citizens Council of Birmingham, Alabama, charged that rock and roll — "the basic, heavy-beat music of the Negroes" — appealed to "the base in man, brings out animalism and vulgarity" and, most important, formed a "plot to mongrelize America."

Other whites expressed their fear of race mixing by harping on the sexual undertones of rock. Testifying before a Senate subcommittee in 1958, Vance Packard — author of *Hidden Persuaders* — cautioned that rock and roll stirred "the animal instinct in modern teenagers" by its "raw savage tone." "What are we talking about?" Packard concluded, quoting an article from a 1955 issue of *Variety*. "We are talking about rock 'n' roll, about 'hug' and 'squeeze' and kindred euphemisms which are attempting a total breakdown of all reticences about sex." *Cash Box* similarly editorialized that "really dirty records" had been "getting air time," and suggested that companies "stop making dirty R & B records." Russ Sanjek, later vice-president of Broadcast Music, Inc. (BMI), which initially licensed most rock songs, summed up the white hysteria over the possibility of white and black sexual relations: "It was a time when many a mother ripped pictures of Fats Domino off her daughter's bedroom wall. She remembered what she felt toward her Bing Crosby pin-up, and she didn't want her daughter creaming for Fats."

A few adults defended the music of their children. In 1958 one mother from Fort Edward, New York, found that rock eased the boredom of her housework: "After all how much pep can you put into mopping the floor to 'Some Enchanted Evening,' but try it to 'Sweet Little Sixteen' by Chuck Berry and see how fast the work gets done. (I know the above is silly, but I just had to write it because it really is true, you know.)" "Rock and roll has a good beat and a jolly approach that keeps you on your toes," she added.

To jazz innovator Count Basie, the uproar over rock reminded him of the racist slurs hurled at his music two decades earlier. After living through the "swing era of the late 1930s when there was a lot of screaming pretty much like the furor being stirred up today," he remembered "particularly one comment in the 1930s which said 'jam sessions, jitterbugs, and cannibalistic rhythm orgies are wooing our youth along the primrose path to hell.' The funny thing is, a lot of the kids who used to crowd around the bandstand while we played in the 1930s are still coming around today to catch us. A lot of them are parents in the PTA, and leading citizens."

But many whites refused to accept the Count's logic. To waylay expected integration, they tried to outlaw rock and roll. The Houston Juvenile Delinquency and Crime Commission blacklisted thirty songs that it considered obscene, all of them by black artists, which included "Honey Love" by the Drifters, the Five Royales' "Too Much Lovin'," "Work with Me Annie" by Hank Ballard and the Midnighters, and Ray Charles's "I Got a Woman." R & B singer Jimmy Witherspoon, living in Houston at the time, felt that "the blacks was starting a thing in America for equality. The radio stations and the people in the South was fighting us. And they were hiring program directors to program the tunes. . . . They banned Little Richard's tune ('Long Tall Sally') in Houston." In Memphis station WDIA banned the recordings of thirty black rock-and-roll singers.

Stations in other major cities started similar campaigns against the new music. In April 1956 at a Nat King Cole concert, the White Citizens Council of Birmingham, equating jazz with R & B, jumped on the stage and beat the performer. Explaining the incident, Ray Charles said it happened because "the young white girls run up and say, 'Oh, Nat!' and they say, 'No, we can't have *that!*' Come on man, shit, that's where it is." At other rock and roll shows, Bo Diddley reminded interviewer Lou Cohen, "we used to have funny things like bomb scares and stuff like that because we were in South Carolina where the K. K. K. didn't want us performing."

THE MUSIC INDUSTRY VS. ROCK 'N' ROLL

The music industry also organized against rock and roll. Crooners whose careers had taken nose dives because of the new music bitterly condemned it. Testifying before Congress in 1958, Frank Sinatra called rock "the most brutal, ugly, desperate, vicious form of expression it has been my misfortune to hear." The black performers — "cretinous goons" — lured teenagers by "almost imbecilic reiterations and sly — lewd — in plain fact dirty — lyrics." By such devious means, he concluded, rock managed "to be the martial music of every sideburned delinquent on the face of the earth." A year earlier, Sammy Davis, Jr. — a black who had achieved success by singing in a style that differed little from Sinatra —

put it more succinctly: "If rock 'n' roll is here to stay I might commit suicide." At the same time, Dean Martin cryptically ascribed the rise of rock to "unnatural forces."

Disc jockeys who lost listeners from their pop and classical programs to rock and roll stations similarly spoke out against their competition. In 1955 Bob Tilton of Madison's WMFM called for "some records for adults that don't rock, roll, wham, bam, or fade to flat tones." To Chuck Blower of KTKT in Tucson, the year 1955 "with the tremendous upsurge of R & B into the pop crop — the almost complete absence of good taste, to say nothing of good grammar — this has been the worst and certainly the most frustrating pop year I have ever known." Generally, a *Billboard* survey in the same year indicated that "many jockeys believe the quality of the pop platter has seriously deteriorated in the past year. . . . Several jockeys are strongly opposed to the rhythm and blues influence in pop music."

Songwriters in the American Society of Composers, Authors, and Publishers (ASCAP) showed an equal disdain of rock. Because the new music usually was written by the performers themselves, professional songwriters began to suffer, and soon complained. Lyricist Billy Rose, then a board member of ASCAP, labeled rock and roll songs "junk," and "in many cases they are obscene junk much on the level with dirty comic magazines." Meredith Wilson, the bandleader of *Music Man* fame, charged that "rock and roll is dull, ugly, amateurish, immature, trite, banal and stale. It glorifies the mediocre, the nasty, the bawdy, the cheap, the tasteless." Mrs. Barbara Lehrman, a listener from Brooklyn, New York, supported Wilson's contention: "Let's give the music business back to the music men," she demanded in a letter to Senator John Pastore. "Let's clear the air of ear-splitting claptrap." To reassert their control, in 1958 ASCAP songwriters initiated a $150 million lawsuit against their competitor, the rock-oriented Broadcast Music, Inc., on the pretext of payola among the jockeys. It eventually ended in a Congressional subcommittee, but did little to squelch the popularity of rock music.

THE BLANCHING OF ROCK

Many record executives more successfully undermined black rockers and their music. Some leaders of the music industry personally disliked rock and roll. RCA vice-president George Marek did not "happen to like [rock] particularly, but then I like Verdi and I like Brahms and I like Beethoven." As Ahmet Ertegun explained, "you couldn't expect a man who loved 'April in Paris' or who had recorded Hudson DeLange in the 30s when he was beginning in the business, to like lyrics like 'I Wanna Boogie Your Woogie,' and 'Louie, Louie.' He had always thought race music and hillbilly were corny, and so he thought rock 'n' roll was for morons."

More important than personal taste, established record executives feared the economic consequences of a new music that they did not control. Since the major companies had dismissed the songs as "race music," black rock and rollers of the early 1950s had signed with new, independent labels. Having a virtual monopoly on rock acts by 1955, these independents siphoned off profits from the majors when white teens started to buy rock and roll records. From 1952 to 1957 the independents increased their share in the popular market by 50 percent, while the profits of such majors as Columbia declined dramatically.

To reverse this trend, larger companies copied or "covered" the songs of black artists with watered-down versions of the originals performed by whites. From 1954 to 1956, Pat Boone — wearing a white sweater and white buckskin shoes — rose to prominence by covering R & B songs. He copied "Ain't That a Shame" of Fats Domino, "At My Front Door," by the El Dorados, "Tutti Frutti," by Little Richard, the Flamingos' "I'll Be Home," "Long Tall Sally," again by Little Richard, and Ivory Joe Hunter's "I Almost Lost My Mind," among many others. Boone's renditions usually toned down the originals. For example, he changed Etta James's "Roll with Me, Henry" to the more bland "Dance with Me, Henry," and took T-Bone Walker's "Stormy Monday," substituting the phrase "drinkin' coca cola" for "drinkin' wine."

The companies enlisted other artists to cover songs from independent labels. The McGuire Sisters copied "Sincerely" from the Moonglows; Dorothy Collins took Clyde McPhatter's "Seven Days"; Perry Como stole "Kokomo" from Gene and Eunice, as did the Crew Cuts, who also took their monster hit, "Sh-Boom," from the Chords. The Chicago-raised LaVern Baker, who in 1955 on Atlantic cracked the R & B market with "That's All I Need" and "Tweedle Dee," fell victim to many cover artists. "Imitation may be the sincerest form of flattery, but the kind of flattery I can do without," dryly noted the singer.

To sell these imitations, Columbia, Capitol, Decca, and RCA marketed them in new ways. The companies placed their product on racks in suburban supermarkets. By 1956, four thousand supermarkets sold $14 million worth of records. In another year, 11,500 of these stores handled records and sold $40 million of them, which accounted for almost 20 percent of all record sales. In addition, first Columbia and then RCA and Capitol started mail-order record clubs to further increase sales.

Many disc jockeys aided big business in the purge of the independent labels. Although a few jockeys such as Alan Freed refused to spin covers, most gladly played "white" music. "It was a picnic for the majors," Ahmet Ertegun of Atlantic Records told an interviewer. "They'd copy our records, except that they'd use a white artist. And the white stations would play them while we couldn't get our records on. 'Sorry,' they'd say. 'It's too rough for us.' Or: 'Sorry, we don't program that kind of music.' " Similarly, Danny Kessler of Okeh records found that "the odds for a black record to crack through were slim. If the black record began to happen, the chances were that a white artist would cover — and the big stations would play the white record. . . . There was a color line, and it wasn't easy to cross."

The industry's leaders even succeeded in banning some black artists from the airwaves. In one instance, CBS television executives discontinued the popular "Rock 'n' Roll Dance Party" of Alan Freed when the cameras strayed to a shot of black Frankie Lymon of the Teenagers dancing with a white girl.

Finally, the introduction of the 45 rpm record by the major companies helped undermine the power of the independents. Leon Rene of the small Exclusive Records outlined the effects of the move: "We had things going our way until Victor introduced the seven-inch vinyl, 45 rpm record, which revolutionized the record business and made the breakable ten-inch 78 rpm obsolete overnight. . . . Competition with the majors, however, forced the independent labels to use the seven-inch 45 rpm records, and they had to reduce the price of R & B records from a dollar-five to seventy-five cents, retail. This forced many independent companies out of business."

Through all of these efforts, businessmen at the heads of the major companies succeeded in suppressing or at least curtailing the success of the independents and their black performers. The McGuire Sisters' copy of "Sincerely" sold more than six times as many records as the Moonglow original. In 1955 and 1956 the covers of such white artists as Pat Boone climbed to the top of the charts while black artists received little fame or money for their pioneering efforts.

By the early 1960s, Wynonie Harris tended bar; Amos Milburn, the Texas rhythm and blues man who recorded "Let's Rock Awhile," "Let's Have a Party," and "Rock, Rock, Rock," became a hotel clerk; and Muddy Waters and Bo Diddley were forced to tour constantly in order to make a living. "With me there had to be a copy," complained Bo Diddley twenty years later. "They wouldn't buy me, but they would buy a white copy of me. Elvis got me. I don't even like to talk about it. I was Chess Records along with Muddy Waters, Koko Taylor, Etta James, Chuck Berry, Little Walter, Howlin' Wolf. Without us there wouldn't have been no Chess Records. I went through things like, 'Oh, you got a hit record but we need to break it into the white market. We need to get some guy to cover it.' And I would say, 'What do you mean?' They would never tell me it was a racial problem." Johnny Otis put the problem succinctly: Black artists developed the music "and get ripped off and the glory and the money goes to the white artists."

THE STORY OF ARTHUR "BIG BOY" CRUDUP

The saga of Arthur "Big Boy" Crudup bears testimony to Otis's charge. Crudup, born in Forrest, Mississippi, and working as a manual laborer in the fields, logging camps, sawmills, and construction projects until he was in his thirties, headed to Chicago in 1941 and signed a contract with RCA, releasing over eighty sides between 1941 and 1956. The songs included "Mean Ole Frisco Blues," "Rock Me Mama," "She's Gone," "That's All Right Mama," and "My Baby Left Me," songs that have been subsequently done by Elvis Presley, Creedence Clearwater Revival, Elton John, Rod Stewart, Canned Heat, Johnny Winter, and many others. But in the late 1950s Crudup quit playing: "I realized I was making everybody rich, and here I was poor."

In 1968 Dick Waterman, an agent and manager for many bluesmen, fought for Crudup through the American Guild of Authors and Composers. He reached an agreement in 1970 with Hill and Range Songs, which claimed ownership of Big Boy's songs, to award the musician $60,000 in back royalties. Crudup and his four children then

Photo by George Wilkinson; used by courtesy of Delmark Records

Arthur "Big Boy" Crudup

traveled from his home in Virginia to New York City and signed the requisite papers in the Hill and Range office, a converted four-story mansion. John Clark, the Hill and Range attorney, took the papers to Julian Aberbach, head of Hill and Range, for his signature, while Waterman, Crudup, and his children "all patted each other on the back and congratulated Arthur that justice had finally been done." But, according to Waterman, "the next thing, John Clark comes back in the room, looking stunned and pale, and says that Aberbach refused to sign because he felt that the settlement gave away more than he would lose in legal action. We all waited for the punch line, for him to break out laughing and whip the check out of the folder. But it wasn't a joke. We sat around and looked at each other." Crudup, who once said "I was born poor, I live poor, and I'm going to die poor," passed away four years later, nearly destitute.

In only a few years, the direction of the 1950s had become clear. Major companies refused to allow independent labels and their black artists to enjoy the success that they deserved. As Mick Jagger of the Rolling Stones once observed: "Music is one of the things that changes society. The old idea of not letting white children listen to black music is *true,* 'cause if you want white children to remain what they are, they mustn't."

Elvis and Rockabilly

Elvis Presley — a kinetic image in white suede shoes. His black zoot-suit pants violently shook as he gyrated his hips and legs. He wore an oversized, white checkered jacket over a jet-black shirt with an up-turned collar, and *no tie*. A sneering, disdainful expression covered Presley's face, and his greased-backed hair fell over his sweat-drenched forehead. A microphone tilted at a 45-degree angle: The singer grabbed it as if he were going to wrench it from its metal base and barked, snarled, whimpered, and shouted into it. Screaming fans. Fans pulling at Elvis's loose pants, his suit, and his shirt, lusting to tear off a piece of the raw energy that burst forth. The energy of a new music that had only partly been heard before — the music of a white country past and the more wild and suggestive beat of the black man. A hybrid that would change the face of popular music. They called it rockabilly.

ROCKABILLY ROOTS

Rockabilly was conceived in the middle South, where black and white cultures stood face to face over a seemingly impassable chasm. Lower class Southern whites, who lived the life of poor white trash and knew the ways of neighboring blacks, delivered a pulsating mixture of black-inspired rhythm and blues and country and western. They were teenagers like Jerry Lee Lewis, who leapt on his piano, banged the keys with his feet, and heaved his jacket, and sometimes his shredded shirt, to the audience; the more subdued Carl Perkins, writer of "Blue Suede Shoes," "Boppin' the Blues," and many other classics; Johnny Cash, who launched his career with "The Ballad of a Teenage Queen," "Get Rhythm," and "Folsom Prison Blues"; Johnny Burnette, the co-founder of the crazed Rock and Roll Trio with brother Dorsey and Paul Burlison; the quiet, bespeckled Texan, Charles "Buddy" Holly; and, of course, Elvis Presley, the pacesetter of the new music, whose raw edge drove the crowds to a frenzied insanity. Despite the warnings of many horrified adults, these poor Southern whites spread the message of rock and roll to millions of clamoring fans and vaulted to the top of the national charts.

Most rockabillys never dreamed of such success. Presley, the king of swagger, the musical embodiment of James Dean's celluloid image, grew up in a thirty-foot-long, two-room house in the poor section of Tupelo, Mississippi. His father, Vernon, sharecropped and worked odd jobs, while his mother, Gladys, did piecework as a sewing machine operator. When Elvis was born in January 1935, one neighbor remembered that his parents "didn't have insurance and the doctor didn't believe in carrying his expectant mothers to the hospital, so Gladys stayed at home." And during Elvis's childhood in Tupelo, noted a friend, the Presleys "lost their house and moved several times. They lived in several houses this side of the highway, on Kelly Street, then on Barry. Later the house on Barry was condemned. They was real poor. They just got by." In 1948 the Presley family moved from Mississippi. As Elvis told it: "We were broke, man, broke, and we left Tupelo overnight. Dad packed all our belongings in boxes and put them on the top and in the truck of a 1939 Plymouth. We just headed to Memphis. Things had to be better."

But in Memphis the standing of the Presleys initially did not improve. Vernon worked for a tool company, as a truck driver, and finally in 1949 landed a job as a laborer at the United Paint Company. Earning less than forty dollars a week, he paid the rent on an apartment in the Lauderdale Courts, a federally funded housing project. Elvis attended nearby Humes High School, "a lower poverty-type school, one of the lowest in Memphis," according to one of Presley's classmates. After graduating from Humes in 1953, he did factory work at the Precision Tool Company and then drove a truck for the Crown Electric Company until he turned to music. Jane Richardson, one of two home service advisors working for the Memphis Housing Authority, summed up the condition of the Presleys during their first years in Memphis: "They were just poor people."

Other rockabilly stars came from similar economically depressed backgrounds. Jerry Lee Lewis, who scored hits in 1957 with "Great Balls of Fire" and "Whole Lotta Shakin' Goin' On," was born in September 1935 on a farm outside Ferriday, Louisiana. His father, the gaunt-faced Elmo, eked out a living with carpentry work and produce from the farm. Harold Jenkins, otherwise known as Conway Twitty, was the son of a riverboat captain. He grew up in Friars Point, Mississippi, a small town only forty miles from Presley's birthplace in Tupelo. Likewise, Johnny Cash was born on February 26, 1932, into a poor country family in Kingland, Arkansas. When Franklin D. Roosevelt's New Deal came to the South, the Cashes moved to Dyess, Arkansas, as

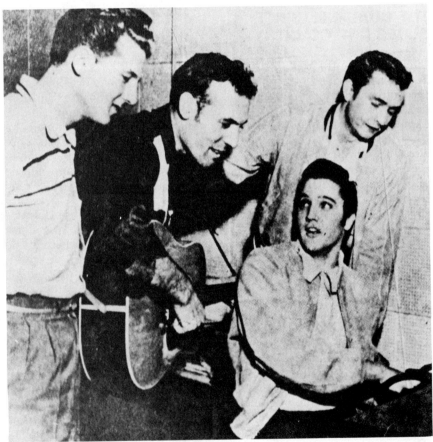

Courtesy of Sun Records

The Million Dollar Quartet of Sun Records. From left to right: Jerry Lee Lewis, Carl Perkins, Elvis Presley, and Johnny Cash

Elvis and Rockabilly **31**

part of a resettlement program for submarginal farmers. Johnny later enlisted in the army and after his discharge sold refrigerators in Memphis. The boredom of the sales job prompted him to write the classic "I Walk the Line." Carl Perkins grew up only a few miles from Johnny Cash — according to Cash, "he on the Tennessee side of the Mississippi, I on the Arkansas side. We both lived on a poor cotton farm." When he wrote "Blue Suede Shoes," Perkins said, "Me and my wife Valda were living in a government project in Jackson, Tennessee. Had had the idea in my head, seeing kids in the bandstand so proud of their new city shoes — you gotta be real poor to care about new shoes like I did — and that morning I went downstairs and wrote out the words on a potato sack — we didn't have reason to have writing paper around."

THE DUAL INFLUENCE: BLUES AND COUNTRY

These poor youths combined the twin musical influences of the rural Southern experience: the blues and country music. Elvis Presley, as did the Delmore Brothers of the 1930s and Arthur "Guitar Boogie" Smith in the 1940s, looked to both black and white music for inspiration. A member of the evangelical First Assembly of God Church in Tupelo, he "used to go to these religious singings all the time. There were these singers, perfectly fine singers, but nobody responded to them. Then there was the preachers and they cut up all over the place, jumpin' on the piano, movin' ever' which way. The audience liked 'em. I guess I learned from them."

Elvis also learned from such bluesmen of the Mississippi Delta as Booker "Bukka" White, Big Bill Broonzy, Otis Spann, B. B. King, John Lee Hooker, and Chester "Howlin' Wolf" Burnett, hearing them in the clubs along Beale Street in Memphis, one of the main thoroughfares of black culture in the South. According to blues great B. B. King, "I knew Elvis before he was popular. He used to come around and be around us a lot. There was a place we used to go and hang out on Beale Street. People had like pawn shops there and a lot of us used to hang around in certain of these places and this was where I met him."

And, of course, the Presley sound was steeped in the country and western tradition of the South — Roy Acuff, Ernest Tubb, Ted Daffan, Bob Wills, and Jimmie Rodgers. In late 1954 Elvis, then called the King of the Western Bop, played the Bel Air Club in Memphis with Bill Black, Scotty Moore, and Doug Poindexter's Starlite Wranglers. At that time, recalled Poindexter, "we were strictly a country band. Elvis worked hard at fitting in, but he sure didn't cause too many riots in them days." Presley's first recordings revealed his dual influences: a "race" number written by Arthur "Big Boy" Crudup, "That's All Right Mama," and a Bill Monroe country tune, "Blue Moon of Kentucky." As Paul Ackerman, *Billboard*'s music editor, pointed out: "Often the difference between a country side and a R & B side is merely the use of strings as against the use of horns. The Presley sound — it is pointed out — might be called R & B without horns but with strings." Presley summed it up himself: "I love the rhythm and beat of good rock and roll music and I think most people like it too. After all, it's a combination of folk or hillbilly music and Gospel singing. And both these forms of music have been popular for a long time."

The Everly Brothers — Don and Phil — also listened to the black blues played on local radio stations and the country sound strummed by their father, guitarist Ike Everly of Brownie, Kentucky. They titled their second LP *Songs Our Daddy Taught Us*. Modeling themselves after their idol, Elvis Presley, the Everlys scored hits in 1957 with "Bye,

Courtesy of Don Everly

The Everly Brothers in the studio

Elvis and Rockabilly **33**

Bye, Love" and "Wake Up Little Susie," and the next year with "All I Have to Do Is Dream," "Bird Dog," and "Devoted to You."

Bill Haley — the Midwesterner who with his group the Comets recorded the rockabilly "Crazy, Man, Crazy" in 1952, did a watered-down version of Big Joe Turner's "Shake, Rattle, and Roll" a year-and-a-half later, and in 1955 soared to the top of the pop charts with "Rock Around the Clock" — attributed his country swing style to his parents and Louis Jordan, the pioneer of the boogie woogie jump beat. "My mother was a piano teacher. My dad, who was from Kentucky, played mandolin. And I suppose that was where the country influence came from." The Comets' pianist, Milt Gabler, added, "We'd begin with Jordan's shuffle rhythm. You know, dotted eighth notes and sixteenths and we'd build on it. I'd sing Jordan riffs to the group that would be picked up by the electric guitar and tenor sax, Rudy Pompanelli. They got a sound that had the drive of [Jordan's] Tympany Five and the color of country and western. Rockabilly was what it was called back then." "We started out as a country western group, then we added a touch of rhythm and blues," Haley later told Robert Hilburn of the *Los Angeles Times*. "It wasn't something we planned, it just evolved. We got to where we weren't accepted as country western or rhythm and blues. It was hard to get bookings for a while. We were something different, something new. We didn't call it that at the time, but we were playing rock and roll." The wildman Jerry Lee Lewis, who never has minced words to make a point, underlined the unique end product of the marriage between R & B and country: "I play rock and *roll*. Don't ever call me a hillbilly. I'm a *rocker*."

Ironically, at least to self-righteous Northerners, it was Southern whites who incorporated the black-inspired R & B into their music. "The breakthrough didn't come, as you might expect, in the North," observed Atlantic Record co-founder Ahmet Ertegun. "No, it was 'prejudiced' white Southerners who began programming R & B. They began playing Fats Domino, Ivory Joe Hunter, Roy Milton, Ruth Brown, Amos Milburn because young white teenagers heard them on those top of the dial stations and began requesting them. What the hell was Elvis listening to when he was growing up?" "Despite the Ku Klux Klan and bloodshed, the Southern white is a helluva lot closer to the Negro psyche and black soul than your liberal white Northerner," added Jerry Wexler, another top executive at Atlantic.

SUN RECORDS AND THE DISCOVERY OF ELVIS

Southern rockabillys started to play their brand of raucous black and white blues at an auspicious time. Sam Phillips, the owner of the Sun Record Company in Memphis, who himself had worked in the Alabama cotton fields, "got turned on to rock and roll immediately, when it was still rhythm and blues. I always felt that rhythm and blues had a special viability." Even as a boy in the fields, Phillips seldom noticed "white people singing alot when they were chopping cotton, but the odd part about it is I never heard a black man who couldn't sing *good*. Even off key, it had a spontaneity about it that would grab my ear."

Since, in his words, "there was no place in the South they could go to record, the nearest place where they made so-called 'race' records — which was soon to be called rhythm and blues — was Chicago," from 1951 to 1954 Phillips recorded several of the best black talents in the Memphis area: Jackie Brenston, who with the Ike Turner band cut "Rocket 88," which was later copied with great success by Bill Haley and the Comets; Howlin' Wolf; Doc Ross; Joe Hill Louis, the one-man band; B. B. King; Rosco Gordon, who himself crossed the boundary separating R & B and rockabilly; and Big Walter Horton.

But the Sun waxmaker developed problems: Many of the best black performers in Memphis, such as B. B. King and Howlin' Wolf, trekked to Chicago, the rhythm and blues capital of the world, and the remaining artists only sold a limited number of discs. Faced with a cash-flow problem, Phillips confided in his secretary that "if I could find a white man who had the Negro sound and the Negro feel, I could make a billion dollars."

Elvis Presley made Sam Phillips's dream come true. In 1953 Presley swaggered into the Sun studios to record the Ink Spots' "My Happiness" as a present for his mother. On a Friday in January 1954 he returned and cut his second disc — a ballad, "Casual Love," and a country tune called "I'll Never Stand in Your Way." Marion Keisker, the secretary at the studio, taped the takes and rushed them to her boss. After a few weeks, Phillips telephoned Presley and made arrangements to cut a version of "That's All Right Mama." The Sun owner then took the record to WHBQ disc jockey Dewey Phillips for his R & B radio show, *Red Hot and Blue*. Dewey received an enthusiastic response to the Presley record and interviewed the singer. In Dewey's words, "I asked him where he went to high school and he said Humes. I wanted to get that out, because a lot of people listening thought he was colored." Within a few days over five thousand orders for the record streamed into the Sun offices, and by July 1954 the song hit the top position in the Memphis charts.

Elvis's first tour of the South was met by an uncontrolled reception. "In his first public show," Phillips remembered, "we played him at a little club up here at Summer and Medenhall. I went out there that night and introduced Elvis. Now this was kind of out in the country and way out on the highway, as they say. It was just a joint. Here is a bunch of hard-drinking people, and he ain't necessarily playing rhythm and blues, and he didn't look conventional like they did. He looked a little *greasy,* as they called it then. And the reaction was just *incredible*."

The mania continued unabated. On July 4, 1955, in DeLeon, Texas, fans shredded Presley's pink shirt — a trademark by now — and tore the shoes from his feet. One female admirer from Amarillo, Texas, got a big gash in her leg at the concert. "But who cares if it left a scar," she told a *Newsweek* reporter. "I got it trying to see Elvis and I'm proud of it. This must be what memories are made of."

Country singer Bob Luman recalled similar hysteria at Kilgore, Texas. "The cat came out in red pants and a green coat and a pink shirt and socks," he told writer Paul Hemphill, "and he had this sneer on his face and he stood behind the mike for five minutes, I'll bet, before he made a move. Then he hit his guitar a lick, and he broke two strings. So

Photo by Alfred Wertheimer, used by courtesy of RCA Records

The young Elvis Presley, 1956

there he was, these two strings dangling, and he hadn't done anything yet, and these high school girls were screaming and fainting and running up to the stage, and then he started to move his hips real slow like he had a thing for his guitar. That was Elvis Presley when he was about nineteen, playing Kilgore, Texas. He made chills run up my back."

"THE KILLER"

Sam Phillips, buoyed by his success with Presley, began to record other young Southerners who had the same gritty sound. A persistent Jerry Lee Lewis ("The Killer") joined the Sun legion in 1956. He told this story about his start there: Jack Clement, the producer at the Sun studio, "told me he didn't have time to make a tape with me, but I told him he was going to do it or I'd whip him. I had driven up to Memphis from Ferriday, Louisiana — 286 miles. I sold 39 dozen eggs to pay for the gas. I said, 'You've got the time. I'm going to play the piano and you're going to put it on tape for Sam Phillips.' He said, 'Well, if you feel that strongly about it, you must be good."

When Phillips returned from a long-deserved vacation at Daytona Beach, Clement put Lewis's "Crazy Arms" on the sound system, and the Sun owner screamed, "where the *hell* did that man come from." "He played that piano with abandon," Phillips later remembered. "A lot of people do that, but I could hear between the stuff that he played and he didn't play, that spiritual thing. Jerry is very *spiritual*. I said, 'Jack, did you get his damn phone number?' He said, 'Yeah, I know where he is.' I said, 'Well, you get him here as fast as you can.'"

In December 1956 Sun issued "Crazy Arms," which entered the lower reaches of the charts. For the next year Jerry Lee backed a few lesser known Sun acts such as Warren Smith on "Miss Froggie" and the insanely wild Billy Lee Riley and his Little Green Men — Billy Lee hanging from the waterpipes with one hand and clutching the microphone with the other during one memorable performance. Lewis helped Riley on "Flying Saucers Rock and Roll" and "Red Hot" and lured two of the Little Green Men to his own camp, drummer James Van Eaton and guitarist Roland James.

With his new band in 1957, Jerry Lee Lewis ripped through an earth-shattering version of "Whole Lotta Shakin' Goin' On" for his second Sun disc, and sold sixty thousand copies regionally soon after its release. But the record, complained Lewis, "was banned" on radio stations across the country for its sexual overtones. Phillips, however, in dire financial straits, decided to put Sun's efforts behind the single. "I knew the only hope to make Sun a successful and big company was that we take Jerry Lee Lewis and put everything behind him and use his talent to create all the other Sun personalities," remarked Judd Phillips, Sam's brother and a Sun executive at the time.

The promotion package included a spot on the popular *Steve Allen Show* — the close rival to the *Ed Sullivan Show* — which showcased

Lewis frantically banging the keys, kicking over the piano stool into the audience, and shaking his mop of curly blonde locks until he looked like Lucifer's incarnation. The teens in the audience erupted while the stagecrew peered in disbelief. After the performance, the switchboard lit up: Scandalized voices screamed their dissatisfaction and shakey-voiced teenagers called to find out more about their new idol. In an uncharacteristic understatement, Lewis related: "Then I got on the Steve Allen Show and it busted wide open." Hits followed with "Great Balls of Fire," "Breathless," and "High School Confidential."

"BLUE SUEDE SHOES"

Lewis's success was matched by a steady stream of Sun rockabilly talents, among them guitarist-songwriter Carl Lee Perkins. Born in Tiptonville, Tennessee, on April 9, 1932, Perkins and his family moved near Jackson, Mississippi, where young Carl found work at a battery factory. Eight years later, in 1953, he bought his first guitar, a $150 Les Paul, and began to perfect a unique style. Since he seldom had the cash for new strings, he once told a reporter, "I'd slide along to where I'd had to tie a knot and push up on a string 'cause I couldn't jump over the knot. Maybe if I'd been wealthy and could have bought new strings, I'd have slid down it and not developed the pushing up on the strings and I'd have sounded like everyone else."

The music Carl applied his technique to resembled that of other rockabillys. He "liked Bill Monroe's fast stuff and also the colored guys, John Lee Hooker, Muddy Waters, their electric stuff. Even back then, I liked to do Hooker's things Monroe style, blues with a country beat and my own lyrics." The result bore a striking similarity to the Presley sound. Bob Neal, then a disc jockey at Memphis radio station WMPS, recalled that he and Elvis saw Perkins perform "in the fall of 1954 and we were both struck by the sound Perkins was getting. It was very similar to Elvis's own." After hearing Presley's first Sun recording, Perkins himself felt that "it was identical to what our band was doing and I just knew that we could make it in the record business after that."

Perkins and his band, which included his brothers Clayton and Jay as well as W. S. Holland, signed with Sun in 1955 and began touring from the back of a truck with another Sun acquisition, Johnny Cash. Admission to watch the traveling show was one dollar. That year the Perkins band released three singles for Sun: "Movie Magg," backed by "Turn Around"; "Let the Jukebox Keep Playing," with the hard-bopping "Gone, Gone, Gone"; and in December 1955, Perkins's smash, "Blue Suede Shoes," which by April 1956 topped both country and western and R & B charts.

For a while it looked as if Perkins would wrestle the rockabilly crown from the still-emerging Elvis. But on March 22, 1956, tragedy

Carl Perkins

struck. On the way to New York City for appearances on the *Ed Sullivan Show* and the *Perry Como Hour,* outside of Delaware, Perkins's car crashed. Although Carl sustained only minor injuries, the accident dealt a damaging blow to the singer's career. "I was a poor farm boy, and with 'Shoes' I felt I had a chance but suddenly there I was in the hospital," he bitterly recalled. Perkins never did attain the stardom of Presley: He in fact may never have reached those heights since, as he later admitted, "Elvis was hitting them with sideburns, flashy clothes and no ring on the finger. I had three kids." Yet Perkins remained a vital force in rockabilly. Ricky Nelson, the 1960s rockabilly crooner of *Ozzie and Harriet Show* fame, "used to listen to the radio and longed to be a recording artist. I wanted to be Carl Perkins." Two years later in 1963, across the Atlantic, another youth — a Liverpudlian by the name of George Harrison — paid tribute to Perkins: He changed his first name to Carl for his stage name in emulation of his idol.

THE SUN ROCKABILLY STABLE

Besides the Big Four of Sun — Presley, Jerry Lee Lewis, Perkins, and Johnny Cash — Sam Phillips supported and nurtured a battalion of lesser-known but nonetheless hell-bent rockabillys. Billy Lee Riley was probably the most promising. The wildman Riley, a part-Indian who played guitar, harmonica, drums, and bass, formed the Little Green Men in 1955. Although he scored hits with "Flying Saucers Rock and Roll" and "Red Hot" and drove crowds to a frenzied pitch with his onstage antics, Riley never achieved major recognition. From his vantage point, he felt that his failure stemmed from the "distribution of Sun discs. They sent out a bath of discs all together and when there was a Perkins release, a Cash release and later Jerry Lee Lewis, the deejays didn't want to be bothered with the rest of the bunch. The public could only afford so many at one time anyway."

Sonny Burgess, another slightly crazed rockabilly in the Sun fold, produced raw rock but failed to garner a national audience. A farmboy from Newport, Arkansas, Burgess heard of Sun's growing reputation and traveled to Memphis in 1955. His music, best exemplified in his minor hit "Red-Headed Woman," which sold ninety thousand copies, combined a country Arkansas heritage and black rhythm and blues: "Yes, I really liked R & B, Fats Domino, Jimmy Reed, Muddy Waters," Burgess told a reporter. Burgess's gritty, R & B-inspired voice ripped a song to shreds and then hurled the remains toward the audience: It possessed the demonic quality of the true rockabilly. Authors Colin Escott and Martin Hawkins called Sonny's music "loosely organized chaos."

Ray Harris, who cut "Come On Little Mama" for Sun in 1956, had the same style. Bill Cantrell, then a Sun employee, contended that "Ray wanted to be another Elvis. He couldn't sing and he wasn't good to look at but he didn't care. Man, he was crazy. You would go to visit him and hear him practicing there on Ogden from two blocks away. He would open the door wearing nothing but his overalls and dripping with sweat. He had an old portable tape recorder and he'd go back to singing and playing and sweating. In the studio he would throw himself around with his arms like windmills. That record 'Come On Little Mama' was a triumph for the guitar man Wayne Powers and drummer Joe Riesenthal. They had to keep up with the guy." *Billboard* just referred to the single as "excitable."

Not all Sun rockabillys possessed the passion of Ray Harris. Sam Phillips tried to force some country artists into the Sun sound despite their dislike of the new music. The most notable was Roy Orbison. In March 1956 Orbison recorded "Ooby Dooby" for Sun, which sold nearby a half million copies and reached number 59 on the *Billboard* charts. The single represented the best showing of a Sun disc besides the singles of the Big Four of Sun. The serious singer, characterized by sunglasses and a high-pitched, ethereal voice, followed with "Rockhouse," but only reluctantly. Said Jack Clement: "The first artist Sam gave me to record was Roy Orbison. I recorded 'Rockhouse' with Roy and it was good but Roy was not into what the Sun studio was capable of back then." Orbison confirmed his dissatisfaction with the rockabilly trend: "I was writing more ballads then [1957], but I didn't bother to ask Sam to release them. He was the boss and there was no arguing. I made some demos of things like 'Claudette' but that was about it. I would never have made it big with Sun. They just didn't have the ways to get into the audience I wanted to go for."

Warren Smith, who gave the rights to "Rock and Roll Ruby" to Sun, similarly saw himself as more of a country artist than a rockabilly. So too with Malcolm Yelvington and his Star Rhythm Boys, who cut sides for Phillips from 1954 to 1958. Said Malcolm: "Rockabilly, I didn't care for at first but at that time it was the only thing going. Country was at an all-time low. I wanted to record like Hank Williams or Moon Mullican but Sam wanted something with a beat to it." The results, though at times half-hearted, were far from disappointing. Even rockabillys like Orbison drove the Southern teenagers wild. By late 1956, then, Sam Phillips had achieved his goal. He had groomed a stable of white country boys who sang with the feeling of black men and the intensity of whirling dervishes, driving white teenage girls over the brink of hysteria.

ROCKABILLY SWEEPS THE NATION

The major record companies soon noticed the local success of rockabilly and tried to capitalize on it. To its Coral subsidiary, Decca Records signed the Rock and Roll Trio, Johnny and Dorsey Burnette and Paul Burlison. Growing up in Memphis, the threesome met in 1953 at the Crown Electric factory, the same company for which Presley drove truck. Initially they played in a Hank Williams style. But when Burlison backed Howlin' Wolf on a radio broadcast in West Memphis, the group started to blend their country roots with the blues.

Beale Street in Memphis "was really happening in those days, and my dad and his friends would go down there a lot and listen to the blues guys," remembered Billy Burnette, the son of Dorsey, who recently revived the rockabilly tradition of his family with a top-selling album of his own. "They'd buy their clothes on Beale Street, at Lansky Brothers, where all the black people shopped. Right outside Memphis, where there was a voodoo village, all black — real mystic kind of people. People who were into music would go over there and get charms and things like that. You know, a lot of real old line Southern people called my dad and my uncle white niggers. Nobody was doing rock and roll in those days except people they called white trash. When my dad and uncle started doin' it, they were just about the first."

The pathbreaking Trio caused riots throughout the South with "The Train Kept a Rollin'," "Rock Billy Boogie," "Tear It Up," and "Rock Therapy." In one incident, reported the Evansville, Indiana, *Courier* in late 1956, "all during Burnette's performance, the crowd of about two thousand persons kept up a continuous howl that all but drowned out the singer's voice." When Johnny Burnette tried to leave the stage, hundreds of wild-eyed girls attacked him and "tore his shirt to bits for souvenirs." According to the *Courier,* "the singer, who had all but exhausted himself in the performance, was in sad shape when he reached the car. 'I shoulda laid off that last 'Hound Dog,'' he panted." In 1956 the Trio decided to quit their jobs and move to New York City with hopes of commercial success. When the young Southerners won first prize on Ted Mack's *Amateur Hour,* Decca added the group to its roster.

The same year, Decca discovered Charles "Buddy" Holly. Holly, a skinny teenager from Lubbock, Texas, who wore thick-rimmed glasses and a shy grin, had been exposed to R & B on radio and through records. But unlike Presley, who attended an evangelical church and grew up close to blacks in Mississippi and Tennessee, Holly was primarily influenced by white country music. By his sixteenth birthday, he already had "a thought about making a career out of western music if I am good enough but I will just have to wait and see how that turns out." Within two years Holly and a friend, Bob Montgomery, regularly played country music on local radio station WDAV and performed at the Big D Jamboree in Dallas. By 1957 when he formed the Crickets (Joe B. Mauldin on standup bass, drummer Jerry Allison, and, at one point, current country singer Waylon Jennings), Holly had perfected a style of rockabilly that was based on country and contained a dash of nearby Mexican sounds, a jumpy R & B rhythm, and Bob Wills-type Western Swing. Some called the music the Tex-Mex sound, which distinguished it from the more heavily R & B-influenced rockabilly of Presley and identified its geographical roots.

Holly took his distinctive sound to the small studio of producer Norman Petty, who had already recorded hits for the Rhythm Orchids — "Party Doll" and "Stickin' with You," released under the names of singer Buddy Knox and bassist Jimmy Bowen. The Crickets first hit the charts with "That'll Be the Day," the title taken from a John Wayne line in the movie "The Searchers." They followed with a series of fresh rockabilly tunes that became rock and roll classics: "Peggy Sue," "Maybe Baby," "Not Fade Away," "Rave On," "Oh Boy," and many others.

Decca included on its growing roster of artists Bill Haley and the Comets, the group that kicked off the commercial mania over rockabilly with Jimmy DeKnight's "Rock Around the Clock." First recorded in 1954, the song became the marching hymn of youth in 1956 after it resurfaced as the theme song of the film *Blackboard Jungle.* In the words of rock critic Lillian Roxon, it "was the first inkling teenagers had that they might be a force to be reckoned with, in numbers alone. If there could be one song, there could be others; there could be a whole world of songs, and then, a whole world."

Capitol Records, trying to make inroads into the new youth market, signed Gene Vincent, the Korean War veteran, who was born Gene

Craddock in the Southern navy town of Norfolk, Virginia. With his band, the Bluecaps, Vincent in 1956 released the unforgettable "Be-Bop-A-Lula." According to the singer, he wrote the classic one day when he "and Don Graves were looking at his bloody comic book. It was called Little Lulu and I said, 'Hell, man, it's bebopalulu.' And he said, 'Yeah, man, swinging,' and we wrote the song. Just like that. And some man came to hear it and he bought the song for $25. Right. Twenty-five dollars! And I recorded it and told my friends that I was going to get a Cadillac, because all rock and roll singers had Cadillacs." From 1956 to 1958, in quest of his Cadillac, Vincent cut "Dance to the Bop," "Bluejean Bop," "Race with the Devil," "She She Little Sheila," and "Crazy Legs," which described the singer's wild performances.

Liberty Records jumped into the rockabilly field with Eddie Cochran. The son of two Oklahoma City country-western fans, Eddie, unlike all other rockabillys, grew up in the Midwest, in the town of Albert Lea, Minnesota. In 1953 his family moved to Bell Gardens, California. While thumbing through the racks of a local record store, Cochran met Jerry Capehart, who would be his songwriter-collaborator throughout his career. In 1955 the duo moved to Nashville, signed with American Music, and recorded "Skinny Jim," which flopped. Trying to secure better distribution for their discs, Capehart flew to Los Angeles and convinced Si Waronker of Liberty Records to invest in the rockabilly talent of Cochran. After releasing a few unsuccessful singles, in late 1958 Cochran alternated between an Elvis-like whimper and a gravel-voiced growl in an anthem of teenage frustration, "Summertime Blues." "Well, I'm a gonna raise a fuss/ I'm a gonna raise a holler/ About workin' all summer just to try to earn a dollar," Eddie boasted to his listeners over a background of clapping hands. The singer continued: "I'm gonna take my problem to the United Nations/ Well, I called my congressman, and he said ho/ Like to help you son but you're too young to vote/ Sometimes I wonder what I'm a gonna do/ There ain't no cure for the summertime blues." Cochran's bopping call to arms struck a chord among teenagers, who were gaining increasing power by their numbers but who were still called "son" and denied the vote. The song neared the top of the charts, and another rockabilly star had been born.

THE SELLING OF ELVIS PRESLEY

RCA Victor lured to its label the performer who reached the most phenomenal heights. In 1955 the company offered Sun Records thirty-five thousand dollars for the rights to Elvis Presley's recorded material. Sam Phillips accepted the money and surrendered all of the Presley tapes that Sun had produced. In January 1956 RCA began to merchandise Elvis. They booked him for six Saturday-night appearances on the Tommy and Jimmy Dorsey *Stage Show,* a half-hour variety program hosted by the two big band leaders that preceded Jackie Gleason's *The Honeymooners*. After the Dorsey shows that included the Elvis segments received high ratings, Ed Sullivan, who earlier had condemned Presley as being "unfit for a family audience," paid the new rock star fifty thousand dollars for three appearances. Shortly thereafter, RCA released "Heartbreak Hotel." As *Billboard* observed, "Presley is riding high right now with network T.V. appearances and the disc should benefit from all the special plugging." A week later the magazine reported that sales of the single had "snowballed," and in a few more weeks it reached the top of the national charts.

Tne new sensation: ad for Elvis Presley, December 3, 1955

In the next few months Presley also hit the charts with a number of songs first recorded by black artists. He scored with singles that had been initially released by Sun and either re-released or re-recorded by RCA. They included Roy Brown's "Good Rockin' Tonight," the Sleepy John Estes and Joe Williams tune "Milkcow Blues Boogie," "Baby, Let's Play House" by Arthur Gunter, and Junior Parker's "Mystery Train." In addition, he had chartbusters with Little Richard's "Tutti Fruitti," the Drifters' "Money Honey," and "Don't Be Cruel" and "All Shook Up" by black songwriter Otis Blackwell, who had penned "Great Balls of Fire" for Jerry Lee Lewis.

The marketing acumen of Colonel Thomas Parker contributed to Presley's dazzling success. Born in 1910, Parker got his start in carnivals. Since the circus life "was a day-to-day living" (the Colonel fondly remembered that when he "found a cigar butt more than an inch long, it was a good day) Parker used his ingenuity to make money. For one of his ploys, he rented a cow pasture and during the night forced the cows to stand on the only road through the field, which also happened to be the exit from the carnival grounds. When customers reached the exit point from the carnival the next day, they could either walk through ankle-deep manure or pay the Colonel a nickel for a pony ride through it.

By 1955 Parker had abandoned the circus and applied his marketing techniques to the careers of such country singers as Roy Acuff, Minnie Pearl, Eddy Arnold, and Hank Snow. A year later the Colonel worked "in the most polished Machiavellian way" on Presley's parents to sign the rockabilly star, according to one of Elvis's neighbors. "Colonel Tom was a salesman, I'll give him that. He sure knew how to sell." Almost immediately the Colonel began to sell Elvis Presley to the media. "The Colonel doesn't sell Elvis to the public, dig?" Jon Hartmann, one of Parker's subordinates later observed. "He sells Elvis to the people who sell to the public, and those are the media people — the television and motion picture personalities, the executives and businessmen who control the networks, the important radio people. It's like an endless trip for the Colonel. Elvis, as a product, always in the state of being sold."

In mid-1956 Hank Saperstein joined Tom Parker in the media blitz. Saperstein had risen in the advertising industry through his successful marketing of Lassie, Wyatt Earp, Ding Dong School, and the Lone Ranger. Not to be outdone by his competitors, he had even stuffed plastic blowguns in cereal boxes to increase the sales of Kellogg Cornflakes. Saperstein recognized the "universality" of the Presley appeal and began to plaster Elvis's name and picture on all types of products. By 1957 Saperstein and Parker had saturated the American market.

If a loyal fan so desired, she could pull on some Elvis Presley bobbysocks, Elvis Presley shoes, skirt, blouse, and sweater, hang an Elvis Presley charm bracelet on one wrist, and with the other hand smear on her lips some Elvis Presley lipstick — either Hound Dog Orange, Heartbreak Hotel Pink, or Tutti Frutti Red. She might then put an Elvis Presley handkerchief in her Elvis Presley purse and head for school. Once she entered the classroom, she could write with her green Elvis Presley pencil, inscribed "Sincerely Yours," and sip an Elvis Presley soft drink between periods. After school she could change into Elvis Presley bermuda shorts, blue jeans, or toreador pants, write to an Elvis Presley pen pal, or play an Elvis Presley game, and finally fall asleep in her Elvis Presley pajamas on her Elvis Presley pillow. Her last waking memory of the day could be the Elvis Presley florescent portrait that hung on her wall. All told, the fan could buy seventy-eight different Elvis Presley products that grossed about $55 million by December 1957. As well as 25 percent of Elvis's performance royalties, Colonel Parker received a percentage of the manufacturer's wholesale price on each item.

REACTIONS AGAINST THE PRESLEY MANIA

Many adults reacted strongly against the Presley mania. In one review Jack Gould, the television critic for the *New York Times,* wrote "Mr. Presley has no discernable singing ability. His specialty is rhythm, songs which he renders in an undistinguished whine; his phrasing, if it can be called that, consists of the stereotyped variations that go with a beginner's aria in a bathtub. . . . His one specialty is an accented movement of the body that heretofore has been primarily identified with the repertoire of the blonde bombshells of the burlesque runway. The gyration never had anything to do with the world of popular music and still doesn't." Jack O'Brien of the New York *Journal-American* agreed that "Elvis Presley wiggled and wiggled with such abdominal gyrations that burlesque bombshell Georgia Southern really deserves equal time to reply in gyrating kind. He can't sing a lick, makes up for vocal shortcomings with the weirdest and plainly planned, suggestive animation short of an aborigine's mating dance."

Others held similar opinions. Jack Mabley of *Downbeat* magazine did not think "the fad of Elvis Presley is going to last much longer than the fad for swallowing goldfish." Similarly, Robert MacDonald, Congressional Representative from Massachusetts, told the House that he viewed "with absolute horror" performers "such as Elvis Presley, Little Richard, Dickey Doo, Conway Twitty, the Royal Teens, and all the other hundreds of musical illiterates, whose noises presently clutter up our juke boxes and our airways." *Time* called Presley a "sexibitionist," while *Look* accused him of dragging " 'big beat' music to new lows in taste." The magazine *America* pleaded with television and radio executives to "stop handling such nauseating stuff" so "all the Presleys of our land would soon be swallowed up in the oblivion they deserve." "Beware Elvis Presley," the magazine cautioned. And Broadway composer Oscar Hammerstein, analyzing "All Shook Up," astutely noted that " 'bug' and 'shook up' don't rhyme. It's sloppy writing."

Some city officials took direct action against the Presley-inspired rock music. In San Antonio, Texas, the city council banished rock and roll from swimming pool juke boxes because it apparently "attracted undesirable elements given to practicing their spastic gyrations in abbreviated bathing suits." Mayor Roland Hines of Asbury Park, New

Jersey, banned all rock concerts in city dance halls. Officials in Jersey City followed Hines's example a few days later. After teenage rioting caused three thousand dollars in damage to the San Jose auditorium, neighboring Santa Cruz barred all concerts in its civic buildings.

Others mobilized against Elvis Presley. In Nashville and St. Louis, angry parents burned effigies of Presley. In Ottawa, Canada, eight students of the Notre Dame convent were expelled for attending a local Elvis show. Yale University students handed out "I Like Ludwig [Beethoven]" buttons to counter the sale of "I Like Elvis" buttons. And a Cincinnati used-car dealer increased business with a sign that read: "We Guarantee to Break 50 Elvis Presley Records in Your Presence If You Buy One of These Cars Today."

Disc jockeys who broadcast classical and pop music also took action. In Halifax, Nova Scotia, station CJCH rigidly forbade the airplay of any Elvis discs. Nashville jockey "Great Scott" burned six hundred Presley records in a public park, and a Chicago station manager smashed Elvis 45s during a broadcast. In Wildwood, New Jersey, another disc jockey started an organization to "eliminate certain wreck and ruin artists" such as Elvis.

Even religious leaders spoke out against Presley. Reverend William Shannon commented in the *Catholic Sun* that "Presley and his voodoo of frustration and defiance have become symbols in our country, and we are sorry to come upon Ed Sullivan in the role of promoter. Your Catholic viewers, Mr. Sullivan, are angry." Although he had never seen Elvis, evangelist Billy Graham was "not so sure I'd want my children to see" him. Reverend Charles Howard Graff of St. John's Episcopal Church in Greenwich Village called Elvis a "whirling dervish of sex," and Reverend Robert Gray of the Trinity Baptist Church in Jacksonville, Florida, believed Presley had "achieved a new low in spiritual degeneracy. If he were offered salvation tonight, he would probably say, 'No thanks, I'm on the top.' " In his sermon "Hot Rods, Reefers, and Rock and Roll," Gray warned the youth in his congregation not to attend the upcoming Presley show in Jacksonville.

A few adults sided with Elvis. Alan Lomax, a collector of American folk songs who had trudged down South with his tape recorder and saved many traditional blues songs, contended that the trend toward rockabilly and Elvis was "the healthiest manifestation yet in native American music." Mae Boren Axton, the schoolteacher who wrote "Heartbreak Hotel" and mothered singer-composer Hoyt Axton, felt that "many rock and roll teenage song hops" and Presley concerts that she had attended allowed youths to release their pent-up aggression in a socially acceptable manner.

ELVIS GOES TO HOLLYWOOD

RCA Victor and Colonel Parker, however, succumbed to majority opinion and toned down Elvis's act. Presley's appearance on the *Steve Allen Show* provides an example. "We'd recognized the controversy that was building around Elvis and so we took advantage of it," remembered Allen. The host put Presley "in a tuxedo — white tie and tails — and [took] away his guitar. We thought putting Elvis in formal wardrobe to sing the song was humorous. We also asked him to stand perfectly still, and we positioned a real hound dog on a stool next to him — a dog that had been trained to do nothing but sit and look droopy." Elvis's respectable behavior on the show, in marked contrast to his earlier appearances from which he gained the title "Elvis the Pelvis," drew criticism from some of his friends. Some supporters leveled even more criticism against Elvis, when in September 1957 the rising star dumped his original band of Scotty Moore, Bill Black, and D. J. Fontana, which had pioneered the distinctive Presley sound.

Presley, however, continued to tone down his act. On subsequent records and in his thirty-one movies, starting with *Love Me Tender* and followed by such films as *G. I. Blues, Flaming Star, Wild Star, Blue Hawaii, Follow That Dream, Kid Galahad,* and *Girls! Girls! Girls!* Elvis for the most part abandoned gut-bucket rockabilly for a soothing ballad style which reinforced his image. The more moderate Presley drew even more fans and sold even more albums.

Like many other lower class youths, Elvis may have compromised his music for the wealth and fame he subsequently received. He got paid about $1 million plus a percentage of the box office receipts for most of his films. He also earned millions of dollars in royalties for the over 250 million records that he sold. In the history of recorded music, only Bing Crosby neared Elvis's mark with about 200 million records sold. Frank Sinatra, the bobby-sox sensation of the 1940s, sold only about 40 million discs. With his money, Elvis bought a fleet of Cadillacs, including one in his favorite color, pink; a forty-thousand-dollar one-story ranch house in Memphis, and then a hundred-thousand-dollar mansion, Graceland, for himself and his parents; and an airplane, a truckload of television sets, and hundreds of other gadgets.

In addition to material wealth, Presley began to receive all types of awards. In 1959 the Mississippi legislature passed a resolution that applauded Elvis as a "legend and inspiration to tens of millions of Americans" who "hence reaffirms an historic American idea that success in our nation can still be attained through individual initiative, hard work and abiding faith in one's self and his creator." A few months later, a joint session of the Tennessee legislature honored Presley.

The rock star, however, paid dearly for his fame. As his popularity increased, Elvis found it difficult to protect his privacy. "Even today [late sixties] I'd be willing to bet a thousand dollars he could draw a hundred people in five minutes anywhere he went," mused Neal Matthews, one of the Jordanaires — Elvis's backup singing group. "And he knows this. It's bound to make him unhappy. He'd like to be able to walk down the street like a normal human being. He can't be a person like anybody else." The "only time he could get out, really, was at night, or if he had the night off. He'd rent a skating rink or a movie house and rent it for the whole night and he and whoever'd be around would go to the

Elvis on stage in his 1968 comeback appearance

skating rink and skate all night until they'd just drop over. Or they'd see two, three movies after the movie theater had closed. That's the only kind of entertainment he had. He couldn't go out."

On his 1969 tour of Hawaii with Minnie Pearl, related Minnie, "there were five hundred women there and as we got out of the taxi, Elvis grabbed my arm and the women broke and mobbed us. I felt my feet going out from under me. . . . You know, everyone wants to be number one, but that one experience was enough to convince me I don't want it." And as Minnie Pearl and her husband enjoyed the Hawaiian sun, "Elvis never got out of his room except to work. They say he came down in the middle of the night to swim. He couldn't come down during the day. He had the penthouse suite on the top of that thing there and we'd get out and act crazy, having the best time in the world, and we'd look up there and Elvis would be standing at the window, looking down at us."

Eventually the isolation began to affect Presley. In 1957 he hurled an expensive guitar into the hallway of a hotel room, breaking it. He also destroyed several television sets, pool cues, juke boxes, and cars. "The temper was the hardest thing to take," one friend recalled. "One day he'd be the sweetest person in the world, the next day he'd burn holes in you with his eyes." As singer Johnny Rivers concluded, Elvis "had created his own world. He had to. There was nothing else for him to do." His retreat into himself ended in drug excess and premature death.

Elvis Presley, then, had been trapped by his own image. The

Elvis and Rockabilly   **49**

gyrating, sneering Elvis, who taunted his audiences and worked them into a fever pitch, had given way to a more haggard performer bloated by drugs and alcohol and adorned by extravagant, Liberace-type costumes, who sang sappy ballads to the well-dressed clientele of Las Vegas nightclubs. On a given night, some of the old magic snuck through the weary flesh, but most of the original vibrancy and vitality had disappeared. Elvis was transformed from an innocent country boy who belted out a new kind of music with animalistic intensity to a well-groomed, multi-million-dollar product. The change, which had begun by 1958 when Presley entered the Army, spelled the end of rockabilly rock. Soon, teenage crooners schooled by Dick Clark would vie for the mantle of the King.

Dick Clark, Philadelphia Schlock, and Payola

A group of young Elvis Presley look-alikes dominated rock music during the late 1950s and early 1960s. Helped by an expanding economy, superpromoter Dick Clark sold a toned-down, respectable rock and roll to the American public. From 1957 to 1963 his *American Bandstand* show and his other recording interests helped to create the Philadelphia sound of Fabian, Frankie Avalon, Paul Anka, and Bobby Darin. This schlock rock, as some have called it, detailed the agony and the ecstasy of teenage romance. And until the payola scandal, Bob Dylan, and the Beatles set it to rest, Philadelphia rock saturated the airwaves and captured the hearts of teens across the country.

AN ECONOMIC BOOM AND A MUSICAL BUST

The creation of Philadelphia rock took place in a prosperous economy. During the decade of the 1950s, the Gross National Product (GNP) rose from about $300 billion to over $420 billion and the average family income increased from about $5,500 to almost $7,000. In 1956 the unemployment rate stood at a little over 4 percent.

The recording industry shared in the general economic growth. By the end of the Clark era in 1963, record companies nationally sold $160 million worth of 45 rpm discs, made about $1.3 billion from television profits, and earned another $500 million yearly from the 500,000 juke boxes that played rock in bars, pool halls, and drive-in restaurants.

Sales figures were high outside the United States as well, as RCA vice-president George Marek observed in 1959: "Rock and roll is popular not only in this country but it has swept the world, the world where there are no broadcasting stations even: It is relatively popular in conservative England, in Australia, India, Germany, wherever you go." In October 1962, for example, "The Young World" by Ricky Nelson, the rockabilly-influenced singer who got his start on his parents' television show, *Ozzie and Harriet,* hit the top of the charts in Japan, and Pat Boone's "Speedy Gonzales" did the same in Israel. A Decca press release of the early 1960s summed up the state of the music business: "The recording industry, a fledgling during the heyday of vaudeville, has shown a steady, remarkable growth until today it stands as a major factor in the world's economy."

Just as the recording business started to expand, most of the rock and roll idols either withdrew from the public or fell into disrepute. In 1957 twenty-two-year-old Jerry Lee Lewis married his thirteen-year-old third cousin, Myra, who was the daughter of Lewis's bass player. It was Lewis's third marriage. Even though a relatively common practice in the rural South — "I know lots of people married to thirteen-year-olds," Lewis said at the time — the marriage caused promoters to cancel the twenty-seven shows scheduled for Lewis's 1957 tour of England. At his first appearance after the incident, the crowd greeted the rockabilly star with silence. "I sho' hope yawl ain't half as dead as you sound," Lewis shouted to the crowd. "Go home, crumb, baby snatcher," the audience yelled back. For over a decade, public censure of Jerry Lee's morals kept him from commercial success.

On January 20, 1958, the King of rock and roll, Elvis Presley, entered the army for a two-year stint and refused to sing for the army on orders from his manager, Colonel Parker. When he received a discharge Presley concentrated on motion pictures, and only in 1968 did he return to the stage.

A mere month after Elvis was inducted, rockabilly singer and songwriter Buddy Holly, the bespectacled youth from Texas who had gained acclaim in 1957 with "Peggy Sue," died in a plane crash near Fargo, North Dakota, in the midst of a tour. J. P. Richardson, the disc jockey known as the Big Bopper, who in 1958 hit the charts with "Chantilly Lace," and the nineteen-year-old sensation Richie Valens (a.k.a. Richard Valenzuela), who had just scored hits with "Come On, Let's Go" and "Donna" were killed in the same accident.

An automobile accident robbed rock and roll of two other talents. On April 17, 1960, after a successful tour of England, Eddie Cochran, Gene

Vincent, and Sharon Sheely, Cochran's girlfriend, who subsequently wrote many of Ricky Nelson's hits, drove to the airport in a chauffeured limousine. En route, near Chippenham, Wiltshire, a tire blew out, the driver lost control, and the car smashed into a lamppost. Within hours Cochran died of multiple head injuries at Bath Hospital. Sheely and Vincent survived, but the accident set Vincent's career back months.

About the same time, two of the pioneers of rock and roll left the arena. In 1959 the flamboyant Little Richard abandoned his jeweled bracelets and wild parties for the ministry of the Seventh Day Adventist Church. Richard had constantly threatened to quit rock. Chuck Conners, the drummer in Little Richard's band, remembered that Richard "had been talking about giving up rock 'n' roll and devoting his life to God for a long time." Then, on his way to Australia, Little Richard looked out the window of his plane and the engines seemed to burst into flames, only squelched by the saving efforts of yellow-colored angels. A few days later, in Sydney on the fifth date of the two-week tour, Richard walked away from rock and roll in the middle of a show and in front of forty thousand fans. As he told it, "that night Russia sent off the very first *Sputnik*. It looked as though the big ball of fire came directly over the stadium about two or three hundred feet above our heads. It shook my mind. It really shook my mind. I got up from the piano and said, 'This is it. I am through. I am leaving show business to go back to God.' " True to his word, Richard deserted his fans for Jehovah. Said the singer: "If you want to live for the Lord, you can't rock and roll too. God doesn't like it." Not until late 1962 during a tour of England did Little Richard again raise the standard of rock.

Shortly after Little Richard left his fans, Chuck Berry was forced from the rock scene by a ruling from a federal court. A fourteen-year-old hatcheck girl accused the rocker of transporting her from New Mexico to St. Louis for immoral purposes. Testimony at the trial, which dragged on for two years, revealed that the girl had been a prostitute when Berry first met her, and that she had come willingly to St. Louis. A judge initially found Berry guilty, but a retrial was scheduled because the magistrate referred to the performer as "this Negro." Nevertheless, the jury in a second trial convicted Berry of a violation of the Mann Act and sentenced him to four years in the Federal Penitentiary at Terre Haute, Indiana. Teenagers soon chanted: "Elvis in the Army, Buddy and Eddie dead, Little Richard in the ministry, and Berry nabbed by the feds."

DICK CLARK AND AMERICAN BANDSTAND

Dick Clark, a marketing genius, tried to create new stars for the chanting rock fanatics. Born in rural New York in 1930, Richard Augustus Clark II attended Syracuse University and studied advertising and radio, getting, in his words, a "sound education in business administration." In 1951 he landed a part-time job as an announcer for station WOLF, and then worked for his father, who was the station manager of WRUN in

Utica. A short while later, Clark decided to take a job at WFIL in Philadelphia, first announcing a radio show of popular and classical music. He later wrote, "I was a great pitchman. I sold pots and pans, vacuum cleaners, diamond rings, Mrs. Smith pies, the works. Eventually I landed the Schaefer Beer account. I did one hell of a beer spot."

In July 1956 Clark moved to WFIL's television station and hosted the Philadelphia *Bandstand* program. Started in October 1952 by disc jockey Bob Horn, the show played records of popular hits to the dancing of local high school students. After adverse publicity over two drunken-driving citations forced Horn off the air, the twenty-four-year-old Clark took over the master of ceremony duties on *Bandstand*.

Dick Clark initially knew little about the rock and roll music that the program highlighted. During his first *Bandstand* appearance as a regular, Clark remembered, he arrived on the "set at two that afternoon with only a foggy notion of what the kids, music, and show were really about." "I don't understand this music," he confessed to record promoter Red Schwartz.

The new moderator of *Bandstand* cared more about the commercial possibilities of the show than the music. "The more I heard the music the more I enjoyed it; the more I enjoyed it, the more I understood the kids," he later related. "I knew that if I could tune into them and keep myself on the show, I could make a great deal of money." Clark — voted by his high school classmates to be the "Man Most Likely to Sell the Brooklyn Bridge" — felt that behind his "bland twenty-nine-year-old face lay the heart of a cunning capitalist." He only wanted to "defend my right and your right to go to a church of our choice, or to buy the record of our choice."

Clark's promotional efforts made the local telecast into a national success. On August 5, 1957, the ABC network televised *American Bandstand* on sixty-seven stations coast to coast to over 20 million viewers. To get sponsors for the show, the announcer "traveled the advertising agency circuit on Madison Avenue" and eventually snagged the lucrative Beechnut Spearmint Gum account. After his achievement, *Advertising Age* predicted that Dick Clark "may replace Arthur Godfrey as the number-one personal salesman."

Besides *American Bandstand,* Clark hosted in 1958 the *Dick Clark Saturday Night Show* — a concert-format program broadcast live from New York City. A year later he put together for television *Dick Clark's Caravan of Stars.* In the announcer's words "it quickly turned into a huge business that has grossed upwards of $5 million a year." He earned another fifty thousand dollars a year from spinning discs at record hops, forming his first corporation — Click Corporation — to channel the profits. He slowly built up interest in such record companies as Chancellor, which headlined Frankie Avalon; Cameo-Parkway, which recorded Bobby Rydell, Charlie Gracie, the Rays, and John Zacherle; Swan Records, whose playlist included songs by Top Ten stars Freddy Cannon and Billie and Lillie; Jamie Records; Chips Record Distributing Corporation;

Courtesy of Dick Clark Television Productions

Dick Clark: the marketing genius behind the Philadelphia Sound

Globe Records; and Hunt Records. He also owned the musical copyrights to over 160 songs — including "At the Hop," "Party Time," "January Music," and "Sixteen Candles" — and controlled the Mallard Pressing Corporation. All told, Dick Clark held at least some share in thirty-three corporations and earned about $576,000 between 1957 and 1969 from these varied off-the-screen sources.

CLARK'S CREATIONS:
INSTANT STARS AND DANCE CRAZES

The announcer used his wealth and influence to create such stars as Fabian. One day in 1957 a South Philadelphia policeman, Dominick Forte, suffered a heart attack on the street. Bob Marcucci, the manager of

Frankie Avalon, offered help and then noticed Forte's fourteen-year-old son, Fabian. Impressed with Fabian's resemblance to Elvis Presley, the manager gave the youth voice and etiquette lessons for two years and then tried to sell his new commodity by buying full-page ads in the trade papers of the music industry. In 1959 Fabian recorded "Turn Me Loose" and "Tiger" on Dick Clark's Chancellor Records. Through Clark's unceasing promotion, the singer sold almost a million copies of the disc. The host of *American Bandstand* gave his support to Fabian in spite of his own opinion that the singer "got screams though he couldn't sing a note."

Clark also molded Ernest Evans, who became known as Chubby Checker, into a star. In the summer of 1960 Clark noticed a black couple on *American Bandstand* "doing a dance that consisted of revolving their hips in quick, half-circle jerks, so their pelvic regions were heaving in time to the music." "For God's sake, keep the cameras off that couple. . . . It looked like something a bellydancer did to climax her performance," Clark screamed to his producer, Tony Mammarella. But the promoter soon realized the commercial potential of the dance and suggested that Cameo Records, a company owned partially by Clark, cover Hank Ballard's 1959 "The Twist." For a singer the company chose Chubby Checker, a chicken plucker at a poultry shop who had attended high school with Fabian and Frankie Avalon. In 1960 *American Bandstand* popularized Checker's "The Twist" until it hit the top of the charts and earned the butcher's helper $822,459 from 1960 to 1962. A new dance craze, started on the program, accompanied the song. To do the dance, instructed critic Lillian Roxon, "you put one foot out and pretend you're stubbing out a cigarette butt on the floor with the big toe. At the same time, you move your hands and body as though you're drying every inch of your back with an invisible towel. That's the twist." The twist craze reached international proportions and spawned a series of records: "The Twist" by Ray Anthony and the Bookends, the Isley Brothers' "Twist and Shout," Ray Henry's "Twist Polka," "Twist with Bobby Darin," Sam Cooke's "Twistin' the Night Away," "Twist with the Ventures," "Twistin' with Duane Eddy," and many others.

Dick Clark marketed other dances and their theme songs on his television show. "Many of these dances," admitted the announcer, "came out of Philadelphia and were associated with songs done by artists on Cameo Records": Bobby Rydell's "The Fish"; the Dovells' "The Bristol Stomp"; Dee Dee Sharp and the "Mashed Potato"; and Chubby Checker with "Pony Time," "Limbo Rock," "Popeye," "The Hitchhiker," and "Slow Twistin'." The dance steps may have reflected the "loneliness and alienation" of "today's youngsters," as David Martin of the University of Southern California argued in his study of rock. Dancer-choreographer Agnes de Mille likewise observed that the dances involved "not a group of couples but a crowd of individuals. . . . These dances are the expressions of total, persisting loneliness and desperation. They are dances of fear." But for Dick Clark, the dance crazes proved to be one more moneymaker.

A RESPECTABLE ROCK AND ROLL

Despite the complaints voiced by some adults, Clark's *American Bandstand* brought a respectability to rock and roll. The promoter featured young, clean-cut singers who crooned about teenage love and contrasted to the James Dean-like hood image of the early Elvis Presley. In 1958 a sheepish fourteen-year-old Paul Anka scored a hit with the ballad "Diana" and later with "Put Your Head on My Shoulder," the melodramatic "You Are My Destiny," "(I'm Just a) Lonely Boy," and "Puppy Love." The same year, the well-groomed Bobby Darin, a close friend of Clark, recorded "Splish, Splash," the first hit by a white artist for Atlantic Records. He followed with "Mack the Knife" and "Dream Lover." In 1959 Bobby Rydell came out with "The Wild One" and "Volare." Teen Freddie Canon hit with "Way Down Yonder in New Orleans," and seventeen-year-old Frankie Avalon did the same with "Venus" and "Why." When he recorded "Venus," Avalon later reported, "Dick got behind it and it sold a million and a half copies. He's the greatest." All of these singers, as well as James Darren, the Dovells, and the Orlons, came from Clark's Philadelphia.

Because most of these performers had not yet reached their twenties, they sang of subjects close to teenage hearts. Dion and the Belmonts sang of young romance in "Teenager in Love," "Teen Angel," "Lonely Teenager," and "Runaround Sue." Neil Sedaka, a classically trained pianist and songwriter who began to record his own material in 1959, turned his attention to the same preoccupation with teenage love in "Oh Carol," "Happy Birthday Sweet Sixteen," and "Breaking Up Is Hard to Do." These songs, and others like them, gave the rock of this period a wholesome image.

The *American Bandstand* show did the same. Clark insisted upon a dress code, forcing boys to "wear a jacket and tie, or a sweater and tie. Nobody dressed that way in real life, but it made the show acceptable to adults who were frightened by the teenage world and their music. Girls couldn't wear slacks, tight sweaters, shorts, or low-necked gowns — they had to wear the kind of dresses or sweaters and skirts they wore in school. No tight toreadors or upturned collars." To further purge sexuality from the airwaves, the announcer refused to "say 'going steady' " and banned the Alligator and Dog dances "as too sexy." "We just didn't deal with sex," Clark later wrote. As rock writer Arnold Shaw concluded, "Clark was, in fact, the great tranquilizer of the era, reassuring parents by his suave manners that rock and roll was not bad and transforming the youngsters on his show into sunshine biscuits."

One of Clark's books on teenage etiquette, *To Goof or Not To Goof*, exemplified his moderation of teenage rebellion. The dust jacket read: "How to have morals and manners and still have fun." The contents dealt with such burning questions "to successful teen-aging" as "where do your elbows go when you're not eating?" "How long should it take to say good night to a girl? To her father?" "Do nice girls call up boys?" and "How far is friendly?" The text could have been written by Emily Post.

THE PAYOLA SCANDAL

Yet, in 1960 Clark fell victim to a campaign against rock music: the payola investigation. Pay-for-play dated to the vaudeville era. "It was an era of outright payola," wrote Abel Green, editor of *Variety*. "From the opening acrobatic act, which plugged *Japanese Sandman, Dardanella* or some other instrumental while making with the hand-to-hand gymnastics, through the rest of the bill, there was little that the then powerful Vaudeville Managers Protective Association and the Music Publishers Protective Associate could do to kayo it." "Historically, payola is an outgrowth of a music business tradition — song plugging," agreed Paul Ackerman, the music editor of *Billboard*.

The payola investigations of the 1950s began with fraud on television. In November 1959 Charles Lincoln Van Doren admitted before the House Special Committee on Legislative Oversight that he had been given answers in advance as a contestant on NBC's "Twenty-One" quiz show. "I would give almost anything I have to reverse the course of my life in the last three years," he told the committee. Reeling from the revelation, the networks discontinued many game programs: NBC cancelled "Tic Tac Dough" and the "Price Is Right"; CBS eliminated all quiz shows from its schedule and fired the president of the network, who had been closely associated with "Quiz Kids," "Stop the Music," and "The $64,000 Question."

The scandal spread to the music industry. First, publishers, who had played their songs on the game shows, became implicated. Then disc jockeys, who had taken money and gifts for spinning certain records, came under scrutiny. In Detroit, station WJBK fired Tom Clay after he admitted to taking $6,000 in a year and a half. After defending payola "as part of American business," WJBK jockey Jack LeGoff lost his job. Don McLeod of the same station was fired two days later. In Boston, three top disc jockeys on WILD — Stan Richards, Bill Marlowe, and Mike Eliot — found themselves unemployed. And in New York, WABC dismissed premier rock announcer Alan Freed when he admitted that he had taken $30,650 from six record companies.

Other announcers confessed to similar misdeeds. Boston jockey Norm Prescott told the House committee that "bribery, payola, has become the prime function of this business to get the record on the air at any cost," and that he had taken almost $10,000 from various record distributors. Another Boston announcer, WBZ's Dave Maynard, admitted that a record distributor had helped pay for his 1957 Mercury station wagon and his 1959 Buick, and had given him $6,817 in cash. Alan Dary, also of WBZ, received cash, a hi-fi, liquor, and carpeting for his master bedroom.

Dick Clark's interlocking interests also became apparent. As Representative John Burnett of Michigan put it: "I think it is pretty convincing that Clark was involved with payola as all other disc jockeys, but on a much larger scale." Congressman Peter Mack of Illinois called him "the top dog in the payola field" and Representative John Moss of

California began to refer to the investigations as "Clarkola." By the end of 1959 the extent of payola in radio and television had become clear: Investigators announced that 207 disc jockeys in forty-two states had taken over $263,000 in payola. President Eisenhower instructed the committee, headed by Oren Harris of Arkansas, to clean up "this whole mess."

Even though disc jockeys who played all types of music took payola, the conservative House of Representatives singled out the jockeys who programmed rock and roll. "Suppose John Smith owns a record company and then buys a broadcast station," suggested the counsel for the committee. "Suppose he dumps its personnel and its good music format to put his own label generally only rock and roll. . . . Now, that's not in the public interest." Without payola, "a lot of this so-called junk music, rock 'n' roll stuff, which appeals to the teenagers would not be played," stressed Congressman John Bennett. "The good music did not require the support, the good music did not require the payment of payola," added Representative John Moss. Such "trash" as rock music had been "pushed" on unsuspecting teens. As rock historian Carl Belz concluded, "the payola hearings would never have taken place if rock had been aesthetically pleasing to the popular music audience. . . . The impetus behind the hearings was undeniably related to an assumption that rock was 'bad music,' that it encouraged juvenile delinquency and that it could only have been forced on the public by illegal business activities."

The battle between ASCAP and BMI, two music licensing concerns, added fuel to the anti-rock hearings. Losing money to rock performers, who wrote their own material, the professional songwriters of ASCAP used the payola investigations as a forum to lash out bitterly against BMI, the licensing agent for R & B and country music, and subsequently for rock and roll songs. The songwriters hired Vance Packard, author of the *Hidden Persuaders,* who tried to demonstrate "that the rock and roll, hillbilly, and Latin American movements were largely engineered, manipulated for the interests of BMI, and that would be the point, that the public was manipulated into liking rock and roll." Rock music, Packard continued, "might be best summed up as monotony tinged with hysteria," which could not be sold to the discerning public without payola. "What do you think is going to happen to rock and roll songs?" asked ASCAP supporter and member Oscar Hammerstein. "There seems to be something funny to me that these songs have been so popular, so much more popular than any other new songs that have been produced, and yet don't live. They die as soon as the plug stops." Such arguments confirmed the fears of most members on the investigating committee, tarnishing the image of even the tone-down rock and roll promoted by Dick Clark.

The payola scandal, coupled with the rise of Bob Dylan and the Beatles, contributed to the decline of Philadelphia rock. In the early 1960s, a social protest movement popularized by Dylan challenged the saccharine songs about teenage love, and the British invasion of

America, spearheaded by the Beatles and the Rolling Stones, posed another threat. When "the Beatles came along," Paul Anka for one "became aware of what limited airplay can do to you, regardless of how good your records and songs are. . . . The British groups grabbed so much airplay we just couldn't break through. I suffered like most Americans that came up with the Presley wave." By 1964 the heyday of Dick Clark had come to a close.

4

Bob Dylan
and the New Frontier

A coffeehouse in Greenwich Village, New York City. Early on a Saturday night in 1962, a twenty-one-year-old singer walked through the door of the well-lit club carrying a guitar case. He was dressed casually: well-worn brown shoes, grey corduroy pants, and a black wool jacket, which covered a plain black T-shirt. A jungle of rumpled hair crowned his head. His lips pressed tightly together and turned up slightly as if he were sneering at the world. He glanced at the tables of patrons, who seemed to be arguing feverishly about some philosophical topic. If anything, the singer looked *serious*.

The deep-set eyes of the young singer also betrayed a nervousness. In fact, earlier he had been so nervous that a friend had filled him with four jiggers of Jim Beam bourbon to give him courage. As the singer slowly moved through the crowd, few seemed to notice. He mounted the stage, opened his case and took out an old, nicked-up six-string acoustic guitar, which he treated like an old friend. Then, he affixed a wire holder around his neck and pushed a harmonica into place. As he sat alone on stage, motionless, a hush descended upon the coffeehouse, which some called a baskethouse because singers passed baskets around after the performance, hoping for spare nickels and dimes. The audience, almost completely white middle-class college students, many of them coming from nearby New York University, politely applauded the singer. For a moment the scene appeared to be very clean-cut and wholesome: boys with closely cropped hair, white jeans, hush puppy shoes, and cardigans; and a few girls dressed in long skirts and low-heeled shoes, and favored with long, well-kempt tresses and rosy cheeks. A picture drawn by Eisenhower gentility and McCarthyite repression. But when the singer began to strum a chord, a flurry of words urgently poured from his mouth: "How many years can a mountain exist before it is washed to the sea?/ Yes 'n' how many years can some people exist before they're allowed to be free?/ Yes 'n' how many times can a man turn his head pretending he just doesn't see?/ The answer my friend is blowin' in the wind, the answer is blowin' in the wind." The singer was young Bob Dylan, who had just recently arrived in New York, and he sang of social protest.

Many youths in the early 1960s raptly listened to Bob Dylan deliver his hymns of social change. As civil rights marchers walked to Selma and as President John F. Kennedy announced plans for a New Frontier, Dylan assaulted American corporate society, racism, and the hypocrisy of the ruling elite with his guitar. His warnings about the evils of modern society, however, were shortlived. When he abandoned the acoustic for the electric guitar, Dylan forsook social protest for songs that delved deeply into his personal problems. By 1964 the "me generation" in America had slowly started to take root and folksongs of protest had become a cult among the radical left.

THE NEW FRONTIER AND CIVIL RIGHTS

From 1962 to 1964, however, Dylan and his compatriots pointed to the inequalities of American life as the source of their alienation. Many Americans suffered the consequences of a depressed economy: In 1960 the unemployment rate stood at about 5 percent. A year later over 8 percent of the labor force, or 5.5 million people, were unemployed.

Yet many looked toward a brighter future. In his inaugural speech of 1960, President John Kennedy — a young, energetic advocate of expansionist Keynesian economics — assured the nation that the United States was standing "on the edge of a New Frontier . . . a frontier of unknown opportunities and perils — a frontier of unfulfilled hopes and threats." The New Frontier, Kennedy ended, "is not a set of promises — it is a set of challenges. It sums up, not what I intend to offer the American people, but what I intend to ask of them." When the United States Steel Company raised their prices after the steelworkers' union had accepted a noninflationary contract, Kennedy forced the company to retract its price hike. His subsequent criticism of big business — "My father always told me that all businessmen were sons-of-bitches, but I never believed it till now" — further endeared him to the American middle class.

The growing civil rights movement offered blacks and sensitive whites hope for future equality among the races. On February 1, 1960, four black students from the Agricultural and Technical College in Greensboro, North Carolina, entered a variety store, made several purchases, and then sat down at the lunch counter, ordering coffee. Although the clerk refused to serve them and told them to leave, the students remained at the counter until the store closed. This method of passive resistance—the sit-in—spread to other cities and resulted in the closing of segregated libraries, beaches, and hotels. On October 19, 1960, for example, a group of blacks marched into the Magnolia Room of Rich's Department Store in Atlanta and refused to leave. Leader Martin Luther King, Jr., was sentenced to four months of hard labor in the Reidsville State Prison for his part in the incident. But as some blacks wrote in the Atlanta *Constitution:* "We do not intend to wait placidly for those rights which are already legally and morally ours to be meted out to us one at a time."

The demonstrations continued. In May 1961 the Congress of Racial Equality, an interracial direct action group founded in 1942, sent "freedom riders" into the South to test segregation laws. In Anniston and Birmingham, Alabama, white racists attacked and brutalized them. Other civil rights groups — the Student Nonviolent Coordinating Committee (SNCC), the Southern Christian Leadership Conference (SCLC), and the Nashville Student Movement — joined the freedom riders and sent a thousand marchers toward Jackson, Mississippi. Over three hundred of the riders, including fifteen priests, were arrested.

On April 3, 1963, protesters led by Martin Luther King, Jr., marched on Birmingham for fair employment and desegregation. Authorities arrested King and 2,500 marchers. When met with renewed protest on May 3, police used dogs, cattle prods, and fire hoses to disperse the protesters. Such brutal tactics sparked marches in forty-three other cities. More demonstrations exploded across the country after the murder in June 1963 of Medgar Evers, the head of the Mississippi NAACP, who was shot in the back outside his home. And on August 28, 1963, over two hundred thousand civil rights adherents, including A. Phillip Randolph, Martin Luther King, Jr., labor leader Walter Reuther, and Roy Wilkens, marched on Washington "for jobs and freedom."

The government slowly responded to the demands for equal rights. The Civil Rights Act of 1960 provided that voting records be preserved for twenty-two months following an election to avoid racist-inspired voting fraud. In October 1962 President Kennedy sent federal troops into Oxford, Mississippi, to protect James Meredith, a black student who had enrolled in the University of Mississippi. A few months later federal officials forced Alabama governor George Wallace to desist in his attempt to personally block the admission of two black students to the state university. In a televised broadcast after the Wallace incident, Kennedy told the nation that the civil rights question was "a moral issue . . . as old as the Scriptures and . . . as clear as the American Constitution." He committed his administration to the proposition "that race has no place in

American life or law." To prove his point, Kennedy selected Robert Weaver to head the Department of Housing and Urban Development — the first appointment of a black to a cabinet position.

THE SURF MANIA

Ironically, amid the fervor of the New Frontier and the furor surrounding civil rights protests, fun-loving surf music saturated the airwaves. In mid-1961 the Beach Boys — leader Brian Wilson, his brothers Carl and Dennis, cousin Mike Love, and Al Jardine, a college friend of Brian — burst forth from Hawthorne, California, with "Surfin' " to kick off the craze. They epitomized clean-cut, middle-class America: Dressed in matching outfits of white slacks and striped sports shirts, the blonde, blue-eyed Beach Boys glorified the mythical dream state of California, where teens enjoyed the endless summer of surfing and hot rods and where there "were two girls to every boy." The band, "the number 1 surfin' group in the country" according to their record label, Capitol, hoped that all youths across the nation could experience the sun and fun of the California Camelot. In "Surfin' U.S.A.," a song patterned almost note for note after Chuck Berry's "Sweet Little Sixteen," the Beach Boys wistfully dreamt about every teen having the opportunity to ride the waves like the blue-eyed, blonde surfriders of California. In "California Girls" they wished all females "could be California girls. The West Coast has the sunshine and the girls all get so tanned/ I dig a French bikini on the Wild Island Gulf by a palm tree in the sand." From 1961 to 1965 the Beach Boys followed with other harmonies that extolled the virtues of the beaches and hot rods in their California fantasyland: "Surfin' Safari," "Little Deuce Coupe," "Surfer Girl," "Fun, Fun, Fun," and the "Noble Surfer." At a time when the bodies of civil rights workers were found mutilated under ten feet of dirt, Brian Wilson felt that "you can always write about social causes, but who gives a damn. I like to write about something these kids feel is their whole world."

Jan and Dean — Jan Berry and Dean Torrance — exhibited a similar preoccupation with fast cars and the ocean and vied with the Beach Boys for the surf crown. Meeting at University High School in Los Angeles, where they had football lockers next to one another, the duo toyed with music until 1961, when they signed with Liberty Records. Jan and Dean, both friends of Brian Wilson, jumped on the cresting surfing craze with "Surf City." According to David Leaf, a biographer of the Beach Boys, "there's a story of Brian Wilson playing Berry and Torrance 'Surfin' U.S.A.' on the piano, with the duo evincing a strong desire to record it. 'No, that one was for the Beach Boys,' quoth Brian. 'You can have this one,' whereupon he played 'Surf City.' Jan and Dean grabbed it and ran all the way to number one. 'Surf City' more than any other single Beach Boys' song epitomized the teenage nirvana aspect of the California mythology. It also set Jan and Dean up for a four-year chart run." Brian Wilson subsequently co-wrote other Jan and Dean hits such

The Beach Boys: kings of the wild surf

as "Drag City," "New Girl in School," and "Ride the Wild Surf." Jan and Dean added "Dead Man's Curve," "Little Old Lady from Pasadena," and "Surfin' Hearse" to their list of accomplishments. As with the Beach Boys, the blonde-haired team created a dreamlike world of unending pleasure through a snappy beat and vocal melodies. Said Dean: "We sang about California and being young. . . . Most of all we had one thing in common: harmony. We liked melody. Lyrics don't mean shit. If melody is there you can sing about a hockey puck."

Once the surf mania hit its peak in 1963, other performers copied the California sound. The surfing fanatic could buy *Surfin' with Bo Diddley*, (which actually contained no appearance at all by Diddley), *Surfin' with the Astronauts, Surfin' with the Challengers, Surfin' Bongos, Surfin' with the Shadows,* the Marketts' *Surfer's Stomp, Surfbeat* by the Surfriders, and *Surf Mania* by the Surf Teens, while a young drag racer had a choice of such titles as *Hot Rod Alley* by Jerry and the Stokers, the Hot Rodders' *Big Hot Rod* or, among many others, *Hot Rod Hootenanny* and *Rods and Ratfinks* by Mr. Gasser and the Weirdos. In 1963 many rock bands wrote about surf and hot rods, ignoring the American black, who had started rock and roll and now desperately struggled for equality. Only singers such as Bob Dylan, with a special brand of protest music, championed the struggling American black.

SONGS OF PROTEST

The foundation for the protest song of the sixties was laid at the turn of the century by the IWW. The International Workers of the World (IWW), popularly known as the Wobblies, first penned protest songs in the United States as part of their drive to achieve equality for American workers. While they marched in demonstrations, the radical unionists sang from the *Little Red Songbook,* first published in 1909 at Spokane, Washington. Organizers Ralph Chaplin and the legendary Joe Hill, a Swedish immigrant who was later executed in Utah for his political beliefs, compiled the songbook. Chaplin's "Solidarity Forever," a protest set to the music of the "Battle Hymn of the Republic," emerged as the Wobbly anthem:

> "They have taken untold millions that they never
>   toiled to earn
> But without our brain and muscle not a single
>   wheel can turn
> We can break their haughty power; gain our
>   freedom when we learn
> That the Union makes us strong
>   Solidarity Forever!"

Woody Guthrie continued the legacy of the protest song after federal and state governments raided and closed IWW offices during the Red Scare that followed World War I. Born in July 1912 to a poor family in Okemah, Oklahoma, Woodrow Wilson Guthrie drifted through the Southwest during his teens. In 1937 he landed a job on the Los Angeles radio station KFVD, where he was always reading radical papers over his program and taking sides with the workers. Within two more years he began writing a daily column for the Communist *People's Daily World* and the *Daily Worker.*

After World War II Guthrie packed his bags and moved to New York City, where he joined the People's Song Group and composed such paeans to the nation's workers as "This Land Is Your Land." "I don't sing any songs about the nine divorces of some millionaire playgal or the ten wives of some screwball," he later explained. "I've just not got the time to sing those kinds of songs and I wouldn't sing them if they paid me ten thousand dollars a week. I sing the songs of the people that do all of the little jobs and the mean and dirty hard work in the world and of their wants and their hopes and their plans for a decent life." The motto emblazoned on Guthrie's guitar summed up his message: "This Machine Kills Fascists."

The Guthrie-type protest song, falling into disrepute during the McCarthy hearings of the 1950s, reemerged in the early 1960s. During that decade the number of college students increased from 3.8 million to 8.5 million. Unlike the more passive collegiates of the Eisenhower era, many of these students took a militant stance. The Students for a Democratic Society (SDS), organized in 1962, declared that

> Loneliness, estrangement, isolation describe the vast distance between man and man today. . . . We would replace the power rooted in possession, privilege, or circumstance by power and uniqueness rooted in love, reflectiveness, reason and creativity. As a social system we seek the establishment of a democracy of individual participation, governed by two central aims: That the individual share in these social decisions determining the quality and direction of his life; and that society be organized to encourage independence in men and provide the media for their common participation.

Similarly, in 1964 at the University of California, Berkeley, students demonstrated as part of the Free Speech Movement, a protest organized to secure the right of political debate at the University and headed by Jack Weinberg and Mario Savio.

Militant students, not satisfied with surf music or hot rod rock, looked for and supported the more cerebral music of protest. As *Newsweek* observed in 1961, "basically the schools and the students that support causes support folk music. Find a campus that breeds freedom riders, anti-Birch demonstrators, and anti-bomb societies, and you'll find a folk group. The connection is not fortuitous." Writer Jerome Rodnitzky, author of *Minstrels of the Dawn,* likewise believed that "the most important factor behind the rise of the protest singer was the general activist climate that permeated collegiate culture in the 1960s."

BOB DYLAN: A SYMBOL OF PROTEST

Collegiate support of folk music led to the mercurial rise of Bob Dylan. Born on May 24, 1941, to the owner of a hardware store in Hibbing, Minnesota, Robert Allen Zimmerman grew up near the Mesabi copper range. Being Jewish in an area that, in his words, "had a certain prejudice against Jews," Dylan felt alienated from his classmates. As an old girlfriend of Dylan's, Echo Star Helstrom, later confided: "The other kids, they wanted to throw stones at anybody different. And Bob was different. He felt he didn't fit in, not in Hibbing." "I see things that other people don't see," Dylan told a reporter from the *Saturday Evening Post*. "I feel things that other people don't feel. It's terrible. They laugh. I felt like that my whole life. . . . I don't even know if I'm normal."

To cope with his feeling of rejection, Dylan turned to performing. In Hibbing, one classmate observed that "he was starting to really dig being a performer. Being up there on stage and have the kids scream over him. . . . I got a strong feeling that he badly wanted the other kids to dig it, to approve of it." The singer's insecurities even surfaced on stage. During his early days on the Greenwich Village scene, recalled an observer, Dylan "was afraid of the audience. Suddenly, at the last minute before he was to go on he would say, 'I don't want to do this. Let's go home.' I'd tell him, 'Bob, you've got to go on,' and he'd say, 'No, I'll do it next Monday.' . . . You had to build up his ego a great deal, pamper him, give him a few drinks."

The music Bob Dylan so hesitantly sang came from various sources. In the eighth grade he began listening to Hank Williams. A few years later he tuned into Gatesmouth Page, a disc jockey from Little Rock, Arkansas, who played Muddy Waters, Howlin' Wolf, B. B. King, and Jimmy Reed. When *Rock Around the Clock* and *Blackboard Jungle* showed in Hibbing, Dylan shouted to a friend outside the theater: "Hey, that's our music! That's written for us." Little Richard and then Elvis Presley became his idols. But after reading *Bound for Glory,* Dylan latched onto his most important influence: Woody Guthrie. "Woody was my god," declared the young singer. He eventually traveled from Minnesota to New York and met a dying Guthrie. Dylan's first album, recorded in October 1961 for four hundred dollars, included a song dedicated to Woody.

In Greenwich Village at such clubs as Gerde's and the Village Gate, Dylan began to sing his own songs of social protest. By 1961, remembered Terri Thal, who was then married to folk guitarist Dave Van Ronk, "he was beginning to think about and talk about people who were being trod upon. Not in any class way, but just that he hated people who were taking people. He had a full conception of people who were being taken, and he did read the newspapers, and that's what came through in 'Talkin' Bear Mountain' and 'Talkin' New York,' both in the Guthrie style of talking blues. Dylan's girlfriend at the time, Suze Rotolo, worked as a secretary for the civil rights group CORE and probably caused Dylan to write 'The Ballad of Emmet Till.' " As someone then in the Village remembered, "Suze came along and she wanted him to go Pete Seeger's way. She wanted Bobby to be involved in civil rights and all the radical causes Seeger was involved in. . . . She influenced Bobby considerably, that way."

Dylan's second album, *Freewheeling,* recorded in May 1963, reflected his social consciousness and on the cover pictured Suze draped on Bob's arm as they ambled down a windswept New York City street on a

A pensive Bob Dylan

grey winter day. On it he included "Blowin' in the Wind," which became an anthem for the civil rights movement. "The idea came to me that you were betrayed by your silence," Dylan told some friends about the song. "That all of us in America who didn't speak out were betrayed by our silence. Betrayed by the silence of the people in power. They refuse to look at what's happening. And the others, they ride the subway and read the *Times,* but they don't understand. They don't know. They don't even care, that's the worst of it." Dylan also composed "Hard Rain's A-Gonna Fall" about the Cuban missile crisis; "Oxford Town," an ode to James Meredith, the black student who attempted to enter the University of Mississippi; "Talkin' World War Three Blues," which painted a humorous but somber picture of life after a nuclear holocaust; and the vitriolic "Masters of War" — "You fasten the triggers for the others to fire/ Then you sit back and watch when the death count gets higher/ You hide in your mansions while the young people's blood flows out of their bodies into the mud." At the time, the singer felt that "there's other things in this world besides love and sex that're important too. People shouldn't turn their backs on them just because they ain't pretty to look at. How is the world ever going to get better if we're afraid to look at these things."

Dylan continued to protest in his next album, *The Times They Are A-Changing,* released in January 1964. Besides the title song, which became a battlecry for those engaged in the emerging social revolution, he wrote about the downtrodden in the "Ballad of Hollis Brown" and the "Lonesome Death of Hattie Carroll," and blasted the establishment in "A Pawn in Their Game." For his efforts, Dylan was featured in *Life* and *Newsweek* and was showered with accolades from the critics and the public. By early 1964, remembered Terri Thal, the audiences attracted to the new sensation formed the "precursor to Beatlemania. Bobby's first big skyrocketing was right there in that Carnegie Hall gig. When it was over and we were all backstage, they began to plot the getaway from all these little girls who were screaming outside. . . . Bobby was terrified over mobs, and that was a mob. Like something I literally had never seen before, little girls hanging on top of the car, and policemen pulling them away so Bobby could get out of there safely." Such popularity brought Dylan greater commercial success: In late 1963 and early the next year, his income jumped to over five thousand dollars a month. "I'm makin' money," Dylan told writer Chris Welles, "but it's botherin' me. The money's wrong. It don't make sense. It's all so weird."

Some questioned Dylan's sincerity, but those close to him came to his defense. John Hammond, the record executive who first put Dylan on vinyl, believed that his discovery "was thinking and talking about injustice and social problems. Bobby really wanted to change things. He was uptight about the whole setup in America, the alienation of kids from their parents, the false values. From my leftist point of view, he was just superb, and it was real." According to protest singer Phil Ochs, Dylan "definitely meant the protest. At one point, he was definitely a leftwinger, a radical, and he meant every word he wrote." Folksinger Dave Van Ronk felt that Dylan "was no opportunist. He really believed it all. I was there."

Dylan's popularization of the protest song made him a symbol in the eyes of his fellow performers. Eric Anderson, known for his "Violets of Dawn," felt that Dylan "and those cats were singing about the Vietnam war when everybody else thought it was still a 'conflict.' The whole scene was generating a lot of vibes, and Dylan had the heaviest vibes of them all. Dylan was sowing the seeds of the decade." To Joan Baez, herself active in the protest movement, "Bobby Dylan says what a lot of people my age feel, but cannot say."

Dylan reinforced his image by a number of public demonstrations.

On May 12, 1963, he refused to perform on the *Ed Sullivan Show* when CBS banned him from singing "Talkin' John Birch Society Blues." In July of the same year he gave a concert with Pete Seeger, Josh White, and Theo Bikel — all radical folksingers of a previous era — to assist black voter registration in Mississippi. In August he took part in the march on Washington for civil rights headed by Martin Luther King, Jr.

THE SINGER-ACTIVISTS

A few other singers took similar action to achieve the goals about which they sang. Texas-born Phil Ochs, the son of a Jewish army physician, attended Ohio State University and there won his first guitar by betting on John Kennedy in the hotly contested 1960 election. A year later he composed his first song, "The Ballad of the Cuban Invasion," about the American invasion of Cuba at the Bay of Pigs and then joined a radical singing group called the Sundowners or, sometimes, the Singing Socialists, with roommate Jim Glover, who later succeeded as half of the pop duo, Jim and Jean. In 1962 Ochs dropped out of Ohio State over the issue of freedom of press for the school paper and journeyed to New York City to start his folk-protest career in earnest. According to Phil, the breakthrough came at the Newport Folk Festival of 1963 "with the Freedom Singers, Dylan, Baez, the songwriters' workshop, where the topical song suddenly became the thing. It moved from the background to the foreground in just one weekend."

Ochs, looking for a forum to propagate his radicalized ideals, immersed himself in the genre and churned out protest songs dealing with the issues of the day: His first album, *All the News That's Fit to Sing*, released by Elektra in April 1964, included "Thresher," "Too Many Martyrs," "The Ballad of William Worthy," "Talking Cuban Crisis," and "Talking Vietnam." Said Ochs: "I was writing about Vietnam in 1962, way before the first anti-war marches. I was writing about it at a point where the media were really full of shit, where they were just turning the other way as Vietnam was being built." Subsequent albums delivered other radical hymns such as "The Ballad of the AMA," "Freedom Riders," "Ballad of Oxford, Mississippi," "Draft Dodger Rag," and I Ain't Marching Anymore."

Phil Ochs backed his words with action. In 1964 when he heard that the bodies of three civil rights workers had been found buried under an earthen dam, he headed to Mississippi. He later traveled to Hazard, Kentucky, to help striking miners in a bloody demonstration directed at mine owners who were trying to ignore the provisions of the Mine Safety Act. Phil's song "No Christmas in Kentucky" became a battlecry among the workers. When Phil and folksinger Tom Paxton played a benefit for the miners, members of the John Birch Society and the Fighting American Nationalists picketed the concert with placards that read "Agrarian Reformers Go Home."

Joan Baez, born in Staten Island, New York, undertook similar protests. The daughter of a Mexican-born physicist and a Scotch-Irish mother, the dark-skinned Baez faced discrimination at an early age. When she lived with her parents in Clarence Center, New York, a town of eight hundred people, she felt that "as far as they knew we were niggers." Such childhood experiences helped Baez to identify with the downtrodden. In 1963 she marched on Washington with Dylan, Odetta, Harry Belafonte, and Peter, Paul, and Mary. The next year Baez helped organize students at the University of California, Berkeley, to protest a ban on student political activity in what became known as the Free Speech Movement, and she refused to pay the percentage of her federal income tax designated for defense spending. In 1965 she founded the Institute for the Study of Nonviolence in Carmel, California, and picketed the White

UPI/Bettmann Newsphotos

Bob Dylan and Joan Baez: the king and queen of folk rock

House to show her disapproval of the Vietnam War. "I don't think the President gives a damn," she told an interviewer. During these demonstrations and others, Baez sang beautifully stirring versions of "Birmingham Sunday," "We Shall Overcome," and "What Have They Done to the Rain."

Tom Paxton also raised his voice in protest. Born in Chicago, a young Paxton traveled to Oklahoma with his family and then served a stint in the army. In the early 1960s he moved to New York City, where he became radicalized. In 1964 he landed a record contract with Elektra and followed the lead of Bob Dylan, offering a series of protest songs in *Ramblin' Boy*. The next year he cut one of his most political albums, *Ain't That News,* which included "Lyndon Johnson Told the Nation," "Buy a Gun for Your Son," "We Didn't Know," and "Ain't That News." Explained Paxton about the title song: "When students by the thousands are demanding free speech and a voice in university affairs; when the poor (again, with the help of the students) are making the first hesitant steps toward organization; when Negroes, disenfranchised for years, are lining up by the thousands to register to vote; when mass demonstrations and teach-ins protest this government's foreign policy; when after the long sleep of the Eisenhower years you find heated dialogues and demonstrations throughout the country — that's news."

DYLAN'S DISENCHANTMENT

Protest music, especially Dylan's involvement with it, faded quickly. As early as 1964, after he was booed by the Emergency Civil Liberties Committee during an acceptance speech for the Tom Paine Award, Dylan started to become somewhat disillusioned with overt political activism. "I agree with everything that's happening," he told writer Nat Hentoff over dinner, "but I'm not part of no Movement. If I was, I wouldn't be able to do anything else but be in 'the Movement.' I just can't sit around and have people make rules for me. . . . Those [protest] records I already made," Dylan told Hentoff, referring to his first three albums, "I'll stand behind them but some of that was jumping on the scene to be heard and a lot of it was because I didn't see anybody else doing that kind of thing. Now a lot of people are doing finger-pointing songs. You know — pointing at the things that are wrong. Me, I don't want to write *for* people anymore. You know — be a spokesman." Dylan began to criticize Joan Baez for her involvement with the Institute for the Study of Nonviolence at Carmel, California. By 1965 Dylan abruptly informed a *Newsweek* reporter that "I've never written a political song. Songs can't save the world. I've gone through all that. When you don't like something, you gotta learn to just not need that something."

In place of social protest, Dylan substituted songs of personal alienation. To Nat Hentoff in 1964 Dylan asserted, "I have to make a new song out of what *I* know and out of what *I'm* feeling. . . . I once wrote about Emmett Till in the first person, pretending that I was him. From now on, I want to write what's inside me." Dylan's music reflected his change in outlook: His first commercial hit — "Like a Rolling Stone" — bitterly ridiculed a socialite who had fallen on hard times. Perhaps because of Dylan's final breakup with girlfriend Suze Rotolo, lost or unwanted love formed the theme of other songs: "It Ain't Me Babe," "All I Really Want to Do," and "She Belongs to Me." Still others told of personal confusion, including the contorted, despondent visions of "Mr. Tamborine Man," "Subterranean Homesick Blues," "It's All Right Ma (I'm Only Bleeding)," and "Desolation Row." By the 1964 Newport Folk Festival, when he set aside his acoustic guitar for the electric, Dylan delivered bitter songs of love, hate, and disorientation. "I wouldn't mind so much if he sang just one song about the war," lamented Irwin Silber, the editor of the radical folk magazine *Sing Out!*

Dylan abandoned protest when he hired Albert Grossman for his manager. Grossman, the organizer of the Newport Folk Festivals, wrenched Dylan away from the politically minded producer John Hammond. He then took "Blowin' in the Wind" and gave it to another one of his acts, Peter, Paul, and Mary (Peter Yarrow, Paul Stookey, and Mary Travers). The group, which had hit the charts with Pete Seeger's "If I Had a Hammer" in 1962, made Dylan's song into a chartbuster.

Dylan, who in his youth had wanted to become "bigger than Presley!" accepted the turn of events and increasingly became more interested in the art of songwriting than in the political message. Hemingway, enthused Dylan at the time, "didn't have to use adjectives. He didn't have to define what he was saying. He just said it. I can't do that yet, but that's what I want to be able to do."

Probably more important than his interest in art and his new manager, the political climate of the nation caused Dylan to become disenchanted with protest. In November 1963 Lee Harvey Oswald assassinated President John Kennedy, a symbol of hope for a generation concerned with economic and racial equality. The shooting shocked many members of the folk community, including Bob Dylan. As folksinger Eric Anderson told it, "you can't separate Dylan from history in the sense of what was going down, the way he reacted to a chain of events. The first being Kennedy's death; I think that got him out of politics. . . . Kennedy, he was sort of like the shadow of the flight. . . and then that bird got shot out of the sky and everyone was exposed, naked to all the frightening elements, the truth of the country. It had flown, that force had lost out. And people were depressed."

Phil Ochs sensed the same feeling of loss. Explaining his ballad "That Was the President," Phil said he saw "a definite flowering-out of positive feelings when John Kennedy became President. The civil rights movement was giving off positive vibrations. There was a great feeling of reform, that things could be changed, that the government cared, that an innovator could come in. . . . Things looked incredibly promising. Then came the Bay of Pigs, the beginnings of Vietnam and the assassination was the big thing. It ruined the dream. November 22, 1963, was a mortal wound the country has not yet been able to recover from." Camelot had vanished.

Shortly thereafter the Great Society of Lyndon Johnson removed some of the demands made by protest musicians. In 1964 Congress and the states passed the twenty-fourth amendment, which outlawed the poll tax. Congress also enacted the Civil Rights Act of 1964, which prohibited discrimination in voting, education, and public facilities; eliminated federal funding to groups that practiced discrimination; and established the Federal Community Relations Service. The same year, federal officials put the Voter Act into motion, registering Southern blacks who had previously been disenfranchised by literacy tests, grandfather clauses, and other such practices. In 1965 Congress passed the Elementary and Secondary Education Act in an attempt to further desegregate the schools.

To aid the poor, Johnson declared a "war on poverty." In 1964 he pushed through a tax cut of $11.5 billion to speed economic growth and supported the Economic Opportunity Act. In the next two years, Congress enacted bills for federally funded education programs and a beefed-up social security system of health care, popularly known as Medicare; established the Department of Housing and Urban Development (HUD); liberalized immigration laws; and gave federal aid to the arts through the National Endowment for the Humanities. It also created rent-subsidy and model-cities programs and an Office of Economic Opportunity (OEO). Headed by one of Kennedy's brothers-in-law, Sargent Shriver, the OEO included a Job Corps for high school dropouts, a Neighborhood Youth Corps for unemployed teens, a Volunteers in Service to America (VISTA) designed to effect domestic change, a Head Start program for disadvantaged youngsters, and the Upward Bound program that sent the disadvantaged to college.

All told, Lyndon Johnson envisioned a Great Society — "a place where the city of man served not only the needs of the body and the demands of commerce but the desire for beauty and the hunger for community." It "asks not only how much, but how good; not only how to create wealth, but how to use it; not only how fast we are going, but where we are headed." Such promises tended at least partially to fulfill the dreams of the protest musicians, and seemingly made further outcries less pressing.

Although a few folk singers such as Phil Ochs continued to demand change and became even more strident, most mimicked Dylan and replaced the protest song with odes to nature, love, and personal deliverance. Some of these artists, jumping on the folk-rock bandwagon that Dylan had built when he went electric, launched their careers with Dylan material. The Byrds — originally Roger McGuinn, David Crosby, Gene Clark, Chris Hillman, and Mike Clarke — luckily lured Bob Dylan to one of their practice sessions in 1964, where the folk bard gave the band permission to record one of his yet unreleased gems, "Mr. Tamborine Man," which pushed the Byrds up the national charts in 1965. Also on *The*

Byrds were electrified versions of Dylan's "Spanish Harlem Incident," "All I Really Want to Do," and "Chimes of Freedom." A month later the zany Turtles charted with "It Ain't Me Babe." Simon and Garfunkel, who in 1957 had attracted notice as Tom and Jerry with "Hey Schoolgirl," reemerged in 1964 with a collegiate image and an album of soft harmonies, *Wednesday Morning, 3A.M.,* that showcased Dylan's "Don't Think Twice" and their own composition, "Sounds of Silence." A husband-wife team, Sonny and Cher, broke the platinum barrier by recording Dylan's "All I Really Want to Do" and a heavily Dylan-influenced "I Got You Babe." At the end of 1965 they had earned almost $2 million. By the same year, the sweet-voiced Judy Collins, who had earlier flirted with such protest songs as "Masters of War," offered her fans such

Courtesy of The Daily *of the University of* Washington

Simon and Garfunkel

Dylan tunes as "Mr. Tamborine Man" and "Daddy, You've Been on My Mind."

According to John Sebastian, the leader of the Lovin' Spoonful, the group that became known for their 1965 "Do You Believe in Magic," Bob Dylan acted as "a force on our music, just like the 'Star Spangled Banner' — we've all heard it." And from Glasgow, Scotland, came a Dylan sound-alike, Donovan Leitch, who softly wafted songs of love and drugged visions to his audiences. By the end of 1965, various groups and performers had recorded forty-eight different Dylan songs, most of them concerned with topics other than protest. According to *Newsweek,* "healthy, cheap, moral or venal, folk rock is what's happening at this moment in the dissonant echo chamber of pop culture."

But folk-rock began to encounter stiff competition. In 1964 the British were invading and conquering America. Soon American teens styled their hair in moptops and joined guitar groups that blasted forth ebullient pop songs as they tried to copy four happy lads from Liverpool.

Courtesy of The Daily *of the University of* Washington

Donovan

The Mods vs. the Rockers and the British Invasion of America

Friday, February 7, 1964. Kennedy International Airport, New York, New York. Outside, a mass of screaming teenagers covered the rooftop on one of the airport wings. The crowd, mostly pubescent girls, had been waiting for more than eight hours in the damp New York winter. They considered themselves lucky. Only those with special passes had been permitted on the vantage point of the roof by the dozens of uniformed security police. Inside the terminal, huddled around the gate, which admitted incoming passengers from London, over nine thousand teenaged girls adorned with bouffant hairdos, over-sized jewelry, and their mothers' make-up, shoved, clawed, and crushed each other in a mad attempt to get to the arrival entrance — a heaving, perspiring mass ready to explode. Only a thin, white nylon rope and a few airport guards separated them from their goal. The minutes passed slowly, and the intensity mounted. A voice from a transistor radio comforted the crowd: "It is now 6:30 A.M. Beatle time. They left London 30 minutes ago. They're out over the Atlantic Ocean heading for New York. The temperature is 32 Beatle degrees."

Four of the passengers on Pan American flight 101 felt uneasy. Said one: "We did all feel a bit sick. Going to the States was a big step. People said just because we were popular in Britain, why should we be there?" Asked another: "America's got everything, George, so why should they want us?" A third: "I was worrying about my hair as well. I'd washed it, but when it had dried, it had gone up a bit." The fourth, the oldest and the leader of the group, sat silent, motionless in his seat. He seldom released his strained emotions outside his music.

As the plane neared its destination, a few wild screams broke a tense silence. Then an entire chorus of animalistic cries from girls on the rooftop alerted the crowd inside of the arrival. The subsequent wails sent tremors throughout Kennedy International, increasing at a deafening rate: the cries of pent-up teenage passion. The girls started to half-chant, half-sing, "We Love You Beatles, Oh Yes We Do."

The plane landed safely and reached the hangar. Scurrying attendants pushed a platform toward the jet, the door swung open and passengers started to descend the steps. Capitol Record employees shoved Beatle kits complete with wigs, autographed photos, and a button saying "I Like the Beatles" at them. At last, four young Englishmen, who sported buttoned-down, Edwardian suits from Pierre Cardin and mushroom-shaped haircuts, walked out. After almost two hundred years, the British had again invaded the United States. This time they would emerge as the victors. The Beatles had arrived in America.

The four lads from Liverpool — John, Paul, George, and Ringo — dashed toward a chauffeured airport limousine. They leapt in the car, locked the doors, and rode toward the terminal. Hundreds of girls hurled themselves at the slow-moving automobile, clinging to the hood, the roof and the sides. They pressed their faces against the windows to catch a glimpse of their heroic loves before they were pulled away by yet another admirer. From inside the car, the United States appeared slightly surreal and, at times, threatening.

The car broke loose from the crowd and headed toward the airport complex. After a short press conference, the Beatles jumped into the limousine and sped down the Van Wyck Expressway, then down Brunswick Street. They reached Manhattan about one hour and thirty minutes later. When the car stopped at New York's plush Plaza Hotel, thousands more swarmed the auto like hungry insects. The Beatles managed to pry the doors open and somehow make it to the hotel lobby, where they were escorted to a twelfth-floor room. There they discovered three screaming girls in the bathtub and called maid service for help. Throughout the night and the next few days, armed guards protected the Beatles from ingenious girls who climbed the fire escapes to the twelfth floor, and from conspiring groups of teens who checked in at the hotel using the names of their well-to-do parents in order to penetrate the inner sanctum of floor number 12. Outside, fans kept a twenty-four-hour vigil, chanting "We Want the Beatles, We Want the Beatles." They inundated their heroes with twelve thousand letters a day.

On Sunday night the new idols from across the Atlantic were to come into full view. Late in 1963, Ed Sullivan, the square-faced, stocky show-business impressario, had witnessed a near-riot at the London airport. Over fifteen thousand screaming fans had descended upon the terminal and had delayed the Queen and Prime Minister Sir Alec Douglas-Home in order to welcome the Beatles back from a trip abroad. Impressed, Sullivan told the *New York Times,* "I made up my mind that this was the same sort of mass hit hysteria that had characterized the Elvis Presley days." He hurriedly located Brian Epstein, the dapper, brilliant manager of the group, and for less than twenty thousand dollars booked the Beatles for three appearances on his show.

On February 9, 1964, Sullivan's hunch proved to be correct. Seven hundred twenty-eight wild teenagers packed into the studio from which the Sullivan show was broadcast. They had battled fifty thousand others for tickets to the show that featured the Beatles. When Sullivan introduced the Beatles — "and now, the Beeeatles!" — the room erupted. Girls with checkered skirts and Macy blouses let out primal screams and pulled their hair, thrusting themselves toward the front of the stage or leaning perilously over the balcony. Some simply fainted. Few noticed that one of the microphones had gone dead. All eyes fastened on Paul bobbing back and forth as he played a left-handed bass guitar; Ringo, smiling as he brushed the drumskins; John, yelling the words over the din; and a rather dour George, the youngest, skinniest member of the group, just looking down at the neck of his lead guitar. The screaming intensified. Explained one girl in the crowd: "You really do believe they can see you and just you alone, when they're up on stage. That's why you scream, so they'll notice you. I always felt John could see me. It was like a dream. Just me and John together and no one else." The show ended amidst the wails. It had been extremely successful. For the first time in television history, over 60 percent of all viewers had tuned into one program and over 73 million people across the nation had witnessed the event. It was bigger than Presley, much bigger than Presley.

The bedlam continued. The Beatles played two twenty-five-minute concerts at Carnegie Hall to twelve thousand fans, who included actress Lauren Bacall and Mrs. Nelson Rockefeller, the wife of the Governor of New York. Actor David Niven and Oscar award-winning actress Shirley MacLaine had been turned away. In fact, Sid Bernstein, the organizer of the shows, had had to surrender his own ticket to Mrs. Rockefeller.

From New York City, after they had twisted at the Peppermint Lounge and flirted with voluptuous bunnies at the Playboy Club, the Beatles rode the King George train to Washington, D.C. On Wednesday, February 11, at 3:09 P.M., amid a storm that left ten inches of snow, the Beatles arrived in the nation's capital. The King George, wrote a reporter for the *Washington Post,* "sat quietly for a few minutes, like a goose sitting in the right frame of mind to produce a golden egg." The band emerged from the train, hurriedly made their way down a platform "behind a wedge of Washington's finest," and reached the main concourse of Union Station. "For hours," the *Post* read, "teenagers had been drifting into Union Station — many of them from National Airport,

Seattle Times

Hysterical Beatle fans, 1964

where the Beatles before the show had been scheduled to arrive. . . . In the concourse, the teenagers, perhaps 2,000 strong, lined the barriers, breathed on the glass, hung through the bars, even climbed the gates." The Beatles, heads down in combat fashion, snaked through the crowd with the help of the police, who pushed and shoved the oncoming torrent of fans. Screamed one girl to the police as they dragged away her friend, "You can't throw her out, she's President of the Beatles Fan Club." Finally, John, Paul, Ringo, and George broke through the crowd into the brisk Washington air and leapt into a waiting limousine. They sped toward the Washington Coliseum, which was jammed with 8,092 wild-eyed teens. "From the moment the Beatles were led to the stage by a phalanx of policemen," the *Post* informed its readers, "the din was almost unbearable." Reporter Leroy Aarons compared the noise to "being downwind from a jet during takeoff." During the performance, frantic, distraught girls began mercilessly to pelt their heroes with jelly beans. Explained George: "It was terrible. They hurt. They don't have soft jelly babies in America but hard jellybeans like bullets. Some newspaper had dug out the old joke, which we'd all forgotten about, when John had once said I'd eaten all his jelly babies."

From Washington, the Beatles flew to Miami, where they were greeted by four bathing beauties, a four-mile-long traffic jam, and seven thousand screaming teens who shattered twenty-three windows and a plate glass door in a tumultuous attempt to touch their idols. The group played for a raucous audience in Miami, then headed toward New York

The Mods vs. the Rockers and the British Invasion of America **81**

City, where they upstaged the President. In an article entitled "LBJ Ignored as New York Crowds Chase Beatles," *Billboard* reported that "President Lyndon B. Johnson visited here late last week, but the arrival was overshadowed by the Beatles invasion. Few were aware of the President's presence in their midst, but no one could miss the fact that Britain's Beatles had descended upon the town. Radio, TV, and all other communication media were filled with Beatle clamor. At Kennedy Airport here, Beatle greeters began lining up at 4 A.M. Friday to await the group's arrival this afternoon."

By the time the Beatles had left New York for London on February 16, the entire nation had been afflicted with Beatlemania. Headlines in the staid *Billboard* told the story: "The U.S. Rocks and Reels from Beatles Invasion"; "Chicago Flips Wig, Beatles and Otherwise"; "New York City Crawling with Beatlemania"; and "Beatle Binge in Los Angeles." During their brief stay, the Beatles sold over 2 million records and more than $2.5 million worth of Beatle-related goods: blue and white Beatle hats; Beatle T-shirts and beach shirts; Beatle tight-fitting pants; Beatle pajamas and three-button tennis shirts; Beatle cookies; Beatle eggcups; Beatle rings, pendants, and bracelets; a pink, plastic Beatle guitar with the pictures of the four lads stamped on it; a plethora of Beatle dolls — inflatable figurines, six-inch hard rubber likenesses, painted wood dolls that bobbed their heads when moved, and a cake decoration in the form of the Beatles; Beatle nightshirts; countless Beatle publications; Beatle ice-cream sandwiches covered with a foil Beatle wrapper; Beatle soft drinks; and Beatle wigs, which Lowell Toy Company churned out at fifteen thousand a day. Selteab (Beatles spelled backwards), the American arm of the Beatle manufacturing giant, NEMS, even drew up plans for a Beatle motor scooter and a Beatle car. From almost every standpoint, the Beatles' visit to America had been the nine most incredible and intense days in rock and roll history.

THE MODS AND THE ROCKERS

This spectacular event had its genesis years before in an economic depression that spawned warring gangs of British lower-class youths. In England by the late 1950s, the babies born immediately after World War II had grown up. "That was the Bulge, that was England's Bulge," Pete Townshend, the lead guitarist for The Who, told a reporter. "All the war babies, all the old soldiers coming back from the war and screwing until they were blue in the face — this was the result. Thousands and thousands of kids, too many kids, not enough teachers, not enough parents." Upon finishing school at fifteen or sixteen, most of these youths unsuccessfully looked for work. In March 1964 Harold Wilson, a Labour Party leader from Liverpool and later Prime Minister, regarded "as deserving of the utmost censure and condemnation a system of society which, year in, year out . . . cannot provide employment for its school-leavers." Newly enacted English conscription laws exacerbated the problem. Ringo Starr thought youth unemployment in the late 1950s mushroomed because the draft "ended, and so at 18 you weren't regimented. Everyone was wondering what to do."

The idle working-class teens began to form rival gangs: the Rockers and the Mods. The Rockers, modeling themselves after the tough Teddy Boys of the early 1950s, bought black leather jackets, tight-fitting pants, and pointed boots or suede shoes. They greased back their hair in a pompadour style and sometimes put on sunglasses in beatnik fashion, roaring down the streets on motorcycles. The Modernists — Mod, for short — on the other hand favored "teenage Italian-style clothes." According to Townshend, himself a Mod, they had "short hair, money enough to buy a real smart suit, good shoes, good shirts; you had to be able to dance like a madman. You had to be in possession of plenty of pills all the time and always be pilled up [especially with Drynamil, an amphetamine also known as 'purple hearts']. You had to have a scooter covered in lamps. You had to have like an army anarack to wear." The demands of fashion in the "incestuous, secretive" society of Mods shifted rapidly. "One outfit might be 12 quid, a week's wages, and the next fucking week you'd have to change the whole lot." "And that was being a Mod," concluded Townshend. As with the Rockers, added the guitarist, the Mods "were nothing. They were the lowest, they were England's lowest common denominators. Not only were they young, they were also lower-class young." "Most Mods were lower class garbagemen, you know, with enough money to buy himself Sunday best."

The gang experience gave many of these youths a sense of belonging. Townshend knew "the feeling of what it's like to be a Mod among two million Mods and its incredible. It's like being — suddenly you're the only white man in the Apollo [Theater in Harlem]. Someone comes up and touches you and you become black. It's like that moment, that incredible feeling of being part of something which is really much bigger than race and much bigger than — it was impetus. It covered everybody, everybody looked the same, and everybody acted the same and everybody wanted to be the same. It was the first move I have ever seen in the history of youth towards unity, towards unity of thought, unity of drive and unity of motive." "Any kid," said Townshend, "however ugly or however fucked up, if he had the right haircut and the right clothes and the right motorbike, he was a Mod. He was a Mod!"

The Mods and the Rockers, each bound together by a common appearance, fought one another for dominance. During the Easter weekend of 1964 at Clacton-on-Sea, Essex, a few hundred "young scooter riders" from the eastern and northeastern parts of London attacked motorcycle gangs of Rockers. According to D. H. Moody, chairman of the Urban District Council, "they insulted passers-by, lay in the middle of the road to stop traffic, jumped onto cars and destroyed and damaged property. The girls were almost as bad and [one witness] had seen five of them try to knock a child off his bicycle." "At one stage," reported the *London Times,* "there was almost a battle on the seafront with missiles of all descriptions being thrown." The police intervened and arrested more than a hundred rioters, who the *Times* called a "collection of uncivilized youths with no respect for persons, property, or the comfort of other people." In explaining the incident, Labour's chief front bench spokesman, Fred Willey, observed that the "general complaint of those who took part was that there was nothing for them to do. They came from housing estates with far too few social amenities and were expected to spend their time in amusement arcades. . . . The present government regarded working-class adolescents as fair game for blatant exploitation by commercial interests."

On May 17 and 18, 1964, trouble broke out in the Kent resort of Margate and at Brighton. Over eight hundred Mods, arriving "on scooters bristling with headlights and badges," fought two hundred leather-jacketed Rockers. The *Daily Express* painted a terrifying picture: "There was dad asleep in a deckchair and mum making sandcastles with the children when the 1964 boys took over the beaches at Margate and Brighton yesterday and smeared the traditional scene with more bloodshed and violence." Fumed Dr. George Simpson, Margate Court Chairman, "these long-haired, mentally unstable petty little sawdust Caesars seem to find courage, like rats, by hunting only in packs." By Tuesday, when the clashes subsided, "at least 40 youths had been arrested," the *Daily Mirror* informed its readers. "And there was blood on the sand."

THE WHO: QUINTESSENTIAL MOD BAND

These warring gangs had definite musical preferences. "The groups that you liked when you were a Mod were The Who," bragged Pete Townshend. "That's the story of why I dig the Mods, man, because we were Mods and that's how we happened." Peter Meadon, the early manager of The Who and the founder of the Mod band the Ace Faces, in 1963 convinced The Who, then called the High Numbers, to adopt a Mod image. Said Meadon: "I had this dream of getting a group together that would be the focus, the entertainers for the Mods; a group that would actually be the same people onstage as the guys in the audience. . . . an actual representation of the people." Roger Daltry fit the image with his "French crewcut" and "Townshend identified with the Mod scene immediately."

In 1964 the High Numbers recorded two Mod anthems for their first single on Fontana Records: "Zoot Suit," a compendium of Mod fashion, and "I'm the Face," a reworking of bluesman Slim Harpo's "Got Love If You Want It." A Fontana press release asserted that it was "the first *authentic* Mod record . . . a hip, tailored-for-teens R & B oriented shuffle rocker . . . with a kick in every catchphrase for the kids of the fast-moving crowd . . . to cause an immediate rapport between the High Numbers and the thousands of young people like themselves. In a nutshell — they are the people." The single, however, only sold around five hundred copies, and the High Numbers parted company with Meadon.

Late in 1964 the band enticed Kit Lambert, the son of classical composer Constant Lambert, and Chris Stamp, the brother of actor Terence Stamp, to become co-managers. According to drummer Keith Moon, the new managers sent band members "to Carnaby Street with more money than we'd ever seen in our lives, like a hundred quid each. . . . We weren't into clothes, we were into music. Kit thought we should identify more with our audience. Coats slashed five inches at the side. Four wasn't enough. Six was too much. Five was just right." The band returned with garb that would become their trademark: Bull's-eye T-shirts; and pants, shirts, and jackets cut from the British flag. Lambert and Stamp renamed the group The Who, and booked them for sixteen consecutive Tuesdays at the London Marquee Club, a Mod hangout owned by Ziggy Jackson, where, according to Moon, the band "blew open the doors of the Marquee to rock." To complete The Who image, Townshend contributed the first of his many compositions, "My Generation," which became the battlecry of the Mods. "That's my generation, that's how the song 'My Generation' happened, because of the Mods," Townshend explained.

The Mods also listened to the Small Faces. Steve Marriott of the Faces remembered that "we started out doing little clubs and weddings, but because we were Mods we were asked to play London clubs like the Flamingo. We were a bit dubious about it, 'cause we weren't very good. . . . But all the London management started watching the Mod following we were getting. The only other band really doing that was The Who, and they were pretty successful."

The members of The Who grew up in the same lower-class neighborhoods as other London Mods. Roger Daltry, lead singer and organizer of the group at the age of fifteen, Townshend, and bassist John Entwhistle were raised in Shepard's Bush, a dilapidated suburb of West London. Before The Who gained notoriety, its members were all manual laborers — Daltry for five years as a sheet metal worker, and Townshend and Entwhistle at various odd jobs. Keith Moon, the ebullient madman of The Who, who met an untimely death in 1978, grew up in Wembley and joined the band when he wandered into the Oldfield Hotel one day to witness their act. Noticeable with his "dyed ginger hair and a ginger cord suit," Moon asked the band if he could play with them during one number. In the words of the drummer, "they said go ahead and I got behind this other guy's drums and did one song — 'Road Runner.' I'd several drinks to get me courage up and when I got onstage I went arrgggGhhhh on the drums, broke the bass drum pedal and two skins, and got off. I figured that was it. I was scared to death. Afterwards I was sitting at the bar and Pete came over. He said: 'You . . . come 'ere.' I said, mild as you please: 'Yesyes?' And Roger, who was the spokesman then, said: 'What are you doing next Monday?' I said: 'Nothing.' I was working during the day, selling plaster. He said: 'You'll have

Pete Townshend of The Who

to give up work . . . there's this gig on Monday. If you want to come, we'll pick you up in the van.' I said: 'Right.' And that was it."

The Who's subsequent sound captured the anger and rebelliousness of the English Mods. Townshend, the writer of most of the band's material, felt that "rock's always been demanding. It is demanding of its performers, and its audience. And of society. Demanding of change." "The world turns if you turn it and that if you don't turn it, it's going to fucking sit there." Because The Who called for change, they challenged adult society with their hard-driving music. In the words of its lead guitarist, The Who's brand of rock 'n' roll "is a single impetus and it's a single force which threatens a lot of crap which is around at the moment in the middle class and in the middle-aged politics or philosophy."

Townshend's guitar-smashing antics and Moon's destruction of his drum kit, "a gesture which happens on the spur of the moment," accentuated the rebellious spirit of the band.

The intensity of The Who's music, however, made commercial success in the United States unlikely. Record executives and the general public, attuned to a more sedated sound, ignored the 1965 tour of The Who in America. Two years later the group made little headway playing back-up to Herman's Hermits, the instant pop sensation that in 1964 hit the charts with "I'm into Something Good" and later with "I'm Henry the Eighth, I Am," "Mrs. Brown You've Got a Lovely Daughter," and "Dandy." Financial success and international recognition for The Who came only in 1969, when the band unveiled its rock opera, *Tommy*. By that time, the Mod movement had long since dissipated.

THE EARLY BEATLES: A ROCKER BAND

One Rocker group, made up of rowdy youths from Liverpool, did not have to wait so long for fame and fortune. Formed in 1959, the Quarrymen, as they were first called, then Johnny and the Moondogs, the Silver Beatles, and finally just the Beatles, started their musical careers in the Cavern Club of Liverpool. The next year they traveled to Hamburg, Germany, to back up singer Tony Sheridan. Within two more years the Beatles had become the rage of England. And by 1964 they had become world-wide celebrities.

The Beatles, like The Who, came from poor families. Abandoned by his father and mother, John Winston Lennon grew up with his aunt Mimi and as a boy joined a Rocker gang that "went in for things like shoplifting and pulling girls' knickers down." Paul McCartney, the son of a cotton salesman, lived in a half house — "they were such small, diddy houses, with bare bricks inside," he later reminisced. The youngest of the Beatles, George Harrison, was the son of a bus driver and began an apprenticeship as an electrician at the age of sixteen. And Ringo Starr, born Richard Starkey, told a reporter that his family had "always been just ordinary, poor working class." When her husband deserted the family, Ringo's mother worked as a barmaid to support her child. At fifteen, Ringo landed a job as a messenger boy for the British Railways.

These four Liverpool youths adopted a Rocker image. To his aunt, Lennon seemed to be "a real Teddy boy." But "I wasn't really a Ted, just a Rocker," Lennon confessed. "I was imitating Teds, pretending to be one. I was never a real one, with chains and real gangs. If I'd met a proper Ted, I'd have been shit-scared." Paul spent hours styling his pompadoured hair and choosing the clothes that fit into Rocker fashion. Worried that his son would "turn out a Teddy boy," Jim McCartney "said over and over again that [Paul] wasn't going to have tight trousers. But he just wore me down." George Harrison rebelled in much the same way. According to his mother, he "used to go to school with his school cap sitting high on top his hair. And very tight trousers. Unknown to me, he'd run them up on my machine to make them even tighter. I bought him a brand new pair once and the first thing he did was to tighten them. When his dad found out, he told him to unpick them at once. 'I can't Dad,' he said. 'I've cut the pieces off.' George always had an answer." As a band the Beatles affected a Rocker image: They wore black-and-white cowboy shirts with white tassles dangling from the pockets, leather jackets, and pointed cowboy boots.

The western attire indicated a major musical influence on the Beatles: American rockabilly. Although they covered such Chuck Berry tunes as "Rock and Roll Music" and "Roll Over Beethoven," the band initially modeled its sound after Elvis Presley. "Nothing really affected me until Elvis," John Lennon remembered. "I had no idea about doing music as a way of life until rock 'n' roll hit me. It was *Rock Around the Clock,* I think. I enjoyed Bill Haley, but I wasn't overwhelmed by him. It wasn't until 'Heartbreak Hotel' that I really got into it." McCartney felt that Presley "was the biggest kick. Everytime I felt low I just put on Elvis and I'd feel great, beautiful. I'd no idea how records were made and it was just magic. 'All Shook Up'! Oh, it was beautiful." When Malcolm Evans, later a road manager for the Beatles, first heard the group at the Cavern Club, he felt that they "sounded a bit like Elvis."

The Beatles showed their appreciation of other rockabilly stars as well. In 1959 as a Silver Beatle, George Harrison changed his name to Carl Harrison after one of his heroes, Carl Perkins. At another time, the foursome called themselves the Foreverly Brothers in honor of the Everly Brothers. *Variety* spotted the influence years later. "Mullarkey," read one story. "The Beatles are dishing up a rock and roll style that was current in this country ten years ago and that is still typical of such groups as the Everly Brothers." The name the group eventually decided upon reflected the rockabilly connection. As John told reporter Jim Steck, "I was looking for a name like the Crickets [Buddy Holly's band] that meant two things. From Cricket I went to Beatles. . . . When you said it, people thought of crawly things; when you read it, it was beat music."

MANAGER BRIAN EPSTEIN

This Rocker band, playing an English brand of rockabilly music tinged with R & B, the English music hall tradition, and washboard-and-fiddle skiffle music became famous through the efforts of Brian Epstein. Epstein, born in September 1934 into a wealthy family, was raised in a five-bedroom house in Childwall, one of Liverpool's most exclusive residential areas. He began a successful career as a salesman in two of his father's stores: a furniture shop and the North End Music Enterprises. "I enjoyed selling as well, watching people relax and show trust in me," he intimated. "It was pleasant to see the wary look dissolve and people begin to think there were good things ahead for them and I would be the provider." After conquering the record retailing business, Epstein turned his attention to the Beatles, a group that he had heard about in one of his music stores. As he told it, "I suppose it was all part of getting bored with simply selling records. I was looking for a new hobby. The Beatles at the same time, though I didn't know it and perhaps they didn't either, were also getting a bit bored with Liverpool." In 1961 Brian Epstein became the manager of the Beatles, getting a 25 percent share of their expected profits.

To make the band more palatable to the general public, Epstein changed their Rocker image. When he first saw them at the Cavern Club, he thought that "they were a scruffy crowd in leather." The Beatles "were not very tidy and not very clean. They smoked as they played and they ate and talked and pretended to hit each other." Brian tried to "clean our image up," John Lennon contended. "He said our look wasn't right. We'd never get past the door at a good place. We just used to dress how we liked, on and off stage. He talked us into the suit scene." Said Epstein himself: "First I got them into trousers and sweaters and eventually into suits." Besides changing their appearance, said Pete Best, the Beatles' drummer before Ringo joined the group, the manager forced the band to "work out a proper program, playing our best num-

Courtesy of Capitol Records

The Beatles

bers each time, not just the ones we felt like playing." After Epstein had finished molding the four Liverpudlians, noticed Malcolm Evans, "the image of the Beatles was so good and nice."

To sell the band, Epstein brought in other professionals from the music business. He interested George Martin, an executive with the Parlophone branch of the Electrical Music Industry (EMI). On September 11, 1962, Martin recorded the Beatles' first British release: "Love Me Do" and "P.S. I Love You." Epstein, who "didn't know how you promoted a record," then enlisted the services of Tony Barrow, a publicity man for Decca Records. By May 1963 the manager had set up the machinery to make the Beatles a national sensation.

THE TOPPERMOST OF THE POPPERMOST

As with some other lower-class youths, the Beatles may have compromised their image for the promises of money and fame. Scarred by the insecurity of his childhood, John "wanted to be popular. I wanted to be the leader. It seemed more attractive than just being one of the toffees." "All I wanted was women, money, and clothes," Paul later confessed. In discussing his financial future with Paul, George said that he "felt he was going to make a lot of it [money]. He was going to buy a house and a swimming pool, then he'd buy a bus for his father." As a group, the Fab Four dreamed of stardom. In 1961, remembered George, "we still used to send up the idea of getting to the top. When things were a real drag and nothing happening, we used to go through this routine: John would shout, 'Where are we going, fellas?' We'd shout back, 'To the Top, Johnny.' Then he would shout, 'What Top?' 'To the Toppermost of the Poppermost, Johnny!' "

The Beatles soon achieved their goal. They first became well known in Liverpool. By late 1962, remembered Maureen Cox, Ringo's first wife, admirers "used to hang around the Cavern all day long, just on the off chance of seeing them. They'd come out of the lunch time session and just stand outside all afternoon, queuing up for the evening show. . . . It was terrible, the mad screams when they came on. They went potty." News spread quickly. More than five thousand squealing teens mobbed a Beatle performance and caused a riot in Manchester. At Newcastle-upon-Tyne, over four thousand diehards lined up in front of a concert hall at three o'clock in the morning in order to secure tickets for an evening Beatle show. Dr. F. R. C. Casson, a psychologist who tried to explain the phenomenon for the readers of the *London Times,* likened "Beatlemania to the frenzied dancing and shouting of voodoo worshippers and the howls and bodily writhing of converts among primitive evangelical sects in the southern states of America." "Beat music," Dr. Casson said, "has a rhythmic stimulation on the brain. A similar result of rhythmic stimulation is seen in some types of epileptic fit which may be caused by rapidly flickering light."

On October 13, 1963, the band gained national exposure when they performed at the London Palladium. Over fifteen million television viewers watched thousands of young Londoners claw at each other to get into the Beatle concert. "From that day on," insisted press agent Tony Barrow, "everything has changed. My job has never been the same again. From spending six months ringing up newspapers and getting no, I now had every national reporter and feature writer chasing *me*." Within two more weeks, on November 4, the Beatles performed for the Queen at the Royal Variety Performance and solidified their reputation. Following the heavy-set singer Sophie Tucker, who Paul called the Beatles' favorite American "group," they elicited screams and moans with "Till There Was You," "Twist and Shout," and "She Loves You." During one number, John asked the audience to clap. "Those upstairs, just rattle your jewelry," he added, looking up toward the royal box. The following Sunday, twenty-six million Britons witnessed the escapade in front of their television sets.

By December 1963 manufacturers started to offer Beatle products — one firm in Peckham selling Beatle sweaters "designed specially for Beatle people by a leading British manufacturer with a top-quality, two-tone Beatle badge." The Beatle fan club swelled to over eight hundred thousand members, and the foursome sold a million copies of two singles which featured "I Want to Hold Your Hand" and "She Loves You." The band's first British album, *Please Please Me,* topped the British charts for over six months. By the end of 1963 the Fab Four had sold eleven million records and eighteen million dollars worth of Beatle goods.

Public opinion responded favorably to the clean-cut Beatles. The *Daily Mirror* argued that "you have to be a real sour square not to love the nutty, noisy, happy, handsome Beatles." From a different political wing, the *Daily Worker* of the British Communist Party commented that the "Mersey sound is the voice of 80,000 crumbling houses and 30,000 people on the dole." Although Conservative politician Edward Heath first criticized the Beatles' language as "unrecognizable as the Queen's English," he later told an interviewer: "Who could have forecast only a year ago that the Beatles would prove the salvation of the corduroy industry" as thousands emulated the band in its trouser style. Prime Minister Sir Alec Douglas-Home called the group "our best export" and "a useful contribution to the balance of payments." Even the Queen complimented the Beatles. "So young, fresh, and vital," she cooed.

Amid such praise, Brian Epstein began to question his marketing tactics. He feared overexposure: "At first sight the endless discussion in the newspapers of the Beatles' habits, clothes, and views was exciting. They liked it at first and so did I. It was good for business. But finally it became an anxiety. How long could they maintain public interest without rationing either personal appearances or newspaper coverage? By a stringent watch on their bookings and press contacts we just averted saturation point. But it was very close. Other artists have been destroyed by this very thing."

The band members started to doubt the value of stardom as they began to pay the price of success. Ringo Starr complained about the loss of friendships and the diminishing control he exercised over his own life. "There were so many groups in Liverpool at one time that we often used to play just for each other, sitting in on each other's sessions, or just listening. It was a community on its own, just made up of groups." But when the Beatles became popular nationally, "it broke all the community up. People start hating each other." Moreover, Ringo felt slighted when George Martin replaced him with a session drummer on "P.S. I Love You." "Nobody said anything. What could the others say, or me? We were just lads, being pushed around. You know what I mean. They were so big, the London record company and all that. We just did what we were told." At about the same time, John believed that the band had relinquished too much control. In Liverpool, he later told an interviewer, the Beatles "felt embarrassed in our suits and being very clean. We were worried that our friends might think we'd sold out — which we had, in a way."

THE BEATLES INVADE AMERICA

Despite their doubts, the Beatles prepared for even greater success in America. Epstein paved the way for the British invasion, convincing Capitol Records to spend fifty thousand dollars on a "crash publicity program." The company plastered five million "The Beatles Are Coming" stickers on buildings, fences, and telephone poles in every state, and printed a million copies of a four-page tabloid about the Fab Four. Capitol executives pressed one million units of a promotional, seven-inch Beatle interview record, which gave radio listeners the impression that the Beatles had personally contacted every disc jockey in the country. They also convinced many of the major weekly publications to run stories on the British foursome before their arrival: *Time* covered the group in its November 15, 1963, issue; *Newsweek* did so three days later; and on January 31, 1964, *Life* published a color spread entitled, "Here Come The Beatles." By February 7, 1964, Brown Meggs, director of Eastern operations for Capitol Records, told the *New York Times* "I have been on full-time Beatle duty since — the date is indelibly imprinted on my mind — January 6 when I returned from vacation. All this came at once, everything happened in a tremendously concentrated period. I'm awfully tired, but Beatles only come once in a decade, if that." Voyle Gilmore, a vice-president of Capitol, summed up the efforts of his company: "There was a lot of hype."

When the Beatles arrived in New York City on February 7, 1964, Beatlemania had swept the United States. Entering the charts at number 83, by February 1 "I Want to Hold Your Hand" had replaced Bobby Vinton's "There! I've Said It Again" in the number 1 slot. The song remained in the top position for seven weeks, quickly followed by "She Loves You," "Can't Buy Me Love," "Love Me Do," and "A Hard Day's Night." To get a glimpse of the band that they had heard on the radio, thousands of screaming teenagers descended upon Kennedy International Airport. Another fifty thousand fans competed for the 728 tickets to the *Ed Sullivan Show* that would headline the Beatles. The lucky few who did manage to witness their heroes in action hysterically yelled and fainted throughout the performance. "What happened in the states was just like Britain," Ringo remembered, "only ten times bigger, so I suppose it wasn't like Britain at all."

Some adults disapproved of the new rage. After the Sullivan show, the *Herald Tribune* called the Beatles "75% publicity, 20% haircut and 5% lilting lament." To the *Daily News,* "the Presleyan gyrations and caterwauling were but lukewarm dandelion tea compared to the 100-proof elixir served up by the Beatles." Disregarding his personal ban on Sunday television viewing, evangelist Billy Graham watched the Beatles on the *Ed Sullivan Show* and believed that the performance revealed "all the symptoms of the uncertainty of the times and the confusion about us." Ray Block, orchestra leader on the Sullivan program, prophesied that the band "wouldn't last longer than a year," and actor Noel Coward said: "I've met them. Delightful lads. Absolutely no talent." Concert critic Louis Biancolli summed up the adverse reaction to the Beatles: "Their effect is like mass hypnosis followed by mass nightmare. I never heard anything like what went around me. I've read about the bacchantes and corybantes in wild Greek rites screaming insensately. They were antique squares compared to these teenage maenads."

Most media commentators, however, welcomed the clean-cut, well-tailored Beatles and their aristocratic manager. *Time* wrote that "the boys are the very spirit of good clean fun. They look like shaggy Peter Pans, with their mushroom haircuts and high white shirt collars, and onstage they clown around endlessly." The *1964 Yearbook* of World Book Encyclopedia singled out the Beatles' "rambunctious and irreverent sense of fun" and the stuffy *Yearbook* of Collier's Encyclopedia likened the foursome to "Little Lord Fauntleroys." *Newsweek* probably best captured the majority opinion when it labeled the Beatles "a band of evangelists. And the gospel is fun. They shout, they stomp, they jump for joy and their audiences respond in a way that makes an old-time revival meeting seem like a wake. . . . The Beatles appeal to the positive, not negative. They give kids a chance to let off steam and adults a chance to let off disapproval. They have even evolved a peculiar sort of sexless appeal: cute and safe. The most they ask is: 'I Want to Hold Your Hand.'" The fun-loving Beatles seemed a perfect antidote to the pessimism that had engulfed America after John F. Kennedy's death a few months earlier.

The "cute and safe" Beatles, appealing to a vast audience, scored fantastic successes in America. The third week of February 1964, contended *Billboard,* "was the week that was the Beatles'. First in the platter polls, first in the press, first in police protection and the first in the hearts of New York teenagers, who upset the mechanics of John F. Kennedy Airport, the Plaza, a CBS-TV studio, Penn Station and Carnegie Hall ever since the foursome arrived from London."

Shortly after their tour of the United States, Beatle John Lennon released his book *In His Own Write,* which nudged Ian Fleming's latest James Bond thriller from the top of the best-seller list and won Lennon an invitation to the prestigious Foyles Literary Lunch on Shakespeare's 400th birthday. Some compared the book to James Joyce's classic *Finnegans Wake.* Almost simultaneously, the Beatles released a full-length motion picture, *A Hard Day's Night.* "The idea was to make it as quickly as possible and get it out before their popularity faded," admitted director Richard Lester. The timing was superb. Even historian and JFK speechwriter Arthur Schlesinger, Jr., lauded the movie as "the astonishment of the month" by a group who embodied the "timeless essence of the adolescent effort to deal with the absurdities of an adult world." In its first six weeks the film earned $5.6 million in rental fees.

A few months later, in 1965, the Beatles returned to the States for another tour: It included a stint at New York's Shea Stadium, where the Fab Four lured fifty-five thousand rabid fans and grossed $304,000 — "the greatest gross ever in the history of show business" up to that time, according to promoter Sid Bernstein.

In Seattle a typical explosion of mayhem erupted over the second coming of the Beatles. When the foursome arrived in town, they faced screaming, clawing teenagers. Escorted by a police motorcade, they immediately sped to room 272 of the seaside Edgewater Inn, which had been secured with barbed wire and sawhorse barricades. While in their room, Ringo, George, Paul, and John sorted through the hundreds of letters from their fans that had been mailed to the Edgewater, ate a few of the cookies and cakes that Beatle diehards had baked, and fished from a window that overlooked the Pacific.

They only emerged from the hotel into the damp Seattle air that night, when they ran from the hotel lobby and jumped into a limousine bound for the Coliseum. Marty Murphy, a twenty-five-year-old switchboard operator at the Edgewater Inn, rode with the Beatles, dragged into the car by Brian Epstein, who desperately needed help with two terrified Beatle secretaries. According to her account, "the limousine started moving. Now I could understand why the Beatles had looked so scared when they arrived. When we got to the barricade, I have never been so frightened in my life. These children had their faces pressed up against the car, all bent out of shape. They were crying, screaming, 'Touch me! Touch me!' They were saying that to me, and they didn't even know who I was. Finally, the limousine got to the Coliseum." When the Beatles leapt onstage and started to play, remembered police officer Noreen Skagen, "I only sort of heard the music; the screaming was just too loud. The Beatles themselves looked very tense, pale, scared. . . . We had to have a regular flying wedge with our then-TAC squad to bring them into the Coliseum and on stage. The entire audience charged the stage when the Beatles were ready to leave. We were constantly dragging hysterical youngsters who had gone berserk. Back then, it wasn't a matter of drugs or alcohol. It was hysteria. The girls were in love. They would say, 'I have to talk to them! You don't understand!' "

Seattle Times

Seattle welcomes The Beatles, 1965

After the performance, the police bundled up the Fab Four in blankets, put them on stretchers and carried them through the crowd to a Red Cross van, which escaped the wild hordes who demanded their heroes. About the entire episode the *Seattle Times* wrote: "Seattle seethed with uncontrollable hysteria, terrifying noice and danger in a real-life nightmare last night. This was the Beatles' show. For 30 incredible minutes, those in the jam-packed Seattle Center Coliseum had the feeling of being sealed in a crazed capsule pitching through the chasms of space." A similar hysteria gripped other cities on the Beatles tour, and by the end of 1965, it had reaped more than $56 million in the United States alone.

Besides publicity and talent, a change in the format of radio programming, which made it easier to market a specific band, contributed to the Beatles' triumphant sweep of America. In 1961 on station KVND of Fresno, California, the fast-talking disc jockey Bill Drake perfected the Top 40 playlist, which reduced the number of songs and the pauses in a radio program. The tunes of a popular group such as the Beatles could then be played over and over. In 1964, during Beatlemania, one record executive in a company that had no Beatle releases complained of the consequences of the Top 40 format: "Stations are playing our records like spot commercials between Beatle tunes." Said Brown Meggs of Capitol: "What sells records is radio. The Beatles got unbelievable radio play. There wasn't a single market in the country in which airplay wasn't simply stupendous."

OTHER BRITISH INVADERS

In the mid-1960s the often-played, well-publicized, talented Beatles conquered the American music market and paved the way for other British groups, some of them linked to Brian Epstein. "The biggest thing the Beatles did was to open the American market to all British artists," contended British promoter Arthur Howes, who planned the early Beatle tours of England. "Nobody had ever been able to get in before the Beatles. They alone did it. I had brought over lots of American stars, but nobody had gone over there." By February 1964, agreed *Variety*, "Britannia ruled the airwaves." "The advent of the [Beatles] now has shattered the steady, day-to-day domination of made-in-America music here and abroad." By the end of 1964 British rock bands had sold over $76 million worth of records in the United States, and *Newsweek* estimated that almost four hundred groups had sprung up in Liverpool alone. Bill Harry, the editor of the English music magazine *Mersey Beat*, explained that "the beat career is the equivalent of becoming a boxer in the beginning of the century — the only way into the luxury world."

Some of the British groups had grown up with the Beatles in Liverpool. Gerry Marsden, a truck driver who was a neighbor of the Beatles, formed a band called the Pacemakers. Under the watchful eye of manager Brian Epstein, Gerry and the Pacemakers climbed the charts in 1964 with a song written for the Beatles, "How Do You Do It?" They also recorded the hits "Ferry across the Mersey" and "Don't Let the Sun Catch You Crying," and starred in the movie *Ferry across the Mersey*.

Members of another Epstein act, Billy J. Kramer and the Dakotas, rose from their humble working-class backgrounds to stardom with "Want to Know a Secret," a track from the Beatles' first album. Billy J. Kramer, a worker for the British Railways, originally sang with a group called The Coasters, but linked up with the Dakotas on the advice of Epstein. Observed *The Big Beat* fanzine in 1964: "The marriage of the zing singing of Billy J. to the true-beat accompaniment of the Daks has proven a brilliant stroke on the part of Epstein. These boys just have to step onto the stage and the fans go wild!" Although producer George Martin was "forced to the conclusion that [Kramer's] was not the greatest voice in the world" (he had to "double-track his voice" during recording sessions), Billy J. Kramer hit the charts with "Little Children," "Bad To Me," and "I'll Keep You Satisfied."

Together with the Beatles, Gerry and the Pacemakers and Billy J. Kramer delivered the Liverpool "Mersey Sound." Alex Korner, who with Cyril Davies gave birth to the British blues scene of the 1960s, found that "there was a certain brashness about the Liverpool music, which stamped it almost immediately — they played it the way they speak English, you know! You could definitely tell a Liverpool group. The Mersey sound was basically a guitar sound: lead guitar, rhythm guitar, bass guitar, and drums was the basic Liverpool set-up."

Groups from other parts of Great Britain invaded America with variants of the Mersey sound. From Manchester, a dingy, smokestacked industrial center much like Liverpool, came Freddie Gerrity and the Dreamers. Quitting his job as a milkman, Freddie and his Dreamers hit the charts in 1964 with "I'm Telling You Now." A year later on American TV's *Shindig* and *Hullabaloo,* the band created a short-lived dance craze — "Do the Freddie."

In 1965 Wayne Fontana and the Mindbenders, another amalgam of poor Manchester youths, scored a hit with "The Game of Love." Fontana (a.k.a. Glyn Geoffrey Ellis), who took his stage name from his record company, quit his job as a telephone engineering trainee and formed a band during an audition at the Oasis Club in Manchester. He named the group The Mindbenders after a horror film that was then playing in a local theater. Besides their 1964 hit, The Mindbenders charted with a sequel, "A Groovy Kind of Love."

The Hollies proved that they had more staying power than most other Manchester bands. The group was started by Graham Nash and singer-guitarist Allan Clarke. The two first met in grammar school and later became the Two Teens. After a few name changes, including the Guytones and the Deltas, the duo added three other members in 1963 and labeled themselves the Hollies after their musical hero, Buddy Holly. Almost immediately, the band produced a string of blockbuster hits: "Ain't That Just Like Me," "Just One Look," "Look Through Any Window," "Bus Stop," and "Stop, Stop, Stop." In 1965, during a tour of America, they drove fans to a frenzied state at New York City's Paramount Theater and on such television shows as *Shindig, Hullabaloo,* and *The Smothers Brothers Show*.

The Dave Clark Five, from the Tottenham section of London, initially posed the most serious threat to the commercial dominance of the Beatles. Grouping together to raise money for Dave Clark's rugby team, the Five trailed the Beatles to America in 1964 and grossed over $750,000, scaling the charts with "Glad All Over." The liner notes on their American debut album predicted that "the Tottenham sound of the Dave Clark Five is on its way towards overthrowing the reign of the Beatles in this country." The next year they copied the Fab Four and branched out into films, which included *Lucy, Get Yourself a College Girl*, and *Having a Wild Weekend*. As critic Lillian Roxon observed, "the whole key to the Five is that Clark is not so much a musician as a businessman and that the whole operation from the start, and still today, of course, has been run as a very efficient business. Everyone else had breakdowns and internal hassles and big creative triumphs. Dave Clark and his musical boys come on like young business executives and always have, and that's what they are."

From the Muswell Hill region of London, a Northern working-class suburb, came the Kinks. In 1964 and 1965 the group — brothers Ray and Dave Davies, Peter Quaife, and Mike Avory — invented power-chord rock and blasted their audiences with such classics as "You Really Got Me," "All Day and All of the Night," and "I Need You." Dave Davies explained to *Melody Maker* that the distinctive sound originated because at that time "I was never a very good guitarist . . . so I used to experiment with sounds. I had a very small amplifier which distorted badly." Besides this innovation, the Kinks tapped their British heritage and delivered a series of witty tunes based upon a skiffle, music-hall sound.

Other, more blues-oriented English groups edged into the American market. The Yardbirds, formed in 1964, featured Keith Relf on vocals and harmonica and a series of premier lead guitarists: first Eric Clapton, then Jeff Beck, and finally Jimmy Page. In 1965 the foursome scored minor hits with "Heart Full of Soul," the Bo Diddley number "I'm a Man," and "For Your Love."

Three years earlier, Manfred Mann (a.k.a. Michael Lubowitz) had teamed with fellow jazz aficionado Mike Hugg to become the Mann-Hugg Blues Brothers. After greeted by wild receptions to their music at the London Marquee Club, the duo added three more members and emerged as Manfred Mann and the Manfreds or, in the United States, as just Manfred Mann. In 1964 the band scored the first of a series of hits, a remake of the Exciters' "Do Wah Diddy Diddy." The band subsequently rehashed such R & B gems as Muddy Waters's "Got My Mojo Working," "Smokestack Lightning" by Howlin' Wolf, and Willie Dixon's "I'm Your Hoochie Coochie Man."

The Animals, a group of poor youths from a mining town in northern England and named for their behavior on stage, played a more convincing brand of British R & B. In 1962 jazz organist Alan Price modified his combo to include lead guitarist Hilton Valentine, bassist Bryan "Chas" Chandler, John Steel on drums, and Eric Burdon, whose voice captured the raw, deep pain of black American bluesmen. Price was pushed in the direction of rhythm and blues by the new musicians,

Photo by Cam Garrett

Jeff Beck of the Yardbirds

especially Burdon, who, according to the *New Musical Express,* had "written out hundreds of lyrics by artists like Mose Allison and Chuck Berry. On the first page he had written the word *Blues* in his own blood. He had cut his finger especially for it." In their first two years the Animals earned a following at the Club-a-Go-Go in their home town of Newcastle-on-Tyne. Price remembered that "we used to play everything from the blues to Chico Hamilton, and it used to swing like the clappers." After moving to London in 1964, the band reworked the black folk song "The House of the Rising Sun" into a blockbuster hit. They then released "I'm Cryin'," "Boom Boom," "Don't Let Me Be Misunderstood," "Bring It on Home to Me," "It's My Life," and "We Gotta Get out of This Place," and triumphantly toured the United States in the fall of 1964.

George Ivan Morrison and his group, Them, were equally dedicated to American R & B. Raised in Ulster by parents who were blues and jazz enthusiasts, Van Morrison grew up listening to the likes of John Lee Hooker, Muddy Waters, Leadbelly, and Sonny Boy Williamson. At fifteen, he dropped out of school and joined a band called the Monarchs, which headlined at the R & B Club in Belfast. In 1964 the stocky, pudgy Morrison formed the Them, which released three now-legendary songs, "Baby, Please Don't Go," "Here Comes the Night," and the unforgettable "Gloria." Although almost defining the updated English version of R & B, the Them received only minimal attention at the time.

The Mods vs. the Rockers and the British Invasion of America **99**

THE ROLLING STONES

A publicist for the Beatles, Andrew Loog Oldham, discovered one of the most successful and talented of the R & B revival bands: the Rolling Stones. As with most other British youths, the Stones became interested in rock music through American rockabilly. Mick Jagger "had been singing with some rock and roll bands, doing Buddy Holly," guitarist Keith Richard remembered. "Buddy Holly was in England as solid as Elvis. Everything that came out was a record smash number one. By about '58 it was either Elvis or Buddy Holly." Richard himself was "really listening to what was coming over the Atlantic. The ones that were hitting hard were Little Richard, and Presley, and Jerry Lee Lewis." He "was rockin' away, avoidin' the bicycle chains and razors in those dance halls." And when *Blackboard Jungle* with the music of Bill Haley and the Comets showed in London, Richard found that "people were saying 'Did ya hear that music, man?' Because in England we had never heard anything: the BBC controls it and won't play that sort of music. But everybody our age stood up for that music and the hell with the BBC."

Members of the Rolling Stones soon began to uncover the blues roots of rockabilly. Keith Richard heard "Broonzy first. . . . Then I started to discover Robert Johnson and those cats." The multi-instrumental Brian Jones, initially the impetus behind the group, one day heard "Elmore James, and the earth seemed to shudder on its axis. . . . The blues was real. We only had to persuade people to listen to the music, and they couldn't help but be turned on to all those great old blues cats." Mick Jagger, who started out by singing in a band called Little Boy Blue and the Blue Boys, similarly "was crazy over Chuck Berry, Bo Diddley, Muddy Waters, and Fats Domino, not knowing what it meant, just that it was beautiful."

One day in London, recalled Richard, "I get on this train one morning and there's Jagger — and under his arm he has four or five albums. . . . He's got Chuck Berry, Little Walter, Muddy Waters." The two talked about their mutual passion for R & B and in a few weeks, with a friend, Dick Taylor, formed a band called the Glimmer Twins, which laid "down some of this Chuck Berry and Little Walter stuff. No drummer or anything, just two guitars and a little amplifier. And suddenly in '62, just when we were getting together, we read this thing about a Rhythm and Blues Club starting in Ealing." Jagger and Richard linked up with another blues fanatic, Brian Jones, and moved into a run-down apartment in the downtrodden district of King's Road. They called themselves the Rolling Stones. After adding drummer Charlie Watts and bassist Bill Wyman, the Stones appeared publicly on July 12, 1962, at the Marquee Club in Soho.

The material chosen by the early Stones indicated their blues orientation. For their first single, recorded in March 1963, they covered

Chuck Berry's "Come On" and Muddy Waters's "I Wanna Be Loved." Their first American album, *England's Newest Hitmakers,* included Slim Harpo's "I'm a Kingbee," "Carol" by Chuck Berry, Willie Dixon's "I Just Wanna Make Love to You," and Jimmy Reed's "Honest I Do." Subsequent albums exposed teenage record buyers to such R & B classics as "You Can't Catch Me" and "Talkin' about You" (Chuck Berry), "Little Red Rooster" (Willie Dixon), "Mona" (Bo Diddley), and "Look What You've Done" (Muddy Waters). The Stones recorded many of these cuts at the legendary Chess studio in Chicago. "Chuck Berry wandered in while we were recording 'Down the Road Apiece,' " a wide-eyed Bill Wyman told a reporter for the *New Musical Express,* "and he said to us: 'Wow, you guys are really getting it on.' Muddy Waters was also there." Even the name of the band — the Rolling Stones — came from a tune penned by Muddy Waters, and in April 1963 the *Record Mirror* characterized the Stones as "genuine R and B. As the trad scene gradually subsides, promoters of all kinds of teen-beat entertainments heave a long sigh of relief that they have found something to take its place. It's rhythm and blues . . . and to the Station Hotel, Kew Road, the hip kids throw themselves around to the new 'jungle music' like they never did in the more restrained days of trad. And the combo they writhe and twist to is called the Rolling Stones."

The Stones, though dedicated to the music of the poor American black felt an overpowering drive to get ahead. According to Jagger, they "were always hustling to get our picture on the cover of *Fab* or *Rave* or *Teen.* As soon as the teenyboppers caught on, we were in for the big scream." Keith Richard, always more graphic, told a *Time* reporter in 1964, "I hope to be sitting in a country house with four Rolls-Royces and spitting at everyone."

This lust for wealth may have come from their middle-class values. Unlike the Beatles and many members of other British bands that invaded America, the Stones came from middle-class homes. Jagger, born on July 20, 1943, was the son of Joe Jagger, a physical training instructor. He grew up in a comfortable home in Dartford, which was — in his own words — "a very protected environment. It was a middle-class home. I was just an ordinary rebellious studious hard-working kid." Jagger even attended the prestigious London School of Economics, where he became radicalized. Although a young tough, Keith Richard was the son of an electrical engineer. The father of Brian Jones worked as an aeronautical engineer and his mother offered piano lessons. Before he helped to form the Stones, Jones made money as an architect's assistant. Likewise, drummer Charlie Watts, the son of a lorry driver for the British Railways, attended Harrow Art School and worked in an advertising agency before joining the Stones. Only bassist Bill Wyman described himself as "a straight working-class type." As Mick Jagger aptly pointed out, "we weren't from poverty families. [And the audience] were people like us . . . more like a college crowd."

THE STONES TURN RAUNCHY

As a strategy to capture a larger following, the Stones and their manager consciously created a contrast to the Beatles: the raunchy, crude, offensive Rolling Stones. At first the band appeared to be like most other British invasion bands. When they performed on *Thank Your Lucky Stars,* a British television program, the Stones wore checkered suits. "You have to make some compromises," Andrew Loog Oldham instructed the group, sounding like his one-time boss, Brian Epstein. "Just to get started in this business you have to compromise a bit." As Keith Richard later told it, the manager "tried to tidy us up. . . . There are photographs of us in the suits he put us in, those dog-toothed checked suits with the black velvet collars."

Oldham's tactics backfired. Looking like any other British band during their first tour of the United States, which started in June 1964, the Stones received scant notice. They first appeared on a segment of *Hollywood Palace* that happened to be hosted by the loveable lush, Dean Martin. After the Stones chugged through their versions of "I Just Want to Make Love to You" and "Not Fade Away," a twisted-faced Martin, eyes rolling upward, asked the audience, "Aren't they great?" He continued: "They're off to England to have a hair pulling contest with the Beatles. . . . Their hair is not that long — it's just smaller foreheads and higher eyebrows." When a trampolinist finished his act, Martin added: "That's the father of the Rolling Stones. He's been trying to kill himself ever since." To a distraught Brian Jones, Dean Martin "was just a symbol of the whole tour for us."

Mostly, the band played to empty seats. In San Antonio, Texas, the crowd clamored for an encore by a trained monkey over one by the Rolling Stones. "We all wanted to pack up and come home," confessed Bill Wyman. The colorful Keith Richard remembered "Nebraska, we really felt like a sore pimple in Omaha. On top of that, the first time we arrived there, the only people to meet us off the plane were twelve motorcycle cops who insisted on doing this motorcade thing right through town. And nobody in Omaha had ever heard of us. We thought, 'Wow, we've made it. We must be heavy.' And we get to the Auditorium and there's 600 people there in a 15,000-seat seat hall."

To avoid a complete disaster, Oldham quickly changed his course of action and manufactured an opposite to the neat, smiling Beatles. "It was perfect, just perfect," Oldham told Jagger after a press conference, at which the Stones had given flippant and insulting replies to American journalists. "They're going to plaster your pictures and your terrible, terrible statements all over the papers. Those dirty Rolling Stones, that's what you are. The opposite of those nice little chaps, the Beatles. It's working, it's sure as hell working. We're gonna make you famous." "The long-haired, dirty-rebel image was pushed on us here in the States," Richard contended. In 1965 Jagger added: "That's what we wanted you Americans to think, that we were dirty and raunchy. That was our image over there. If those dumb American birds dig that kind of shit, why shouldn't we do it?"

To refine the image, Oldham engineered a few changes. He downgraded piano player Ian Stewart to roadie. "Well, he just doesn't look the part, and six is too many for [fans] to remember the faces in the picture," Oldham told Richard at the time. The manager shaved a few years off the ages of each Stone in their official biography, making them teens again. He then convinced his label, London Records, to blitz the media. Read one ad in *Billboard,* "They're great? They're outrageous! They're rebels! They sell! They're England's *hottest.*"

The rest of the media soon picked up the cue. In 1964 the *News of the World* carried an article headlined "Would You Let Your Daughter Go Out with a Rolling Stone?" and pictured the band as "symbols of rebellion . . . against the boss, the clock, and the clean-shirt-a-day routine." The Stones, it continued, looked like "five indolent morons, who give one the feeling that they really enjoy wallowing in a swill-tub of their own repulsiveness." Even *Melody Maker* and the *New Musical Express* described the group as "the ugliest pop group in Britain" and "the caveman-like quintet."

The music of the Stones also began to change. Pressured in part by Andrew Oldham, who, according to Richard, "had never listened to an R & B record in his life," Richard and Jagger pushed aside the versatile Brian Jones and began to concentrate on their own material, which relied more on pop conventions than the blues. In their first three albums, Jagger told interviewer Ed Rudy, the Stones found "that American songs are better for ourselves. The songs that Keith and I write . . . we give to other people. They're mostly ballads." But by their fourth LP, *Out of Our Heads,* which was recorded in July 1965, the band had started to move away from R & B toward the more commercial, pop sound of "Satisfaction," "Play with Fire," "The Last Time," and "Under Assistant West Coast Promotion Man." By the 1966 *Aftermath,* Jagger-Richard compositions such as the murky incantations of "Paint It Black" and the misogynist venom of "Under My Thumb" and "Stupid Girl" had almost totally replaced R & B material.

The new sound and satanic image of the Stones dovetailed with their second tour of America in the autumn of 1964 and made it a smashing success. Their October performance on the Ed Sullivan program ended in such chaos that the host babbled: "I promise you they'll never be back on our show. . . . Frankly, I didn't see the Rolling Stones until the day before the broadcast. They were recommended by my scouts in England. I was shocked when I saw them. It took me seventeen years to build this show; I'm not going to have it destroyed in a matter of weeks. Now the Dave Clark Five were nice fellows — they are gentlemen and performed well." *Newsweek* pegged the Stones as a "leering quintet" obsessed with pornographic lyrics. One concerned woman wrote to *Time* magazine: "We like the Beatles because they have rhythm, enthusiasm, and a good sound. After listening to the groans,

The Rolling Stones on the "Ed Sullivan Show"

pants, and frankly dirty words of the Rolling Stones and a few other sick groups, one begins to wonder where they dig up a DJ to play such garbage."

Such adult criticism of the band predictably pushed rebellious American teenagers into the Stones' camp. Keith Richard at the time felt an "energy building up as you go around the country. You find it winding tighter and tighter, until one day you get out halfway through the first number and the whole place is full of chicks screaming. We'd walk into some of these places and it was like they had the Battle of the Crimea going on — people gasping, tits hanging out, chicks choking, nurses running around." "There was a period of six months in England we couldn't play ballrooms anymore because we never got through more than three or four songs every night," added Richard. "Chaos. Police and too many people in the places fainting. They used to tell us, 'There's not a dry seat in the cinema.' And the bigger it got, America and Australia and everywhere it's exactly the same number." Beatle George Harrison noticed by 1966: "It's become the in thing for adults to say the Beatles are good or the Beatles are funny, it's in for adults to like us. So the real hip kids — or the kids who think they are — have gone off us. The in thing for those kids now is to be a Stones fan, because their parents can't stand the Rolling Stones." The income of the band reflected their growing popularity: It skyrocketed from about $150 a week in early 1963 to almost $800 a week a year later. By 1967 the Stones had become millionaires.

THE PRICE OF SUCCESS

The Rolling Stones, as well as the Beatles, found the intensity of success overwhelming. The frantic pace of touring and churning out two or three albums a year eventually led Keith Richard, who needed some escape from the pressure, to heroin addiction. Success had the same effect on Richard's common-law wife, Anita Pallenberg, and Marianne Faithfull, Jagger's rich girlfriend, who in 1964 gained musical notice with her version of "As Tears Go By" and fifteen years later delivered the bitter, cutting testament, *Broken English*. In 1966 Mick Jagger suffered a nervous breakdown. And for Brian Jones, who turned to drugs and alcohol after he lost his influence in the Stones, stardom ended in 1969 at the bottom of a swimming pool.

George Harrison felt that in Liverpool the Beatles "were doing shorter hours, but it was still as enjoyable. We were part of the audience. We lived our lives with them. We never rehearsed an act. . . . Then came touring, which was great at first, doing an even shorter, more polished act and working out new songs. But it got played out. We got in a rut, going round the world. It was a different audience each day, but we were doing the same things. . . . No one eventually enjoyed touring. You can't really. Once you've got to manufacture it, it doesn't work." He vowed never to do it again: "Never in this life or any other life. I mean, a lot of the time it was fantastic, but when it really got into the mania it was a question of either stop or end up dead." The usually sanguine Paul McCartney told a reporter that "to go from being a kid living on the street on some council-estate [public-housing] project to become very famous is a big change. Living with all the trappings of that isn't an easy adjustment; your privacy has to go a bit. It is a bit humiliating sometimes."

John Lennon gave the most bitter assessment: "I came out of the fuckin' sticks to take over the world it seemed to me. I was enjoying it, and I was trapped in it, too. I couldn't do anything about it, I was just going along for the ride. I was hooked, just like a junkie." One "has to completely humiliate oneself to be what the Beatles were." Added Lennon, who with McCartney formally disbanded the band in 1970: "Since I was 22, I was always 'supposed to.' I was supposed to write a hundred songs by Friday, supposed to have a single out by Saturday, supposed to do this or that. I became an artist because I cherished freedom — I couldn't fit into a classroom or an office. Freedom was the plus for all the minuses for being an oddball! But suddenly I was obliged to a record company, obliged to the media, obliged to the public. I wasn't free at all!" The guitarist contended that "I was always waiting for a reason to get out of the Beatles from the day I filmed *How I Won the War* [in 1966]. I just didn't have the guts to do it. The seed was planted when the Beatles stopped touring and I couldn't deal with not being onstage. But I was too frightened to step out of the palace. That's what killed Presley. The king is always killed by his courtiers. He is overfed, overindulged, overdrunk to keep him tied to his throne."

The Beatles had paid the price of success, but had risen to dizzying heights that no other rock performer had scaled. From 1964 to 1966 their music — along with the sounds of other British bands that invaded America — blasted from the radios of almost every American teenager. Yet by 1966, even though they still commanded a huge following and easily sold a million copies of each record they produced, the Beatles had to contend with a new force that exploded on the rock scene in a rainbow of colors — the psychedelic movement.

6

****

Acid Rock

****

"Everybody's relaxing and not afraid to speak out and not afraid not to wear a tie to work," asserted Marty Balin, one of the founders of the Jefferson Airplane, which took off in San Francisco during the mid-1960s. "The one word I can think of is love, even though that sounds like a cliché, but that's where it's at, it's uninhibited, coming out emotion. It's like the twenties. The twenties were really a start and at the end of it, they had all these great creative different things come out of it. I really feel it's the same. It's the most moving generation since the twenties. In creativity. And out of this are going to come many wonderful artists and people and thinkers. Even the philosophy of the day is being changed by what's happening now."

Speak out. Love. Creativity. Moving generation. Happening now. Words of a new era. In the wake of the British invasion, hundreds of middle-class, college-educated youths clustered around San Francisco Bay to disseminate these ideas. They hoped to demonstrate to the country, and eventually to the world, that love could replace war, sharing could replace avarice, and community could replace the emphasis on the individual. These San Francisco visionaries strove for nothing less than a total transformation of American social mores, and they demanded change immediately. As Jim Morrison, lead singer of the Doors, screamed: "We want the world, and we want it *now*."

A new hybrid of rock and roll propagated these "hippie" values: Called acid rock after a strange new drug, LSD, which circulated among the bands, the music broadcast the word of hippiedom from the epicenter, San Francisco, to the hinterlands. Unlike the lower-class British invaders who used music to entertain ("There's no message in our music; it's just for fun," smiled Dave Clark), the West Coast bands played for a purpose: The groups — the Jefferson Airplane, the Doors, the Grateful Dead, Quicksilver Messenger Service, Big Brother and the Holding Company, the Seeds, and countless others (1,500 by one count) — were the leaders of a youth movement that consciously withdrew from what they considered to be the corrupt, crumbling edifice of America's 9-to-5, workaholic society. As an alternative, they tried to build a community of love and understanding. From 1965 to 1967 the vanguard of rock and roll had a mission.

THE BEATS

In San Francisco the year 1965 began with a social upheaval, which had its origins with the Beats, who had wandered from their homes in New York City to San Francisco's North Beach more than a decade earlier. In 1951 Jack Kerouac, the Columbia football star turned writer, planted the seeds of the Beat Generation when he bummed around the country with the ever-energetic, ever-adventurous Neal Cassady and told of their travels in *On the Road*. The same year, poet Lawrence Ferlinghetti left New York for San Francisco because "it was the only place in the country where you could get decent wine cheap"; two years later he opened the prime beatnik haunt in North Beach, City Lights Bookstore. In 1953 Allen Ginsberg migrated to San Francisco on the advice of his friend Neal Cassady, and two years later organized the first public appearance of the Beat Generation — a poetry reading advertised as "Six Poets at the Six Gallery," at which Ginsberg premiered his controversial poem "Howl." In 1957 Kerouac finally published *On the Road,* to the critical acclaim of the *New York Times.*

The Beats formulated a countercultural philosophy based upon tenets of Eastern religion. Their metaphorical name — Beat — suggested the quest for a beatitude that could be discovered in Zen Buddhism. It also referred to the patron saints of the movement, the drifters, who shed the trappings of institutional society and gathered in places such as the New York City Bowery. Although appearing "beat down" and downtrodden to "straights," the bums symbolized the freedom that the avant-garde so dearly cherished. As one writer put it, the beatniks "chased the unwashed American dream." Finally, the term reverberated to musical connotations — to the cool, disengaged jazz of

Poet Allen Ginsberg: a bridge between the Beats and the Hippies

Miles Davis, Lennie Tristano, and Gerry Mulligan that wafted from the coffeehouse hangouts of the Beat writers.

Congregating in San Francisco's City Lights Bookstore and New York City's Greenwich Village, these countercultural literati lambasted the hypocrisy in American society. Beat comic Lenny Bruce satirized the marketing of the Lone Ranger and the wiles of the Avon lady. In his *Naked Lunch* (1959), William S. Burroughs, the literary genius who had inherited the Burroughs adding machine fortune, wove together powerful, graphic images of a decaying society: "Smell of chili houses and dank overcoats and atrophied testicles. . . . A heaving sea of air hammers in the purple brown dusk tainted with rotten metal smell of sewer gas." Ginsberg delved into the same cesspool of American life with such drug-inspired poems as "Howl," which the San Francisco Police Department declared obscene, banned, and confiscated. *Naked Lunch* met the same fate.

In place of traditional bourgeois values, the Beats preached a cultural relativism. "We love everything," explained Kerouac. "Billy Graham, the Big Ten, Rock and Roll, Zen, apple pie, Eisenhower — we dig it all." Since no value was absolute, morality depended upon the individual. As one Beat argued, "I stay cool, far out, alone. When I flip it's over something *I* feel, only me." Such an ethos led to experimentation with sex and drugs, especially marijuana and amphetamines, which Kerouac mentioned in *Dharma Bums*. Writer Burton Wolfe put it this way: "They had no interest in building a greater America, in fighting Communism, in working at a career to buy hundred-dollar suits and dresses, color television sets, a house in the suburbs, or a flight to Paris. In fact, they laughed at those goals. Some brew, a few joints, a sympathetic partner in the sack, a walk in the park, an afternoon of lying in the sun on the beach, a hitchhike trip to Mexico — this was all there was."

The anti-institutional values of the Beats generated damaging criticism from more traditional quarters. Right-wing F.B.I. director J. Edgar Hoover, turning literary critic in 1959, reviewed Lawrence Ferlinghetti's poem "Tentative Description of a Dinner Given to Promote the Impeachment of President Eisenhower" and concluded, "it appears that Ferlinghetti may possibly be a mental case." A month later the Alcoholic Beverages Commission declared "Beatnikland" a "problem area" and refused to issue any more liquor licenses. Other, more violent critics bombed the women's restroom at the Co-Existence Bagel Shop, a favorite gathering spot for the San Francisco Beats. The Bagel Shop, along with The Place, closed down shortly thereafter. By the end of 1959 Eric Nord, one of the most visible West Coast Beat writers, told a courtroom, "the Beat Generation is dead. I don't go to North Beach anymore."

THE REEMERGENCE OF THE BEATS: THE NEW YORK CONNECTION

Some of the Beats, however, reappeared on the cultural scene in the early 1960s to foster the psychedelic movement. On the East Coast, at St. Mark's Place in Greenwich Village, Beat poets Ed Sanders and Tuli Kupferberg started the Fugs. The band caricatured American society, in the process using the verse of William Blake in "How Sweet I Roamed from Field to Field" and the prose of William S. Burroughs in "Virgin Forest." Allen Ginsberg described the countercultural message of the group in the liner notes on the Fugs' second album. "The United States is split down the middle," he contended. "On one side are everybody who make love with their eyes open, maybe smoke pot and maybe take LSD and look inside their heads to find the Self-God Walt Whitman prophesied for America. . . . Who's on the other side? People who think we are *bad*. . . . Yogis and Beatles say there is no other side. 'We can get along.' Can we? NOW sings Sanders and the Fugs come camping and screaming along, out in the open where every ear can hear the soul politics ecstasy message — They've put it in Front. . . . The Fugs came to tell the truth that was only dreamy till they opened their mouths for Whitmanic orgy yawp. Group Grope, Dirty Old Man, Skin Flowers and Frenzy! Teenagers rise up and understand. When they scream 'Kill for

Peace' they're announcing publicly the madness of our white-haired crazy governments." The poet concluded: "The Bible says that when Christ comes back, 'every eye shall see.' Now every ear can hear, and when the Fugs break thru the monopoly blockade and their image is broadcast on National Television, every kid in America and most white-haired old suffering men will turn them on with Relief at last and every eye shall see."

Also from New York came the Velvet Underground. In 1965 avant-garde artist Andy Warhol stumbled upon the band, then called the Falling Spikes, at the Cafe Bizarre in New York's Greenwich Village and immediately signed them for his multimedia extravaganza, the Exploding Plastic Inevitable. He added actress Nico to the foursome, but center stage definitely belonged to Velvet leader Lou Reed, who named the group after the title of a pornographic paperback. Reed had studied at Syracuse University with Beat poet Delmore Schwartz, and his songs reflected the connection between the Beats and the emerging psychedelic consciousness: They dealt with the down-and-out themes of Beat fiction — heroin addiction in "I'm Waiting for the Man" and the rushing "Heroin," and cocaine in "Run, Run, Run." In the Velvet's second album, Reed led the listener through the adventures of a girl named Candy, who roamed the cultural underground assisted by her junkie boyfriend. It was Beat writing translated into rock music.

THE HAIGHT-ASHBURY SCENE

The most direct bridge between the Beats and the "hippies," as *San Francisco Examiner* writer Michael Fallon first called them in September 1965, could be found in San Francisco. There, a number of prominent Beats helped to create the Haight-Ashbury scene. At the first hippie gathering held at Longshoremen's Hall on the Wharf, wrote journalist Ralph Gleason, "SNCC buttons and peace buttons abounded, stuck onto costumes straight out of the Museum of Natural History. . . . Long lines of dancers snaked through the crowd for hours holding hands. Free-form improvisation ('self-expression') was everywhere. The clothes were a blast. Like a giant costume party." Amid the revelry whirled a long-haired, bearded, and ever-present Allen Ginsberg.

For three days in late January 1966, Beat writer Ken Kesey, author of *One Flew over the Cuckoo's Nest* (1962), and his band of free spirits known as the Merry Pranksters hosted the Trips Festival. For the event, they enlisted the services of the Grateful Dead and Big Brother and the Holding Company, set up five movie screens, on which they projected a mind-boggling combination of colors and shapes, and spiked the punch with a little LSD, a concoction that became known as the kool-aid acid test. The preparations resulted in a "mind-blowing" experience. At the festivities, Kesey stalked the floor dressed in a space helmet and a jump suit. Eyewitness Ralph Gleason saw one man "bandaged all over, with only his eyes peeking out through dark glasses, carrying a crutch and wearing a sign: 'You're in the Pepsi generation and I'm a pimply freak.' Another long-haired exotic dressed in a modified Hell's Angels' leather jerkin that had 'Under Ass Wizard Mojo Indian Fighter' stenciled on his back. Several varieties of Lawrence of Arabia costumes wandered through." At one point Neal Cassady, the Beat High Priest, who in many ways was the catalyst for the other Beats (he appeared in Kerouac's *On the Road* as Dean Moriarty and inspired the Indian in Kesey's *One Flew*), "stood for a while upstairs and then swung out and over the back of the balcony railing, scaring everyone who saw him, as they expected him to slip and fall to the floor." Cassady would re-appear at countless Grateful Dead concerts to deliver amazing free-associational monologues as a prelude before the performances. He would also sit at the helm of the psychedelic bus that took Kesey and the Merry Pranksters on a symbolic trip across the country and that later inspired the Beatles' Magical Mystery Tour.

Other Beats helped put together the "First Human Be-In," which took place in Golden Gate Park on January 14, 1967. Allen Ginsberg, painter Michael Bowen, playwright Michael McClure, poetess Lenore Kandal, and poet Gary Snyder staged the multicolored community gathering, which attracted twenty thousand people on an unseasonably warm January day. Hippies danced on the grass to the sounds of the Grateful Dead, the Jefferson Airplane, and Quicksilver. "The costumes were a designer's dream, a wild polyglot mixture of Mod, Paladin, Ringling Brothers, Cochise and Hell's Angels' Formal," wrote Ralph Gleason in the *San Francisco Chronicle*. "The poets read. Allen Ginsberg (who may yet be elected president) chanted and Gary Snyder sat on the stage and joined in. Bells rang and balloons floated in the air. A man went around handing out oranges and there were sandwiches and candy and cookies. No one was selling anything."

When news of these remarkable events spread across Kansas, Florida, Wisconsin, and other parts of the country, the psychedelic ranks in San Francisco began to swell. Jay Thelin, the co-owner of The Psychedelic Shop, which served as the briefing center for hippie initiates in the city, recalled the rapid influx of youths into the Haight-Ashbury district that occurred by early 1966: "Like, Wow! There was an explosion. People began coming in from all over and our little information shop became sort of a clubhouse for dropouts and, well, we just let it happen, that's all." The hippie movement had blossomed out of the ground prepared by the Beat Generation.

THE HIPPIE CULTURE

The hippies, like the Beats, struck out verbally against bourgeois values. "The standard thing is to feel in the gut that middle-class values are all wrong," remarked one hippie. "It's the system itself that is corrupt," added another. "Capitalism, communism, whatever it is.

These are phoney labels. There is no capitalism or communism. Only dictators telling people what to do."

To replace modern corruption, many hippies turned to simpler civilizations of the past for role models. Attempting to recapture a lost innocence, some tried to recreate the popular image of the noble American Indian. They slipped into moccasins and sported fringed deerskin jackets, headbands, feathers, and colorful beads. Even though most Native Americans, like Rupert Costo, President of the American Indian Historical Society, felt that the hippies represented a "certain insidious and subtle exploitation of the Indian which is the worst of all," the psychedelic generation persisted in a cult of tribalism. Steve Levine, editor of the *San Francisco Oracle,* one of the many countercultural newspapers that serviced and shaped the Hashbury scene, philosophized that "the white-eye who once annihilated the buffalo must now, in action-reacted, be saved from slaughtering himself by the Indian incarnate."

Others followed the example of the Beats and looked for salvation in the mystery of the Orient. As one San Francisco free spirit put it: "The society feeds us machines, technology, computers, and we answer with primitivism: the *I Ching,* the *Tibetan Book of the Dead,* Buddhism, Taoism. The greatest truths lie in the ancient cultures. Modern civilization is out of balance with nature." Zen popularizer Alan Watts became a cult figure, some teens joined Hare Krishna, and weekend hipsters shuffled Tarot cards for portents of the future.

Drugs became the most popular avenue to at least temporarily withdraw from a competitive, computer-chipped American society. Many rolled marijuana into joints or smoked the weed Indian-style, in pipes. Others favored the more expensive, more potent hashish. Still others became disciples of defrocked Harvard professor Timothy Leary, and swallowed sugar cubes containing the hallucinogen LSD. Legal until October 6, 1966, "acid" fragmented everyday perception into a multitude of melting shapes and vibrant colors. Related Leary: "The first thing you notice is an incredible enhancement of sensory awareness. Take the sense of sight. LSD vision is to normal vision as normal vision is to the picture of a badly tuned television set. Under LSD, it's as though you have microscopes up to your eyes, in which you see jewel-like, radiant details of anything your eye falls upon. . . . The organ of the Corti in your inner ear becomes a trembling membrane seething with tattoos of sound waves. The vibrations seem to penetrate deep inside you, swell and burst there. . . . You not only hear but *see* the music emerging from the speaker system like dancing particles, like squirming curls of toothpaste." By the end of the decade over fifteen million of these magic capsules had been distributed single-handedly by Augustus Owsley Stanley III, Owsley to his friends, who became known as the King of Acid. In 1966 an official from the Food and Drug Administration estimated that over 10 percent of all college students had ingested LSD.

Many users contended that the drug experience resulted in al-

Timothy Leary: the guru of LSD

tered, introspective states that expanded consciousness. In September 1966, comfortably lying on a mattress in his headquarters, a 64-room mansion in Millbrook, New York, High Priest Timothy Leary outlined the various states of consciousness to *Playboy:* "The lowest level of consciousness is sleep — or stupor, which is produced by narcotics, barbituates and our national stuporfactant, alcohol. The second level of consciousness is the conventional wakeful state, in which awareness is hooked to conventional symbols: flags, dollar signs, job titles, brand names, party affiliations and the like. . . . In order to reach [the third level], you have to have something that will turn *off* the symbols and open up your billions of sensory cameras to the billions of impulses that are hitting them. The chemical that opens the door to this level has been well known for centuries. . . . It is marijuana. . . . But we must bid a sad farewell to the sensory level of consciousness and go on to the fourth level, which I call the cellular level. It is well known that the stronger psychedelics such as mescaline and LSD take you *beyond* the senses into a world of cellular awareness. During an LSD session, enormous clusters of cells are turned on, and consciousness whirls into eerie panoramas for which we have no words or concepts." Added Jay Thelin, "grass and LSD are the most important factors in the community. You should acquaint yourself with all of the consciousness-expanding drugs. I turn on every Sunday with acid, and I smoke grass everyday, working continuously with an expanding consciousness." Drug use, agreed Yippie leader Jerry Rubin, signified "the total end of the Protestant ethic: screw work, we want to know ourselves. Of course the goal is to free oneself from American society's sick notion of work, success, reward and status."

Youths in the Haight culture also sought to expand their awareness by challenging other social norms. James Simon Kunen, the author of *The Strawberry Statement,* considered his long hair to be a symbol of protest against middle-class values: "As for bad vibrations emanating from my follicles, I say great. I want the cops to sneer and the old ladies to swear and the businessmen to worry." Bluejeans, tattered clothing, startling paisley prints, and wide-striped pants signified a similar spirit of countercultural revolt.

Influenced by their Beat predecessors, many hippies experimented with different sexual relations. They staged "love-ins" across the country and entered into communal living arrangements that were free of sexual restrictions. "Super Zap Them with Love" read a sign on the San Souci Temple, a commune in Los Angeles. Prompted in part by the advent of the birth control pill, these communal living arrangements undermined the nuclear family and threatened the sanctity of private property.

Through such countercultural transformations, the hip community hoped they could provoke other Americans to question and eventually to reject "straight" society. "The true meaning of psychedelics," Ken Kesey argued, "is to know all of the conditioned responses of men and then to prank them. This is the surest way to get them to ask questions, and until they ask questions they are going to remain conditioned robots." "I'm a troublemaker," he continued, "I'll try to stir up things wherever I go, in whatever I do. That's what the whole hippie movement is about: to do outrageous things that cause people to ask questions." A spate of newspapers — the *Oracle,* the *Berkeley Barb,* the *Los Angeles Free Press,* the *Village Voice,* and the *East Village Other* — ceaselessly propagated Kesey's notion of social change by example.

In place of the decaying establishment, the hippies envisioned an uninhibited, cooperative community. The Diggers, most of them former members of the San Francisco Mime Troupe, who named themselves after the seventeenth-century society of English agricultural altruists, owned six farms and provided free food, shelter, and transportation to needy hippies in San Francisco, Los Angeles, Boston, and New York

City. The Prunes in Cleveland and the Berkeley Provos did the same. Others organized cooperative business ventures: In San Francisco on November 23, 1966, the *Examiner* told its readers that "the hip purveyors of paintings, poetry, handcrafted leather and jewelry along Haight Street, having been blackballed by the Haight Street Merchant's Association, have formed their own Haight Street Merchant's Association, HIP for short."

Other adventurous hippies banded together in thirty communes across the nation. At Drop City near Trinidad, Colorado, for example, twenty-two Midwest hippies built and lived in geodesic domes constructed from automobile hoods. Roughly forty miles from San Francisco near Sebastopol, over fifty hippies communally farmed the 31-acre Morningstar Ranch, growing vegetables for the Diggers. Morningstar founder Lou Gottlieb, who held a Ph.D. in musicology and once played in the folk group the Limelighters, wished the Ranch would become "an alternative for those who can't make it in the straight society and don't want to. . . . This sort of thing could be a beautiful alternative for people who are technologically unemployable and for other people it would be a retreat where they could come and re create, I mean really re-create themselves. I can see ten Morningstars in every state, where people from straight society would come to live for a while in the 'alternative society,' a whole different culture based on noncompetition."

ACID ROCK: THE TRIP BEGINS

A legion of rock bands, playing what became known as acid rock, stood in the vanguard of the movement for cultural change. The *Oracle* defined rock music as a "regenerative and revolutionary art, offering us our first real hope for the future (indeed, for the present) since August 6, 1945." It represented a "way of life, international and verging in this decade on universal; and can't be stopped, retarded, put down, muted, modified or successfully controlled." Chet Helms, the transplanted Texan who opened the Avalon Ballroom because he "liked to dance" and who later became the manager of Big Brother and the Holding Company, "was very interested in the scene's potential for revolution. For turning things upside down, for changing values." Even the handbills distributed to promote the Trips Festival in January 1966 hinted that "maybe this is the ROCK REVOLUTION."

Not surprisingly, psychedelic music had its basis in the protests of Dylanesque folk. Marty Balin of the Airplane told a reporter, "I began as a folk musician. I went to New York and I heard Dylan when he was at Gerde's. And I was very impressed by, I don't know what it was, his youth I guess, his exuberance. . . . So I decided to come up here and started up here [San Francisco]. I went through a million different guys and then I saw Paul [Kantner]. He was walking into a folk club. I just saw him, and I said, 'That's the guy.' I just knew it. He had a twelve-

Poster for a Jefferson Airplane show at the Fillmore

string and a banjo and he had his hair down to here and an old cap." The duo asked a few other musicians to join their band and then, according to lead guitarist Jorma Kaukonen, the group was "thinking of names, trying to think of some sort of name that would imply a whole different way of looking at things." They settled on the Jefferson Airplane.

Jerry Garcia chronicled the journey of the Grateful Dead from a band of folkies to a rock and roll outfit. Said the bushy-haired, bearded lead guitarist about himself: "When the whole folk music thing started, I got caught up into that. . . . When Joan Baez's first record came out I heard it and I heard her finger picking the guitar, I'd never heard anything like it before so I got into that and I started getting into country music, into old time white music. Mostly white spiritual stuff, white instrumental music and I got into finger style, the folk-music-festival scene, the whole thing. And I was very heavy into that for a long time and I sort of employed a scholarly approach and even went through the South with tape recorders and stuff recording bluegrass bands. I spent about three years playing bluegrass banjo, that was my big thing and I almost forgot how to play the guitar during that period of time. And then I got into a jug band, we got a jug band going and I took up the guitar again and from the jug band it was right into rock and roll. . . . I was sort of a beatnik guitar player." "Bob Weir, who plays rhythm," continued Garcia, "did the whole folk-blues coffeehouse thing. That was his thing. And he also played jug and kazoo in the jug band when we were playing. And he's a student, you might say. His musical leader was Jorma [Kaukonen]." Concluded Garcia: "Like here on the West Coast, the guys that are into rock 'n' roll music have mostly come up like I have . . . like me and Jorma for example . . . up through folk music."

Other acid-rockers rose through the ranks of folk. Peter Albin, the impetus behind Big Brother and the Holding Company, had his musical interest aroused by folk, bluegrass, and country blues. David Frieberg, the unofficial leader of Quicksilver Messenger Service, learned guitar in 1963 amidst the folk craze, and fellow band member, drummer Dino Valenti, had worked for several years as a folk singer in Greenwich Village. In 1964 Country Joe McDonald "came to become a folksinger with the beatniks in San Francisco" and formed a jug band shortly before he teamed up with the Fish to deliver his politically minded brand of psychedelic rock. Likewise, lead guitarist Robby Krieger of the Doors had started a jug band during his stay at the University of California at Santa Barbara.

But unlike the mild-mannered drone of Dylan, these reborn folkies amplified their message to glass-shattering levels. Jerry Garcia thought of it as "a sensory overload. . . . It's very loud." The San Francisco bands also favored extended, sometimes excruciatingly long guitar solos that twisted around every note of the scale. They completed the transformation from folk to acid rock by adding a distorted guitar feedback, some blues riffs, a dash of country-western, and a fascination with Indian ragas. The result was the heralded San Francisco sound.

ROCK 'N' ROLL REVOLUTION

The psychedelic army perceived their music as a means to explode the social fabric of American society. Jim Morrison, lead singer of the Doors (formed in 1967 by Morrison along with Chicago-born rhythm and blues pianist Ray Manzarek and two members of the Psychedelic Rangers, Robby Krieger and John Densmore) professed an interest "in anything about revolt, disorder, chaos." "When I sing my songs in public," he told the *New York Times,* "that's a dramatic act, but not just acting as in theater, but a *social* act, real action." Grace Slick of the Jefferson Airplane wanted "a whole turnaround of values."

John Sinclair, organizer of the White Panther Party and manager of the Motor City Five (MC 5), one of the non–San Francisco psychedelic bands that began to sprout up throughout the country, was "totally committed to the revolution, as the revolution is totally committed to driving people out of their separate shells and into each other's arms." Rock and roll music, he contended, "is the spearhead of our attack because it's so effective and so much fun. We have developed organic

Courtesy of Elektra/Asylum Records

The Doors

high-energy rock and roll bands, who are infiltrating the popular culture and destroying millions of minds in the process. Our music and our economic genius plunders the unsuspecting straight world for money and the means to carry out our program, and revolutionize its children at the same time."

Sounding like a hoarse-voiced black preacher, Sinclair delivered one of the most rousing exhortations in rock history to kick off an MC 5 concert: "Brothers and sisters, I want to see a sea of hands out there, let me see a sea of hands. I want everybody to kick up some noise. I want to hear some revolution out there, brothers, I want to hear a little revolution!" The crowd, clapping when the MC 5 manager had started, became agitated. Sinclair continued: "Brothers and sisters, the time has come for each and everyone of you to decide whether you are going to be the problem or whether you are going to be the solution. You must choose, brothers, you must choose. It takes five seconds, five seconds of decision, five seconds to realize your purpose here on the planet. It takes just five seconds to realize that it's time to *move,* it's time to *get down with it.* Brothers, it's time to testify, and I want to know, are you ready to testify? *Are you ready?"* screamed Sinclair to a wild crowd that was jumping on the auditorium chairs. "I give you a testimonial — the MC 5!" The band immediately launched into an ear-splitting version of "Rambling Rose." To those in the audience, the revolution had arrived.

DRUGS, SEX, AND ROCK 'N' ROLL

The acid rockers promoted drugs and sex in their program for cultural revolution. Many West Coast bands gave themselves drug-related names — the Jefferson Airplane, the Thirteenth Floor Elevators, the Loading Zone, the Weeds, the Seeds, and the Doors, the last a takeoff on Aldous Huxley's pro-drug book, *The Doors of Perception.* Other groups wrote songs about marijuana, including the Fugs' "I Couldn't Get High," "Doin' Alright," and "Marijuana." Still others extolled the virtues of LSD: One day, Jerry Garcia of the Dead tried acid "and that was the end of that whole world. The whole world just went kablooey. . . . It just changed everything, you know." Jim Morrison of the Doors simply screamed, "break on through to the other side." Even the concert experience, enhanced by light shows of melting shapes and dazzling colors, simulated the altered consciousness induced by drugs. By 1969 a distraught Art Linkletter, whose daughter had overdosed on LSD, charged that at least half of all rock songs were "concerned with secret messages to teenagers to drop out, turn on, and groove with chemicals." A year later, the always quotable Vice-President Spiro Agnew complained that much of "rock music glorified drug use."

The Jefferson Airplane delivered the drug anthem of psychedelia — "White Rabbit": "One pill makes you larger and one pill makes you small/ And the ones that mother gives you don't do anything at all/ Go ask Alice, when she's ten feet tall," sang Grace Slick while the Airplane churned out a sinister, electric drone in the background. She continued: "When the men on the chess board get up and tell you where to go/ You just had some kind of mushroom and your mind is moving low/ Go ask Alice, I think she'll know." Then Slick launched into her fabled piercing vibrato: "When logic and proportion have fallen on a soggy bed/ And the white knight's talking backwards and the red queen's on her head/

Photo by Joel Brodsky; used by courtesy of Elektra/Asylum Records

The young lion: Jim Morrison of the Doors

Remember what the dormouse said, FEED YOUR HEAD, FEED YOUR HEAD."

Sex also preoccupied the acid rockers. The Fugs, never hiding their intentions, belted out "Boobs Alot," "Group Grope," and "Dirty Old Man." Their name itself raised the eyebrows of the sexually inhibited. Reveling in the same theme, the Doors hit the charts with "Love Me Two Times." The sweet-voiced Morrison pleaded with his audience: "Love me one time, my knees got weak/ Love me one time, I cannot speak/ Love me two times, girl, love speaks throughout the week." Then he raised his voice: "Love me two times, baby, love me twice today/ One for tomorrow, one just for today." The singer ended the song with a primal scream that sent shivers down the spine. The Doors also released "Hello I Love You," "Love Her Madly," and their biggest hit, "Light My Fire." Morrison, who characterized himself as an "erotic politician," faced legal charges when he supposedly exposed himself on stage in Florida. The outspoken Grace Slick, who delivered such songs as "Somebody to Love," confessed, "it doesn't matter what the lyrics say, or who sings them. They're all the same. They say, 'Be free — free in love, free in sex.' " "The stage is our bed and the audience is our broad," echoed Marty Balin of the Airplane. "We're not entertaining, we're making love."

By expanding the collective consciousness through drugs to achieve uninhibited love, the vanguard of psychedelia hoped for a tight-knit community, exemplified in their own living arrangements. The members of the Grateful Dead, for example, lived communally in the Haight District at 710 Ashbury Street. Quicksilver Messenger Service roomed together in a house near the Dead headquarters. During the first few years of their existence, the Jefferson Airplane lived together in the Haight.

This emphasis upon a collective identity extended to the concert hall. David Getz, drummer for Big Brother and the Holding Company, remembered that "the whole philosophy of the Psychedelic scene was to consciously avoid making anyone the star, focusing more on the inter-action between the audience and the band, and trying to create some-thing together. That's how the energy happened."

PSYCHEDELIA CONQUERS THE RECORDING INDUSTRY

Dedicated to cooperation, many psychedelic bands renounced the com-mercialism inherent in the recording industry. Many San Francisco bands, observed Max Weiss, owner of Fantasy Records, "are good but a little crazy. They are absolutely non-commercial." In particular, Jerry Garcia of the Grateful Dead resented "being just another face in a corporate personality. There isn't even a Warner 'brother' to talk to. The music business and the Grateful Dead are in two different orbits, two different universes." The Dead, added Stephen Stills of Buffalo Springfield and later of Crosby, Stills and Nash, "were the first people, I don't know whether it was acid or what, to come to that realization where they really didn't give a shit whether they made it or not." Paul Kantner of the Jefferson Airplane expressed the same distaste for the record industry: "The record companies sell rock and roll records like they sell refrigerators. They don't care about the people who make rock or what they're all about as human beings any more than they care about the people who make refrigerators."

In reaction, bands such as the Grateful Dead and the Airplane began to stage concerts for free. "We don't do what the system says — make single hits, take big gigs, do the success number," Dead manager Rock Scully told an interviewer. "The summer of '67, when all the other groups were making it, we were playing free in the park, man, trying to cool the Haight-Ashbury." Eric Clapton, then lead guitarist for Cream, was favorably impressed by the gesture. "The first thing that really hit me hard was the Grateful Dead were playing a lot of gigs for nothing," he remembered of his first visit to San Francisco. "That very much moved me. I've never heard of anyone doing that before. That really is one of the finest steps that anyone has taken in music yet, aside from musical strides. I guess that sums it up, what I think about San Francisco, what the Grateful Dead are doing. There is this incredible thing that the musical people seem to have toward their audience: they want to give."

San Francisco rock also bypassed established commercial channels through FM radio. Insignificant until the mid-1960s, FM took off in the Bay area on station KMPX due to the efforts of disc jockey Tom Donahue. According to the rotund, bearded jockey, "somewhere in the dim misty days of yore, some radio station statistician decided that regardless of chronological age the average mental age of the audience was 12½, and Top 40 AM radio aimed its message directly at the lowest common denominator. The disc jockeys have become robots performing their inanities at the direction of programmers who had succeeded in totally squeezing blips and bleeps and happy, oh yes, always happy sounding cretins who are poured from a bottle every three hours." To eradicate the "rotting corpse stinking up the airwaves," the San Francisco jockey started to air songs that lasted more than three minutes; began to spin entire albums; discontinued the breakneck delivery of the Top 40 disc jockeys; and played songs by the new groups of the Bay area. As much as anything else, FM airplay popularized psychedelic rock.

By 1967 acid rock had taken over the airwaves. Bands such as the Grateful Dead, the Doors, and especially the Jefferson Airplane edged into *Billboard's* top slots, and the San Francisco sound dominated rock. In 1967 the lovable, mop-topped Beatles jumped on the psychedelic bandwagon and released two albums, *Magical Mystery Tour* and *Sgt. Pepper's Lonely Hearts Club Band. Sgt. Pepper's* included the cryptic "Lucy in the Sky with Diamonds," LSD for short, which wove a tale of strange rocking-horse people who ate marshmallow pies and lounged under tangerine-colored trees and marmalade-flavored skies. Later that year, the bubbly Paul McCartney admitted that he had taken LSD, and George and Pattie Harrison, wearing heart-shaped granny glasses and paisley frocks, took a ceremonial tour of the Haight district.

Other bands followed in the Beatles' footsteps. The Rolling Stones followed psychedelic suit with *Their Satanic Majesties' Request,* complete with a three-dimensional cover. The epitome of the white blues growler, Eric Burdon, turned hippie. Of his R & B past, the Animal told *Melody Maker,* "It wasn't me singing. It was someone trying to be an American Negro. I look back and see how stupid I was." Adorned in vibrantly colored shirts and love beads, Burdon sang such odes to hippiedom as "San Franciscan Nights" and "Monterey." The Beach Boys fell under the spell of the Maharishi Mahesh Yogi. Even Dick Clark changed with the times and masterminded a movie, *The Love Children,* which starred a young Jack Nicholson and featured music from such psychedelic bands as the Seeds and the Strawberry Alarm Clock.

THE DECLINE AND FALL OF HIPPIEDOM

Counterculture rock and hippiedom itself, however, had a short-lived heyday. In the Hashbury district, businessmen began to exploit the hippie craze: During the first months of 1967, over twenty shops opened their doors to accommodate the tourist traffic. The Pall Mall Lounge began to market "Love Burgers," and one store in Haight Ashbury began to sell hippie costumes to weekenders — scraggly wigs for $85 and beards for $125. Even the Greyhound Bus Company started a "Hippie Hop" in San Francisco, advertised as "the only foreign tour within the continental limits of the United States." "Haight Street is no longer fun," complained Tavi Strauch, a hippie proprietor. "Many of us are getting away from it because of all the plastic hippies and tourists that are fouling up the whole scene. They've made a mess of it."

On October 4, 1967, Jay Thelin closed the Psychedelic Shop, a hub of the Bay area counterculture, and posted a sign on the front door: "Be Free — Nebraska Needs You More." Two days later, a procession of original hippies in the Haight district loaded a coffin full of beads, peace signs, flowers, and other symbols of their lifestyle and publicly burned it, announcing the "death of hippie, loyal son of media."

Other aspects of hippie culture either turned sour or became part of the American mainstream. Drugs, used by many hippies to increase awareness and sensitivity, changed regular users into mindless shells and wasted addicts. Some youths of the "me generation" — as Tom Wolfe called it — repeatedly tried to delve deeper and deeper into their own consciousness until they became isolated and detached from their own bodies. In the street venacular, these hippies "burned out." Others became hooked on the drugs that seemed to promise freedom. By 1967 addiction to methedrine or "speed" ran rampant in the Haight Ashbury district, and Dr. Ellis D. ("LSD") Sox, the San Francisco public health director, reported that the city spent $35,000 a month for treatment of the drug abuse. Hospitals also treated an increasing number of youths who had overdosed on LSD and heroin. Some of the major figures in the Haight drug culture fell prey to the guns of gangland. On August 3, 1967, John Kent Carter, a dealer known as "Shob," was found murdered, his arms hacked off at the elbows. Three days later, police found William "Superspade" Thomas in a sleeping bag with a bullet through his head at the bottom of a cliff in Marin County.

The saga of Skip Spence perhaps provides the most moving testimony to the perils of the drug subculture. Alexander "Skip" Spence was the drummer for the Jefferson Airplane on their initial two albums, composing "Blues from an Airplane" for the first LP. Trained as a guitarist, Spence then formed the pathbreaking psychedelic band, Moby Grape. *Rolling Stone Record Guide* wrote of the group's first effort: "Moby Grape made only one good album but what an album it is. That its debut LP is as fresh and exhilarating today as it was when it exploded out of San Francisco during 1967's Summer of Love is testament to the band's visionary concept of electric American music." Rock and roll excess, especially drugs, followed Spence to the top. Confided Skip, "acid was like heaven, a moment of God, inspiring, tragic. I must have taken it a hundred times, a thousand times." One day Spence reached too high. He woke up in a hospital: "An overdose where I died and was brought back to life." Today residents of San Jose can watch a scraggly, unwashed ex–rock star spend the seven-dollar-a-day allowance the state offers him. At night, when he does not confine himself to the psychiatric ward of the San Jose hospital, Spence stays alone in a dingy rundown room in Maas Hotel. Sometimes he speaks to Joan of Arc. Once in a while, Clark Kent pays a visit "because he's civilized, decent and a genius." And out a few thick, intense San Jose summer nights, his "master" materializes with startling revelations. Says Spence, delivering his own autobiography, "I'm a derelict. I'm a world savior. I am drugs. I am rock and roll."

While the drug subculture self-destructed, the hippie openness about sex progressively blended into the general American society. In 1948 Norman Mailer resorted to the word "fugging" in the *Naked and the Dead,* and five years later the movie industry denied its seal of approval to Otto Preminger's *The Moon Is Blue* because one of the actors uttered the word "virgin." But by 1969, according to *Time*: "Writers bandy four-letter words as if they had just completed a deep-immersion Berlitz course in Anglo-Saxon" and "the corner drug store sells *Fanny Hill* along with Fannie Farmer." In 1970 the Federal Commission on Obscenity and Pornography recommended wiping out all restrictions on the acquisition of hard-core pornography by adults.

At the same time, sexual activity increased across the nation. As a result of affluence, geographic mobility, and the greater availability of birth control devices, sexual intercourse became more common. "The 60s will be called the decade of orgasmic preoccupation," noted Dr. William Masters, the director of the Institute for Sex Research at Indiana University. He explained that "people talk more freely about sex nowadays, and young people are far more tolerant and permissive regarding sex. But we don't think there have been changes that we could truly call revolutionary. Our studies indicate that there has been a continuation of pre-existing trends, rather than any sudden revolutionary changes. For instance, premarital intercourse has increased but it hasn't shot up in any inflationary way; it has been on the rise ever since the turn of the century."

THE COMMERCIALIZATION OF ACID ROCK

Even acid rock, the music of the counterculture, melted into the American mainstream, falling victim to major record companies that employed slick marketing techniques to sell the psychedelic sound. As Joe Smith, President of Warner-Reprise, told a reporter, "We found we couldn't sell the Grateful Dead's records in a traditional manner. You couldn't take your ad in *Billboard* and sell a record that way. . . . The packaging was important. The cult was important. Free concerts where you handed out fruits and nuts were important" as well as exposure on the underground club circuit, the campuses, and FM radio. Gil Frieson, then vice-president of A & M Records, assembled a Standard American Promotional Package — "billboards on Sunset Strip and Broadway, full page advertising in the underground press, the trades, and various other outlets; radio spots and a promotional tour with all expenses paid by the label." Some companies hired "freaks" such as Derek Taylor of A & M (who helped organize the Monterey Pop Festival) and Andy Wickham of Warner-Reprise to mediate between the label and the temperamental musicians. Most record executives followed the dictum of Colonel Sanders when dealing with artists of the counterculture: When asked if he liked hippies, the chicken magnate once replied to Country Joe McDonald — "dey eats chicken, don't they?"

Smaller businessmen also cashed in on acid rock. In 1965 Wolfgang Wolodia Grajanka, a thirty-five-year-old emigre who had changed his name to Bill Graham, decided to organize the psychedelic groundswell in San Francisco into a business. Moving quickly from being the manager of the Mime Theater troupe to being the organizer-promoter of acid rock shows, Graham eventually opened the Fillmore West Theater in the heart of San Francisco's black ghetto and became the manager of the Jefferson Airplane. Graham did not enjoy the psychedelic sounds. "My musical taste certainly wasn't in that area at the time," he later told *Rolling Stone*. "I've never been a great fan of high volume rock and roll, and a lot of it was nonsensical to me." Not a champion of the music, the promoter took pride in his organizational abilities. Ken Kesey remembered Graham dashing around the Trips Festival with a clipboard and pen, ranting about logistical problems. Said Graham about himself: "I was always, 'Well, I took your ticket and you came here expecting something, and I want to have that. I want the food to be hot and the drinks to be cold.' " By the end of the decade, Graham's organizational abilities had made him a millionaire: He grossed over five million dollars a year from his two Fillmore operations and owned a national talent-booking agency as well as two record labels, San Francisco and Fillmore.

Other budding entrepreneurs followed Graham's lead and opened ballrooms in almost every other major city in the country: the Electric Factory in Philadelphia, the Boston Tea Party, Chicago's Kinetic Playground, the Grand Ballroom in Detroit, and the Electric Circus in New York City. Such enterprising ventures put cash in the pockets of the owners and promoters and brought counterculture rock closer to the American consumer.

Rock bands were susceptible to commercialization partly out of necessity. "In order for a group to survive, man," David Crosby contended, "to really cook and get it on, they gotta be some kind of success. And that means they have to sell in the marketplace, just to have fuckin' amps, and dope, and food." Bill Siddons, the manager of the Doors, agreed: "It's funny, the group out there on stage preaching a revolutionary message, but to get the message to the people, you gotta do it in the establishment way. And you know everybody acquires a taste for comfortable living."

Many acid rockers were accustomed to comfortable living, growing up in middle-class homes. Grace Slick's father was an investment banker in Chicago who sent her to the exclusive Finch College, where, in her words, she became a "regular suburban preppy" and then a model before she joined the Jefferson Airplane; fellow Airplane member Jorma Kaukonen was the son of an official in the United States foreign service; David Crosby's dad, Floyd, won an academy award in cinematography for his work on *High Noon;* Jim Morrison, the son of a rear-admiral, attended the theatre arts department at UCLA, where he met pianist Ray Manzarek and drummer John Densmore; the mother of John Cipollina, the guitarist for Quicksilver Messenger Service, played concert piano, and his godfather, Jose Itúrbi, was a well-known classical pianist; and Peter Albin of Big Brother grew up in suburban San Francisco, the son of a magazine editor-illustrator. As Hunter Thompson, the father of "gonzo" journalism, wrote, most hippies were "white and voluntarily poor. Their backgrounds were largely middle class; many had gone to college."

In the late 1960s the middle-class, college-aged adherents to the psychedelic banner faced a challenge to their dreams. The acid rock army, armed with flowers and well-meaning platitudes, soon confronted the M-1 rifles of National Guardsmen. The brightly colored hopes of hippiedom, swathed in paisley and rainbow hues, turned into a dark nightmare of burning cities and war-torn campuses.

7

The Violent Years: The White Blues and the Soul Explosion

Four o'clock on a muggy, steamy Sunday morning in Detroit, July 22, 1967. A crowd of young blacks clustered around a pack of police squad cars on Twelfth Street, the heart of the city's West Side ghetto. As each of the blacks pressed against sweaty backs and arms to get a better view of the action, blue-shirted, white-faced policemen herded seventy-four captives into paddy wagons. The arrested blacks had been accused of drinking after-hours booze at the United Community League for Civic Action, which also offered sermons on the spreading gospel of Black Power. After finishing their job, the policemen jumped into the squad cards, revved the engines, and started to move out of the area. Someone in the crowd flung a full wine bottle through the air: It shattered the windshield of Tenth Precinct Sergeant Arthur Howison's Ford. Howison slammed on the brakes and leapt onto the street. He was pelted first by a few stones, then by a barrage of rocks and bottles. The police officer ducked back into the car and sped off, followed by the angry mob.

The crowd multiplied as it made its way down Twelfth Street until it had grown to three thousand agitated men, women, and children. Someone grabbed a brick from the pavement and threw it through the window of a grocery store. People swarmed toward the jagged opening: They poked out the rest of the glass in the window frame with sticks, jumped into the store, and began gathering armloads of meat, bread, and canned goods. One man struggled with an entire side of beef. "I've always wanted to be a butcher," he told an onlooker.

Around daybreak some teens upturned a line of garbage cans and set the trash on fire. Another man hurled a homemade firebomb into a shoe store that already had been sacked. Summer breezes fanned the flames, which spread to adjoining buildings. Within a few hours, columns of fire engulfed East Detroit and spread across Woodward Avenue into the west part of the city. Williams's Drug Store and Lou's Men's Wear, along with hundreds of other buildings, disappeared in flames. "It looks like 1945 in Berlin," reported a dejected Mayor Jerome Cavanaugh.

Rioting and looting continued for the next four days. Enraged blacks ravaged thousands of stores, searching for food, clothing, furniture, and liquor. They only spared storefronts that had been marked "Soul Brother" or "Afro All the Way." Fires set by the rioters gutted fourteen square miles of Detroit, causing an estimated $500 million in damages. "Man, this is crazy," one older black told *Newsweek*. "We're burnin' our own houses up. Where these poor people going to live now?" "This is madness," echoed another homeowner. "Why do they have to burn our houses? That's not right. Goddamn. And there's not a house burning in Grosse Point [a white, middle-class suburb of Detroit]. This has got to stop." But other blacks in the Motor City, unemployed and confined to dilapidated slums, were impatient for the reforms promised by the Civil Rights Act of 1964 and predicted more trouble. Said one twenty-two-year-old boy: "We're tired of being second-class. We've been asking too long. Now it's time to take. This thing ain't over. It's just beginning."

The authorities responded to the rioting with armed force. During the first day of troubles, Mayor Cavanaugh unleashed his 4,000-man police force on the ghetto. When police proved inadequate, Michigan governor George Romney mobilized 7,300 state troops and National Guardsmen armed with tear gas, grenade launchers, M-1 rifles, submachine guns, M-48 tanks, and Huey helicopters. "I'm gonna shoot anything that moves and is black," vowed one young Guardsman. The next day, President Lyndon Johnson airlifted Task Force Detroit, a 4,700-man paratrooper unit commanded by Lt. General John L. Throckmorton, who had served as a deputy to General William Westmoreland in Vietnam. All told, an army of 16,000 government men marched into Detroit to quell the tumult. The city had become an armed camp divided into war zones, cordoned off by barbed wire and patrolled by helmeted troops in their khakis.

After the fires had been stamped out and the smoke had cleared, the authorities counted 42 dead, 2,250 injured, and 5,557 arrests. Most of the casualties were black men. On national television President Johnson pleaded that the "violence must be stopped — quickly, finally and permanently. There are no victors in the aftermath of violence. . . . We have endured a week such as no nation should live through: a time of violence and tragedy."

The flames of Detroit, however, spread to other areas. Other Michigan cities erupted: riots in Pontiac, Saginaw, Flint, Grand Rapids, Albion, and Kalamazoo. Incited by Black Power activists such as H. Rap Brown, who threatened, "if America don't come around, we're going to burn America down," riots broke out in urban areas across the nation. During the last days of July looters sacked stores in the black neighborhoods of Phoenix, Hartford, Passaic, Poughkeepsie, and South Bend. The next month four nights of violence ripped Milwaukee, leaving four dead and over a hundred injured. Blacks in nearby Chicago took to the streets, and riots scarred Providence and Wichita. By the end of August race riots had torn apart over seventy cities and had left a trail of eighty-six dead, thousands injured, and blocks of charred rubble. The press called it the "Long Hot Summer."

On April 4, 1968, the murder of black leader Dr. Martin Luther King, Jr., triggered another wave of violence. "When White America killed Dr. King," sneered black militant Stokely Carmichael, "she declared war on us. . . . We have to retaliate for the deaths of our leaders. The executions of those deaths are going to be in the streets." Carmichael proved to be prophetic. A few hours after the King assassination, Washington, D.C., burst into flames. As described by *Newsweek,* the more than seven hundred fires in the national capital, the worst conflagration in the city since the British burned it during the War of 1812, "made Washington look like the besieged capital of a banana republic, with helmeted combat troops, bayoneted rifles at the ready guarding the White House, and a light machine-gun post defending the steps of the Capitol." President Lyndon Johnson activated over fifteen thousand troops — more than twice the size of the U.S. garrison that defended Khe Sanh in Vietnam — to quiet the disorders: In three days of rioting, the death toll reached ten and property damage exceeded $13.3 million.

Other black urban areas exploded upon receiving news of the King assassination. In Kansas City six rioters died and sixty-five were injured. Chicago's riot left eleven dead, ninety-one injured, and miles of burned-out buildings. By the end of the week, 168 cities had erupted into violence; 5,117 fires had been started; about two thousand shops had been ransacked; forty million dollars worth of property had been destroyed; and thirty-nine people, mostly black, had died. It took almost 73,000 Army and National Guard troops to quell the disturbances. In 1967 and 1968 many American blacks had dramatically reasserted their collective identity, an identity born in slavery and shaped by a century of discrimination: They called the reclaimed identity *soul.*

As the inner cities burst into violence, the optimistic mood of white, college-aged youths blackened. Young reformers flooded into Chicago for the 1968 National Democratic Convention armed with backpacks and flowers, only to be met by the guns and clubs of Mayor

Daley's police force. Police arrested 668 protesters, most of them students. A few months later students at the University of California, Berkeley, tried to remove a chain that university officials had roped around a grassy lot known as People's Park. National Guardsmen gassed the unsuspecting students from a helicopter and killed one, wounded thirty, and arrested eight hundred others. Even the conservative *Time* magazine called the reaction a "crushing repression."

Courtesy of The Daily of the University of Washington

Student protest on campus

More of the seven million university students across the country marched in protest: Disturbances occurred at state universities in Maryland, Delaware, and Minnesota. At the University of Wisconsin in Madison, students protested the war in Vietnam by building 435 crosses, planting rows of them in front of the main administration building. The organizer of the demonstration wanted to show that "students really are faced with death." On October 15, 1968, more than one million students and their sympathizers marched on Washington, D.C., to seek a moratorium to the war in Vietnam. By 1969 more than 700,000 students had banded together in 350 chapters of the radical Students for a Democratic Society (SDS). Congress reactivated the House Committee on Un-American Activities to investigate the organization.

The intense, radicalized mood of many American youths, shaped to a large extent by the war in Vietnam, precipitated a change in rock music. The sounds of San Francisco, marked by wandering airy guitar solos, gave way to the slashing, piercing guitars of such British bluesmen as Eric Clapton and Alvin Lee, the cutting sound of American blues enthusiasts like Johnny Winter, and a rhythm and blues revival that featured such legends as B. B. King, Muddy Waters, and Howlin' Wolf, who provided a context for the white guitar heroes. Young rockers also began to listen to an updated version of fifties rhythm and blues called soul music, a reflection of the new black identity that was tempered in the fires of Detroit.

THE PSYCHEDELIC BLUES

Jimi Hendrix, a poor, half-black, half-Indian from a broken home in Seattle, bridged the gap between psychedelia and the urban blues. On the one hand, Hendrix appeared to be the quintessential flower child: The cover photo on his first album, *Are You Experienced?*, captured the wild costumes of the guitarist and his group the Experience — Mitch Mitchell on drums and Noel Redding on bass. Hendrix wore bright yellow pants slung at the hip and a red, pink, and yellow paisley shirt under a white vest, which had two openings around the chest that let two red eyeballs peek out. Around his neck Hendrix sported a vibrant orange, tufted scarf. Redding favored a double-breasted, yellow felt sportcoat with flowers emblazoned on it, and Mitchell had white-and-blue-striped trousers, a yellow scarf and a white, red, and yellow tie-dyed shirt. The group stood against a backdrop of blood-red trees. Hendrix, one of the premier guitarists in an age of guitar heroes, also perfected psychedelic feedback. He played his music at deafening levels and muttered a stoned-out banter at concerts. A few song titles such as "Are You Experienced?" and "Stoned Free" further identified Hendrix with the love children.

Yet Jimi Hendrix unleashed an updated version of the gut-wrenching electric blues. He started his musical education with such R & B greats as Little Richard, the Isley Brothers, James Brown, Jackie

Wilson, Curtis Knight, and B. B. King. In late 1966 Hendrix formed the Experience and amazed an audience at the Paris Olympia as he twisted, rolled, shook, and writhed in perfect time to every half-note of a thunderous electric blues. The next few months the guitarist staged similar shows for spectators at Stockholm's Tivoli, the Sports Arena in Copenhagen, and the Saville Theater in London. Hendrix broke into the American scene in 1967 at the Monterey Pop Festival, a showcase for new talent. He finished his set with a thrashing, tortured version of the Troggs' "Wild Thing." As the last notes of the song blasted the audience from a column of nine amplifiers and eighteen speakers, Hendrix ceremonially doused his guitar with lighter fluid and set it on fire, a violent act that catapulted him to stardom. Explained Hendrix of his antics: "Lots of young people now feel they're not getting a fair deal. So they revert to something loud, harsh, almost verging on violence; if they didn't go to a concert, they might be going to a riot." In an article about Hendrix, which referred to the Experience as a "triptych of smirking simian faces" led by the "hirsute Hendrix, called 'Mau Mau' in one British paper," *Newsweek* commented that "the Experience's destruction is inevitable rather than accidental, the surfacing of a violent streak that has always run through rock and roll, the spontaneous and impulsive violence of the young."

Besides the violence lurking around every corner, Hendrix reflected the deep despondency of American teens. His first album offered such tales as "Manic Depression," "Purple Haze," and the gloomy "I Don't Live Today." Released in 1968, Hendrix's second LP, *Axis: Bold as*

Courtesy of Alan Douglas and Warner Brothers Records

Jimi Hendrix on tour, 1966

Love, drifted further from hippiedom toward the blues. By the time of his death in 1970, Hendrix had almost totally deserted the psychedelic banner for his blues roots and jazz.

Other blues guitar heroes, affecting a hippie image, hit the American scene in 1967 and 1968. The group Cream appeared on stage in eye-boggling outfits, but played sorrowful riffs that came from the London and Scottish slums, where members Eric Clapton, Jack Bruce, and Ginger Baker had been raised. The trio had individually started out in various blues units: Drummer Ginger Baker had driven the Graham Bond Organization; Jack Bruce had played his six-string bass for Graham Bond, Manfred Mann, and John Mayall; and Clapton had added his piercingly shrill guitar sound to the Yardbirds and John Mayall's Bluesbreakers before joining Cream. Cream's first album, *Fresh Cream,* relied upon the blues for inspiration: It included Muddy Waters's "Rollin' and Tumblin'," "I'm So Glad" by Skip James, and "Four until Late" by legendary bluesman Robert Johnson. *Disraeli Gears,* the group's second LP, included a greater number of original compositions, but was still based on the blues tradition. After hearing the album, Rose Clapp, Clapton's grandmother who had raised him, felt that Eric had "always been a lonely boy and his music still gives me that feeling about him." Said the guitarist about himself: "Rock is like a battery that must always go back to the blues to get recharged." After attending a May 1968 Cream concert, Ian Whitcomb wrote in the Los Angeles *Times* ". . . there were no antics — no planned trouser-splitting — from Eric Clapton, Ginger Baker, or Jack Bruce; just great cataleptic hunks cut from the aged blues and pummeled out, slit up, reshaped, thoroughly examined by the violent guitars and drums."

Other groups produced a similar ear-shattering blues. Alvin Lee, the blues fanatic who fronted Ten Years After, first drew attention to his guitar mastery when he backed up John Lee Hooker at the Marquee Club in London. In 1967 Lee joined forces with pianist Chick Churchill, drummer Ric Lee and bassist Leo Lyons. The first Ten Years After album, covered with psychedelic art and a blurred picture of the paisley-clothed band, delivered a biting version of British blues, including covers of Sonny Boy Williamson's "Help Me" and Willie Dixon's gem "Spoonful." The group developed their blues roots on subsequent albums. Blue Cheer, recording three albums in 1968, also blasted forth a psychedelic blues. Laughed manager Gut: "They play so hard, they make cottage cheese out of the air." The Blues Magoos, who recorded the album *Psychedelic Lollipop,* likewise used the trappings of hippiedom to clothe their blues-oriented music.

THE REBIRTH OF THE BLUES

During the late sixties, some young American blues performers who had never toyed with psychedelia started to become popular when their blues dovetailed with the serious mood of young rock and rollers. Steve

Miller had traveled from his home state of Texas to the University of Wisconsin in Madison and there formed a white blues group, the Ardells, with Boz Scaggs and Ben Sidran. In the early sixties, he migrated to Chicago, the blues capital of the world, where he organized a blues band with Barry Goldberg. "Texas and then Chicago," Miller told a reporter, "where I spent some time learning Chicago blues and by the time I got to San Francisco [in 1966] I realized I had picked up a whole lot of Chicago blues." In San Francisco the guitarist formed the Steve Miller Blues Band that sounded, in the words of a reviewer, like "huge sheets of steel violently shaken." In 1968, after appearing at the Monterey Pop Festival, the band signed with Capitol Records and released *Children of the Future*. The next year Miller finally won critical approval and commercial success with *Sailor*.

Another Texan, Janis Joplin, drifted from her middle-class home in Port Arthur to San Francisco, where she sang in bars and coffeehouses. At the time, remembered Joplin, "they were playing that 50s crap on the radio. It seemed so shallow, all oop-boop. It had *nothing*. Then I heard Leadbelly and it was like a flash. It *mattered* to me. . . . When I started singing, blues is all I sang." Joplin, who felt that "I haven't been loved," joined Big Brother and the Holding Com-

Photo by Aaron Rappaport; used by courtesy of Capitol Records

Steve Miller

Courtesy of The Daily *of the University of* Washington

Janis Joplin belting out the blues

pany in 1966 and transformed one of the original psychedelic bands into a blues unit that showcased her saddening, razor-sharp cries of anguish. As with so many of the young American blues artists of the late sixties, Joplin first surprised the rock and roll world at the 1967 Monterey Pop Festival. The next year her first Columbia release, *Cheap Thrills,* reached the million-dollar mark in sales within a few months and her reputation started to grow. But despite the raves of journalists and financial success, Joplin continually felt the blues: "Someday," she confided to an interviewer, "I'm going to write a song about making love to 25,000 people in a concert and then going to my room alone."

The band Canned Heat and blues veteran Johnny Winter also began to attract fans. Brought together in 1965 by singer Bob "The Bear" Hite and guitarist Alan Wilson, Canned Heat initially had trouble finding work. "Nobody would hire us because we were blues," complained Hite, who in the sixties rabidly collected over seventy thousand

Photo by Ebet Roberts; used by courtesy of Alligator Records

Johnny Winter

blues records. In 1968, however, after the group surfaced at the Monterey Pop Festival, the band began to gain recognition. Liberty Records signed them, and they hit the upper reaches of the charts with the single, "On the Road Again."

Johnny Winter experienced the same turn of events. For years Winter had played sleazy beer joints in Texas. But in 1968 Larry Sepulvado, reviewing the blues scene in Texas for *Rolling Stone,* called Winter "a hundred-and-thirty pound cross-eyed albino with long, fleecy hair, playing some of the gutsiest fluid blues guitar you have ever heard." After reading the article, East Coast club owner Steve Paul rushed to Houston and signed the guitarist. A year later Johnny Winter's Columbia debut hit the record stores. "I'd been put down for years for singing the blues and suddenly everyone liked me and wanted to hear me," shrugged Winter in 1969.

John Fogerty formed one of the most popular American R & B groups of the era, Creedence Clearwater Revival, a band that mixed together Chicago R & B with early rockabilly into a driving concoction, which Fogerty labeled "swamp music." As a youth, the gravelly voiced singer and guitarist saw "things through lower class eyes" and was "always ashamed. I never brought my friends home. My room was in the basement — cement floor, cement walls." In his San Francisco home during the beat era and amid the stirrings of hippiedom, Fogerty sat in his room and listened to Muddy Waters, Howlin' Wolf, Elvis Presley, and Carl Perkins. He started a few groups in his teens, and in 1967 he and his brother Tom, Stu Cook, and Doug "Cosmo" Clifford established Creedence Clearwater Revival. The band covered such rhythm and blues classics as "I Put a Spell on You" by Screaming Jay Hawkins and Little Richard's "Good Golly Miss Molly" and repeatedly scored hits with a string of unforgettable originals such as "Proud Mary," "Born on the Bayou," "Keep On Chooglin'," "Bad Moon on the Rise," and "Down on the Corner."

As Fogerty continued to write, he increasingly turned to social commentary in such songs as "Effigy" and "Fortunate Son." In the strutting, explosive "Fortunate Son," he snarled: "Some folks are born, made to wave the flag/ Ooh, they're red, white and blue/ And when the band plays 'Hail to the Chief'/ Ooh, they point the cannon at you/ Some folks inherit star-spangled eyes/ Ooh, send you down to war/ And when you ask them how much should we give/ The only answer's more more more/ It ain't me, it ain't me, I ain't no military son/ It ain't me, it ain't me, I ain't no fortunate one." The lyrics almost perfectly mirrored the sentiments of young rockers, who feared being drafted and sent to an unpopular and escalating war in Vietnam. By the end of the sixties bands such as Creedence, Canned Heat, and Cream dominated the airwaves. Noticed *Time* in May 1969, "The pop scene has become a roaring, pulsating paradox of sound — the white man singing the black blues."

In 1968 and 1969 some legendary R & B performers who had provided the base for such bands as Creedence finally started to make some money for their efforts. In late 1968 Mike Bloomfield, the Chicago-born guitarist who had formed the blues-funk unit Electric Flag, convinced Bill Graham to book B. B. King at the Fillmore West. "The last time we played there it was 95 percent black in 1963," said King, who the year before had eked out a living by playing 342 one-night stands. "This time it was 95 percent white. I was shocked. Mike Bloomfield introduced me as the greatest bluesman. I didn't know if I should go out there. When I finally did, they gave me a standing ovation. I wanted to cry. Words can't say how I felt." Added King, commenting on his fans at the Fillmore, "Perhaps blues expresses what they can't say."

Young rock and rollers also rediscovered guitarist Albert King, the self-proclaimed half-brother of B. B. Albert King had worked as a field hand, a service station attendant, and a bulldozer operator for twenty-five years to support his R & B career. During the late 1960s he at last began to reap the reward of such songs as "Ooh-ee Baby," "Let's Have a Natural Ball," and "Travelin' To California." Growled the six-foot-four-inch, 250-pound King in 1969, "My days of paying dues are over. Now it's my turn to do the collecting." The guitarist spoke for others, such as Muddy Waters, Howlin' Wolf, and John Lee Hooker, who started to be recognized among the rock and roll crowd. Young rockers, intently searching for the roots of the blues, had begun to rediscover the pioneers of R & B.

SOUL MUSIC

Rock and rollers also began to listen to an updated version of R & B called soul music. The term *soul* had been used by American blacks during the fifties to suggest a black identity. In a vague sense, it defined the essence of being black in America. Bebop musicians had soul: in 1957 hornman Lou Donaldson recorded *Swing and Soul;* the next year saxophone great John Coltrane released *Soultrane;* trombonist Bennie Green cut *Soul Stirring* (1958) and *Hornful of Soul* (1959); trumpeter Blue Mitchell played *Blue Soul* (1959); and saxophonist Johnny Griffin led a *Big Soul-Band* (1960). When bop gave way to hard bop during the early sixties, Eldridge Cleaver noted in *Soul on Ice* that many referred to the sound as "soul music."

Around 1965, as the black ghettos of Watts and Harlem erupted in violence, many blacks started to equate soul with the struggle to reassert black dignity in the face of continued discrimination. "Soul is sass, man," wrote Claude Brown, author of *Manchild in the Promised Land*. "Soul is arrogance. Soul is walkin' down the street in a way that says, 'This is me, muhfuh. . . . Soul is that uninhibited, no, *extremely* uninhibited self-expression that goes into practically every Negro endeavor. That's soul. And there's a swagger in it, man." Rock critic Arnold Shaw came to the same conclusion in *The World of Soul:* "Soul is black, not blue, sass, anger and rage. It is not just feeling but conviction. Not just intensity but involvement. A force as well as a style, an accolade as well as identification. It is an expressive explosiveness, ignited by a people's discovery of self-pride, power and potential for growth." Emphasizing the value of the black heritage, blacks began to regard collard greens, black-eyed peas, and sweet potato pie as soul food. Fellow blacks became soul brothers and soul sisters, and rhythm and blues became soul music.

Some of the "soul" performers had been involved in R & B long before it underwent a name change. James Brown, "Soul Brother Number One," released his first record, "Please, Please, Please," with his Famous Flames in 1956. Two years later he scaled the R & B charts with "Try Me," and in 1960 he released "Think." By 1963 when he recorded the now legendary album *Live at the Apollo,* Brown had perfected a stunning stage act complete with a backup band and vocal group known as the James Brown Revue: The singer leapt on stage wearing skin-tight black pants, a half-unbuttoned dark-blue satin shirt, and a purple cape. Without missing a beat, his head jerking to the music, he suddenly jumped in the air, landed in a perfect split, and bounced back to his feet. Before the audience recovered, Brown was snaking across the floor or twirling in mid-air. The fans screamed for more from "Mr. Dynamite."

Ray Charles, considered to be the "Genius of Soul" in the mid-sixties, initially gained fame in R & B. Born Ray Charles Robinson in

Seattle Times

James Brown: Soul Brother number 1

1930, Charles traveled from his hometown of Albany, Georgia, to Seattle in 1947 to play cocktail-swing piano in the Nat King Cole style at such venues as the Elks Club, the Rocking Chair, and the Black and Tan. In 1949 he cut his first disc on the Swingtime label, "Confessing the Blues," and two years later followed with the R & B hit "Baby, Let Me Hold Your Hand." He toured the next few years with blues growler Lowell Fulson, R & B singer Ruth Brown, black comic Moms Mabley, and Eddie "Guitar Slim" Jones. In 1952 Atlantic Records, a leading company in the R & B field, bought Ray's contract from Swingtime for two thousand dollars. During late 1953 in New Orleans, remembered then Atlantic vice-president Jerry Wexler, Wexler and Atlantic president Ahmet Ertegun "ran into Ray at Cosimo's famous small studio, and Ray asked us to please do a session with him. . . . This was the landmark session because it had Ray Charles originals, Ray Charles arrangements, a Ray Charles band." The session produced the single "Don't You Know." The singer-pianist quickly followed with "I've Got a Woman," one of his most notable hits. During the rest of the fifties, he scored repeatedly with "Blackjack," "Come Back," "Fool for You," "Greenbacks," and "This Girl of Mine" in 1955; "Drown in My Own Tears," "Hallelujah, I Love Her So," "Lonely Avenue," and "Mary Ann" the next year; and "Right Time" and "What'd I Say" in 1959. By the turn of the decade Ray Charles had firmly established himself as a major figure in R & B.

Wilson Pickett, although not as prominent in the fifties as Ray Charles, had roots in early R & B. One day in 1959, as Pickett lounged on his porch strumming a guitar and singing, Willie Scorefield, a member of the R & B group the Falcons, happened to pass by. According to Pickett, Scorefield walked up to him and said, " 'Man, you got a good voice,' and invited me to come to the next rehearsal. That's when I found I could sing rhythm and blues." In the next few months Pickett wrote and recorded with the Falcons the hits "I Found a Love" and "You're So Fine."

Otis Redding, recognized as "The King of Soul" by some, initially drew his inspiration from Little Richard. In an unlikely success story, which took place in 1962, Redding drove some friends, Johnny Jenkins and the Pinetoppers, to the Stax studio in Memphis for a recording session. As Redding told it, "they had 30 minutes left in the studio and I asked if I could do a song." "He did one of those heh, heh baby things," recalled Stax president Jim Stewart. "It was just like Little Richard. I told them the world didn't need another Little Richard. Then someone suggested he do a slow one. He did 'These Arms of Mine.' " Impressed by the song, Stewart signed Redding and released it. In 1964 Redding cut *Pain in My Heart,* a mixture of Little Richard screamers and Sam Cooke-type ballads.

Most soul artists, like R & B performers in the fifties, started their careers in the church. Wilson Pickett had sung in small-town gospel groups before he joined the Falcons; he described his own style as "a gospel melody, not nothing pretty, a funky groove with lines that mean something." James Brown had played organ and drums during the forties for various gospel outfits, and Otis Redding had sung in a church choir as a young boy. As youngsters both Sam Moore and Dave Prater (later teaming up as Sam and Dave), had joined Baptist choirs and had toured with gospel groups in their teens. Ray Charles's music reflected his religious upbringing: He changed the Pilgrim Travelers' "I've Got a New Home" to "Lonely Avenue," shortened "Nobody But You, Lord" to "Nobody But You," and exulted in gospel screams in "Hallelujah, I Love Her So." Remarked Eric Burdon of the Animals, Ray "knows which church songs to take to his music and he changes the words slightly and makes hits out of them. By changing the words, I mean taking out the words 'God,' 'Christ' and 'Lord' and putting in their place 'woman,' 'honey' and 'child.'" Added bluesman Big Bill Broonzy about Ray Charles, "he's cryin', sanctified. He's mixing the blues with the spirituals. He should be singing in a church."

Aretha Franklin, the chunky, five-foot-five-inch dynamo dubbed "Lady Soul," had a direct connection to the church. Her father, the Reverend Clarence L. Franklin, served as the pastor of Detroit's 4,500-member New Bethel Baptist Church and recorded over seventy albums of fiery, blues-drenched sermons. Two white-uniformed nurses commonly stood guard at the aisles of New Bethel Baptist to aid parishioners who were overcome by the emotionally draining message of the minister. As a youth Aretha came into contact with such gospel greats as James Cleveland and Mahalia Jackson, and at a funeral of an aunt she witnessed Clara Ward belt out a powerful rendition of "Peace in the Valley." At that moment, the minister's daughter later recollected, "I wanted to become a singer." Aretha began to learn gospel from James Cleveland: "He showed me some real nice chords and I liked his deep, deep sound. There's a whole lot of earthiness in the way he sings, and what he was feelin', I was feelin', but I just didn't know how to put it across. The more I watched him, the more I got out of it." Soon Aretha joined a traveling gospel troupe organized by her father, and she premiered in it until signing with Columbia Records. The soul of Aretha Franklin had matured in the church.

Rhythm and blues, nurtured in church choirs, became known as soul music in the mid-sixties as many black Americans discovered a sense of self-esteem. In July 1965 station WOL in Washington, D.C., attracting primarily black listeners, began to call itself "soul radio," and local disc jockey Fred Correy labeled himself "Soulfinger." *Soul* magazine commenced publication. James Brown, releasing *Papa's Got a Brand New Bag* in 1965, underwent a transformation from "Mr. Dynamite" to "Soul Brother Number One." In 1965 and 1966 Otis Redding perfected his style with *Soul Album, Dictionary of Soul,* and *Otis Blue (Otis Redding Sings Soul),* the last including the hit "Respect."

Atlantic Records recorded most of the soul artists who swept the inner cities of America. In 1965 Wilson Pickett left the Double LL label and moved to Atlantic. That year he cut "In the Midnight Hour" in

Memphis. Wicked Pickett, as he became known, followed it with "634-5789," "Funky Broadway," "Land of a Thousand Dances," and "Mustang Sally." Percy Sledge, the Alabama farm boy who had chopped cotton as a youth, joined the Atlantic stable and in 1966 topped the R & B charts with "When a Man Loves a Woman." Sam and Dave, the "Double Dynamite" soul duo from Miami, were signed by Atlantic's Jerry Wexler. In 1965 they hit with "You Don't Know Like I Know." The next year they scored with "Said I Wasn't Going to Tell Nobody," "You Got Me Hummin'," "When Something Is Wrong," and their trademark, "Hold On, I'm Coming." Atlantic also distributed Stax-Volt artists, who included Otis Redding.

During 1965 and 1966 Atlantic sold its soul acts primarily in the black ghettos. Otis Redding, for example, broke attendance records at shows in Harlem and Watts, and in 1966 grossed $250,000 on a month-long rhythm and blues tour. But in 1966 few whites listened to the "King of Soul." Percy Sledge's "When A Man Loves a Woman" stood on top of the R & B charts but initially attracted little attention from young whites. James Brown bought a bright red Sting Ray, a fleet of Cadillacs, and a wardrobe of 150 suits and 80 pairs of shoes from the money he had amassed from an almost exclusively black audience. In the mid-sixties, while white rock and rollers listened to the Beatles, acid rock or white covers of R & B songs, blacks took pride in a gritty soul sound performed by blacks. "It's SOUL, man, SOUL," exclaimed black disc jockey Magnificent Montague in *Billboard*. "Now what is soul? It's the last to be hired, the first to be fired, brown all year-round, sit-in-the-back-of-the-bus feeling. You've got to live with us or you don't have it. The Black Brothers are the mainstay of our pop music today. Artists like John Lee Hooker, Otis Redding and others are heavy soul — one thing our English friends can't imitate."

MOTOWN

Around 1967 soul music began to become part of rock and roll. Ironically, Motown Records readied white America for the acceptance of soul. Motown had been started by black songwriter Berry Gordy, Jr., in 1959 after he quit his job as a chrome trimmer on a Detroit assembly line and borrowed seven hundred dollars to set up a studio in an eight-room apartment on run-down Grand Avenue in Detroit. Gordy tasted his first success in 1959 with a group of Detroit teens, Smokey Robinson and the Miracles. They sold sixty thousand copies of "Way over There" and almost two years later released a follow-up hit, "Shop Around." Buoyed by these hits, Gordy signed other young, black Detroiters to his company: the Supremes, the Marvelettes, Martha and the Vandellas, Stevie Wonder, and the Temptations.

In the early sixties, Motown built a hit-making machinery that rivaled the nearby auto assembly lines. Gordy, calling his operation "Hitsville U.S.A.," hired songwriters Lamont Dozier and brothers Eddie and Brian Holland, who collaborated on catchy, hook-filled tunes that took the popular charts by storm. The trio composed "Heat Wave" in 1963 for Martha and the Vandellas, then a secretary at the Motown office. After achieving success with the song, they changed a few aspects of "Heat Wave" and produced "Quicksand." The songwriters abandoned the idea only after the third rewrite, "Live Wire," stopped at number 42. The Holland-Dozier-Holland team applied their strategy to other Motown acts. The Supremes' "Baby Love," for example, sounded very similar to "I Hear a Symphony" but contained subtle differences that gave it a singular character. And the formula worked. By 1965 Motown enterprises — a conglomeration of eight labels, a management service, and a sheet music publisher — grossed more than eight million dollars yearly.

Berry Gordy became a millionaire by making sure his acts appealed to a white as well as a black audience. The Supremes — Diana Ross, Florence Ballard, and Mary Wilson — had grown up together in the Brewster-Douglass housing project in Detroit's ghetto. When the group first approached Motown as the Primettes, Gordy suggested to the girls that they finish high school. In 1961, after the girls had completed twelfth grade, Gordy signed them and immediately started to mold them into a form acceptable to white America: He sent them to International Talent Management Incorporated, a finishing school for Motown artists. There, Maxine Powell, owner of Powell's Finishing and Modeling School, taught the youngsters the principles of etiquette and the art of the inoffensive interview. Cooed Diana Ross, "everyone with the [Motown] family has to go to class — a finishing school for beauty and charm, a choreography class and a vocal class. Everyone goes, even if they don't have to sing or dance. They have to learn these different aspects of the business to improve their stage presence." "You have to be very strict with young artists," added Berry Gordy. "That instills discipline." The Motown president then linked the reprogrammed Supremes, complete with straightened hair, slinky dinner gowns, and refined manners, with Holland-Dozier-Holland, who in June 1964 provided the blockbuster hit "Where Did Our Love Go." The single headed the pop charts and established the Supremes as stars alongside Andy Williams, Jack Jones, and Eydie Gorme. Gordy, continuing to push the Supremes to the forefront, garnered spots for the group on the *Ed Sullivan Show, Hullabaloo, The Dean Martin Show, Hollywood Palace,* and *Shindig,* and the Supremes phenomenon snowballed. They charted with "Come See about Me," "I Hear a Symphony," "Nothing but Heartaches," "Stop! In the Name of Love," "Back in My Arms Again," "My World Is Empty without You," "You Can't Hurry Love," and "You Keep Me Hanging On." In one period during 1965–66, the Supremes placed five consecutive singles in the number-one spot of the pop charts. Berry Gordy had created a hit machine by bleaching the ghetto from three Detroit teenagers.

The Motown mogul similarly transformed the male counterpart of the Supremes, the Temptations. Gordy first changed the name of the group from the Primes to the Temptations. Then he replaced their processed hair styles with carefully cropped Afros; discarded casual clothes for top hats and tails; inserted such standards as "Ole Man River" in their repertoire; and added the precise choreography of Motown dance-master Cholly Atkins to the group's stage show. In January 1965 the refurbished Temptations — Eddie Kendricks, David Ruffin, Melvin Franklin, Paul Williams, and Otis Williams — hit the top of the pop charts with "My Girl" and followed in the next few months with a series of showstoppers.

Gordy pressed most of his other acts into a predesigned mold and only rarely allowed the gospel roots and the R & B experience of Motown artists to surface. (For exceptions, listen to Gladys Knight and the Pips' "I Heard It through the Grapevine" and Jr. Walker's "Shotgun.") In Motown's heyday during the mid-1960s, Gordy provided a black counterpart to the Beatles: cute, safe, and well-groomed acts, which delivered hummable, finger-snapping tunes. (One of Motown's artists, Mary Wells, who topped the charts with "My Guy," had toured England with the Beatles in 1964, and during the same year the Supremes cut an album of Beatle songs, *A Bit of Liverpool*.) The Motown empire, called a "whiter shade of black" by rock writer John Landau and named "The Sound of Young America" by Berry Gordy himself, was built upon clean-cut, white-sounding blacks who produced a series of fast-selling pop gems. From 1964 to 1967 Motown scored fourteen number-one pop singles and released forty-six more singles that reached the Top Fifteen.

Although churning out hit after hit of pure pop, Motown had an importance for the white acceptance of the much more gritty soul music of such artists as James Brown and Aretha Franklin. Berry Gordy had established one of the most commercially successful black-owned enterprises, and certainly the most successful black-owned record company. His highly visible family management showed white Americans that blacks could operate a major music business. And no matter how much the Motown acts sounded like white pop singers, they were still black. The Motown stable of artists proved to be the first group of black performers who had been accepted en masse by mainstream white America. After the achievements of Motown, noted rock critics Joe McEwen and Jim Miller, "never again would black performers be confined to the fabled chittlin' circuit; never again would black popular music be dismissed as a minority taste."

BLACK SOUL IN WHITE AMERICA

In addition to Motown, some white rock groups prepared the way for the acceptance of black soul. In 1965 the Rolling Stones released the LP *Out of Our Heads,* which included the Otis Redding tunes "That's How Strong My Love Is" and "Mercy, Mercy." The liner notes mentioned Redding by name. The Animals, always paying tribute to R & B, covered Ray Charles's "I Believe to My Soul" and "Hallelujah, I Love Her So."

Mitch Ryder and the Detroit Wheels screamed the essence of the soul message to dancing white fans in the 1966 albums *Breakout* and *Take a Ride*. Besides the now classic "Devil with a Blue Dress," "Jenny Take a Ride," and "Little Latin Lupe Lu," the LPs included Wilson Pickett's "In the Midnight Hour" and "Please, Please, Please" by James Brown. The sound of the Detroit Wheels "is the music of the soul played through the very nerve ends," aptly read the liner notes to *Breakout*.

The inner city explosions of 1967 and 1968 also made many Americans, especially those raised during the civil rights era, more aware and more interested in black culture. The 1967 riots in Detroit caused a white backlash in some quarters but for others the trouble led to a better understanding of black Americans: Discrimination "hurts them real bad. I'd probably be rioting right with them," a Texas salesman told *Time.* "It degrades [the black man] which no one likes. Therefore it is natural [for them] to fight back," echoed a California truckdriver. Mrs. Margaret Lamb, a widow from Owensboro, Kentucky, told *Time:* "It makes you wonder that they do as good as they do the way people treat them sometimes. You see things that make you wonder why they put up with it."

Besides realizing the plight of black America, many whites even adopted elements of black culture. Some began to look for soul food restaurants. Students, protesting for their own causes, showed support for militant Black Power groups such as the Black Panthers. Black studies classes in history, psychology, English, and anthropology sprouted up on many campuses. And young rockers started to buy soul records. The year "1967 saw the greatest emergence of the blues in recent pop history. It was the year in which rhythm and blues became the music of the charts and the year in which 'soul' became the popular music of America," exclaimed Jon Landau.

White rock and roll crossed over to black soul with Aretha Franklin. Aretha had signed with John Hammond of Columbia in 1960. Mitch Miller, the Columbia executive who had assailed rock in the fifties, gave her voice lessons, hooked her up with Barbara Streisand-arranger Bob Mersey, and assigned her such sappy material as the showtune "If Ever I Would Leave You" and Al Jolson's "Rock-A-Bye My Baby with a Dixie Melody." By 1966 a dissatisfied Aretha had found only moderate success and was in debt to Columbia.

Late that year, when her contract with Columbia expired, Jerry Wexler of Atlantic signed the singer. As Wexler told it, "one day, I happened to be in Muscle Shoals doing a Wilson Pickett session, and I got a call from [a friend] in Philadelphia. All she said was 'Call this number, *now!*' It was Aretha. I had never spoken to her, but I called her and that was it." Within a few months, Aretha recorded for Atlantic *I Never Loved a Man the Way That I Love You,* which included the single "Respect." "Respect" had been an R & B hit for Otis Redding two years earlier, but in 1967 it took on an added importance. The song, belted out by the Detroit-native Aretha Franklin, hit the streets as the ghetto of the Motor City exploded into flames: It seemed to epitomize to whites the renewed self-pride that blacks had discovered. The song sold over one million copies in ten months.

"Respect" opened the floodgates. In 1967 Aretha again hit the charts with "Dr. Feelgood," "A Natural Woman," "Baby, I Love You," and "Chain of Fools." She won the Best Female Vocalist of the Year Award. Early the next year Detroit mayor Jerome Cavanaugh declared Aretha Franklin Day, and Aretha solidified her reputation among whites as the soul spokeswoman with her rendition of "Think": "You'd better think, think about what you're trying to do to me/ Think that your mind's gonna let yourself be free/ Oh, Freedom, Freedom, Freedom, ya, Freeeeeedom." In 1967 Wilson Pickett's *Greatest Hits,* which included "In the Midnight Hour," started to sell among rockers. Sam and Dave scored a crossover success with *Soul Men,* and *Billboard* published the first of an annual supplement, "The World of Soul." Otis Redding, who had died in December 1967 when his twin-engine Beechcraft plane plunged into an icy lake outside Madison, Wisconsin, won posthumous accolades for "Dock of the Bay." The King of Soul, who had received little attention from the white media during his lifetime, was named Best Male Vocalist of 1968. Rock radio began to play Percy Sledge's "When a Man Loves a Woman," and Atlantic Records began to accumulate a fortune. *Time* calculated that "Manhattan-based Atlantic, with such singers as Aretha, Wilson Pickett and Sam and Dave, can now sell more records in a week (1,300,000) than it did in six months in 1950." Remarked Jerry Wexler in 1968: "The young white audience now digs soul the way the black does." Soul, along with the white blues and a revival of fifties R & B, had become the music of rock and roll.

WOODSTOCK AND THE ROCK FESTIVALS

The blues of white youths seemed to fade at the end of the decade, when a ray of light appeared to burst forth from Woodstock, New York. From 1967 to 1970 at least 2.5 million people attended thirty major rock festivals in such places as Seattle, Dallas, and Atlantic City. For three days in August 1969 on Max Yasgur's 55-acre dairy farm in the Catskills, the Woodstock Music and Art Festival attracted more than four hundred thousand people. Some trekked to Woodstock to hear the music — a hodgepodge ranging from such folk-rockers as Melanie, Arlo Guthrie, and Richie Havens to blues-based performers like Jimi Hendrix, Ten Years After, Canned Heat, and the Butterfield Blues Band. Some came to be with their friends; others made the trip out of curiosity. Together, wrote one observer, the festival-goers descending on Woodstock moved "steadily down route 17-B, like a busy day on the Ho Chi Minh Trail."

Though pictured by the media as a spontaneous gathering of footloose, carefree flower children, Woodstock represented a well-calculated business venture. The planning and promotion of the festival had been masterminded by two astute businessmen — John Roberts, a young millionaire who had graduated from the University of Pennsylvania, and Joel Rosenman, a Yale Law School graduate and the son of a prominent Long Island orthodontist. Along with Mike Lang, organizer of the Miami Pops Festival, and Artie Kornfeld, head of Contemporary Products at Capitol Records, they set up the music, the food, the sale of hip souvenirs such as Che Gueverra posters, and the future movie and recording rights to the festival. Although "we were promoting a celebration of the Aquarian Age, and our patrons fancied themselves as street people and flower children," contended Rosenman, "we were a New York corporation capitalized at $500,000 and accounted for by Brout Issacs and Company, tenth largest body of CPAs in New York City." Woodstock, at its inception, had been a business enterprise publicized heavily by the media.

The festival at Altamont Speedway near San Francisco held a few months later crushed any illusion of Woodstock as the herald of a golden age of peace and harmony. Drawn by a free concert staged by the Rolling

Courtesy of Alan Douglas

Hendrix at Woodstock: The end of an era

Stones, who wanted to outdo Woodstock, over three hundred thousand fans flocked to the site. During the event hundreds required treatment for drug overdose, including one youth who jumped off a freeway overpass after ingesting some LSD. (One man had died of a drug overdose at Woodstock.) Horrified spectators watched as the Hell's Angels motorcycle gang, hired to keep order in exchange for five hundred dollars worth of beer, stabbed to death a black eighteen-year-old from Berkeley, one of four deaths at the concert. In a repeat performance of Altamont a few months later, more than fifty thousand youths paid twenty-eight dollars each to attend a "Celebration of Life" on the banks of Louisiana's Atchafalaya River, where the Galloping Gooses motorcycle gang employed as a security force chain-whipped concertgoers. Three people died amid the festivities.

KENT STATE AND THE END OF AN ERA

The youth of America stood frozen in shock on Monday, May 4, 1970. After President Richard Nixon had announced that American troops had been sent into Cambodia, students at Kent State University in northeastern Ohio took to the streets. The first night they hurled bottles at police cars, smashed store windows, and doused trees with gasoline, setting them on fire. The next day protesters firebombed the one-story ROTC building on the Kent State campus. Mayor Leroy Satrom asked Ohio Governor James Rhodes to activate the National Guard. Rhodes, who described the students as "worse than the 'brownshirt' and Communist element . . . the worst type of people that we harbor in America," responded with nine hundred troops armed with M-1 rifles, submachine guns, and cannisters of tear gas. On the third day of troubles, Guardsmen chased a mob of students to a knoll near Taylor Hall. Suddenly, without warning, sixteen National Guardsmen knelt on one knee and leveled their guns at the crowd. Asserted journalism professor Charles Brill, who witnessed the action: "They all waited and they all pointed their rifles at the same time. It looked like a firing squad." The soldiers pumped thirty-five rounds from their M-1 rifles into the protesters standing seventy-five feet away. "It's about time we showed the bastards who's in charge," sneered one Guardsman. The gunfire killed four students and wounded ten others. "My God! My God! They're killing us," screamed one Kent State freshman.

The murders at Kent State caused an immediate reaction in colleges and universities across the nation: Students sacked the treasurer's office at the University of South Carolina; a half-million-dollar fire blazed at Colorado State; 124 students were arrested in a fight with state troopers at the University of Colorado; protesters occupied the ROTC building at the University of Nebraska; three weeks of rioting ravaged the Berkeley campus; in rioting at the University of Maryland state troops injured 138 and arrested 200; students at the University of Wisconsin, chanting "we're gonna open up a second front in Madison," took over the Army Mathematics Research Center and were responsible for twenty major firebombings; 75,000 students marched on Washington, D.C., and gathered in front of the White House; and more than two hundred colleges and universities shut down for at least one day, some for the rest of the year.

After initial outbursts of violence, a sense of helplessness enveloped many American youths. Said one youth at the post–Kent State demonstration in Washington, D.C.: "The people here understand that we are surrounded by fully armed troops and that if we start anything, we'd be destroyed." For the first time in a decade, rebellious youths who had hoped for a better world felt that they had reached a dead end.

Shocking news of the deaths of prominent rock figures during the next few months deepened the hopeless mood of rockers. On July 3, 1970, Jim Morrison of the Doors, who had slowly become an alcoholic, died of a heart attack in his bathtub. Jimi Hendrix passed away on September 18, a victim of an overdose of sleeping pills. Only a few weeks later, on October 3 at the Landmark Hotel in Hollywood, authorities confirmed the death of Janis Joplin from an overdose of heroin. And by July 1971 both the Fillmore East and the Fillmore West, symbols of the naively hopeful psychedelic era, had closed their doors. By the beginning of the 1970s many youths who only a few years before had vowed to work for sweeping social change listened to the guns of Kent State and disappeared into the American mainstream. The violent years had come to a close, and rock and roll would change with the times.

8

Corporate Rock

"I've always said that Rod isn't a rock star. He's a growth industry," remarked Billy Gaff, the manager of blues-croaker-turned-pop star Rod Stewart. "Rod is essentially very conservative. He doesn't invest in football clubs or crazy movie- or record-financing schemes. The tax shelter scams are all a little scary, so we stick to art and real estate."

Other rock stars of the 1970s had a similar penchant for high finance. While many rockers of the previous decade had perceived their music as a means to bring about social change, most rock acts of the seventies abandoned any pretense of protest and chased the millions of superstardom. The record industry, anxious to expand its frontiers, made the dream of superstardom possible: Major record companies sold an ever increasing number of discs in the United States and abroad through more creative and efficient marketing methods. In a rerun of the Dick Clark era they promoted acts with sparkling white teeth, gimicky dazzle, and little substance, who grossed billions of dollars. In the seventies, enterprising musicians and record companies worked together to build rock 'n' roll into a big business.

THE DREAM IS OVER

By the early 1970s the wellspring of hope that had bubbled up in the sixties had evaporated. John Lennon told an interviewer that "the dream is over. I'm not just talking about the Beatles. I'm talking about the generation thing. It's over, and we gotta — I have personally gotta — get down to so-called reality." Leaving behind his overt political activism — his "Give Peace a Chance"; a week-long bed-in with Yoko at the Amsterdam Hilton to protest for peace; a billboard campaign, "War Is Over! If You Want It"; an abortive Toronto Peace Festival; and a new calendar, which "will regard the New Year 1970 as Year One A.P., for After Peace" — Lennon and his wife, artist Yoko Ono, retreated to various country and urban estates. Eric Clapton, scarred by a bout with heroin, threatened to quit the music business. In 1974 he told a reporter from *Time* that "the same thing that makes a man pick up his guitar and

Courtesy of Arnold Stiefel Management

Rod Stewart: rock star as growth industry

play is the same thing that makes him take any drug he can find. Music is really escapism. It's shutting yourself off from everything else, going into a cupboard and staying there." Asked what he had planned for himself in the next ten years, Clapton replied: "I would like to be alive."

Even though many rock giants of the sixties went into hiding, their music persisted in bastardized forms during the next decade. "The seventies was a polished-up version of a lot of things coming out of the fifties and sixties," ironically remarked singer Linda Ronstadt, who herself rose to fame on rehashed renditions of rock classics. "I think we refined them past their prime: like racing horses that have been over-bred — they run fast but their bones break."

HEAVY METAL

Heavy metal music, one of the most propulsive forces behind seventies rock, adopted a traditional rhythm and blues format, cranked up the volume, and added a macho stage show to whip its young male fans into a wild frenzy. It rose from the ashes of such guitar heroes as Hendrix, Clapton, and Alvin Lee, originating in the run-down sections of the British and American industrial heartlands.

Led Zeppelin emerged as the premier heavy metal band, formed in 1968 by Jimmy Page from the remnants of the legendary Yardbirds. Page, a poor youth from a working-class slum of London who had played brilliant session guitar for the likes of the Rolling Stones, the Kinks, and The Who, met session bassist John Paul Jones during their work on Donovan's *Hurdy Gurdy Man*. The duo decided to form a band and added drummer John Bonham and the treble-voiced Robert Plant. Said Page: "Four of us got together in this two-by-two room and started playing. Then we knew — we started laughing at each other. Maybe it was from relief, or maybe from the knowledge that we could groove together. But that was it. That was just how well it was going. . . . The statement of our first two weeks together is our album. We cut it in 15 hours, and between us wrote 8 of the tracks." The self-titled LP unveiled a slashing, amplified blues, including Willie Dixon's "You Shook Me" and "I Can't Quit You Baby," a never released Yardbirds gem, "Dazed and Confused," and a reworked version of Howlin' Wolf's "How Many More Years," now called "How Many More Times." "When Robert and I first got together we realized that we could go in two possible directions — heavy blues or an Incredible String Band trip," Jimmy Page told an interviewer in the early 1970s. Commercially, Led Zeppelin took the correct path: In 1973 the group stormed through the United States, breaking attendance records previously held by the Beatles and grossing more than three million dollars. The band earned thirty million dollars total that year. Two years later fifteen thousand fans waited for twenty-four hours outside Madison Square Garden for tickets to an upcoming Zeppelin show, and in Boston Led Zeppelin fanatics rioted at the box office and caused $75,000 in damage.

Other heavy metallers from Great Britain crashed into America. AC/DC exploded on the American scene from Australia a few years after the Led Zeppelin debut. Like the members of Zeppelin, the musicians in AC/DC grew up in working-class neighborhoods and owned a musical debt to Chicago rhythm and blues. "I started out listening to a lot of early blues people, like B. B. King, Buddy Guy, and Muddy Waters," pointed out the knicker-clad lead guitarist Angus Young. "I liked blues players." The group first delivered its rumbling, deafening, chord-crashing electric blues in 1975 with *High Voltage*. At the end of the decade they latched onto the preoccupation with demons and a hellish otherworld that tormented many older bluesmen (for example, listen to Howlin' Wolf's "Evil" or Robert Johnson's "Me and the Devil Blues") and merged it with their numbing style of R & B to create the heavy metal classic, *Highway To Hell*.

In 1969 a group of Birmingham toughs changed their name from Earth to Black Sabbath and pounded out a similar concoction of the occult and heavy metal. The next year they hit the charts with the album *Paranoid* and a series of singles — "War Pigs," "Electric Funeral," "Iron Man," and "Sabbath, Bloody Sabbath." "I don't profess to be a messiah of slum people," insisted vocalist John "Ozzy" Osbourne, "but I was a back-street kid, and that little demon is still in there, shoving the hot coal in. The aggression I play is the aggression I know. And it's obviously aggression a lot of people have." Added guitarist Tony Iommi, "If we come across doomy and evil, it's just the way we feel."

Riding on the coattails of Led Zeppelin, other British metallers assaulted the American market. Uriah Heep, headed by guitarist Mick Box and keyboard player Ken Hensley, charted in 1972 with *Demons and Wizards*. A year later *Uriah Heep Live* sold over a million copies in the States. Revamping their musical image in 1970, Status Quo turned to heavy metal and released the album *Piledriver*. By 1975 the band had climbed to the top of the charts with *On the Level*. And Deep Purple, fronted by guitarist extraordinaire Richie Blackmore, banged out a series of heavy metal classics on Tetragammaton Records. They continued their metallic output into the mid-seventies with such albums as *Fireball* (1971), *Machine Head* (1972), *Made in Japan* (1973), and *Burn* (1974).

American-bred heavy metallers jumped in on the action. From Flint, Michigan, came Grand Funk Railroad, masters of "loud white noise" in the words of Rod Stewart. The band was pieced together from the remains of Terry Knight and the Pack, with Terry Knight acting as the manager. During March 1969 in Buffalo, New York, Knight wanted to see what the new band "could do to a crowd. I was amazed," the manager remembered. "They had to close down the place. One girl had taken off her blouse and was heading for the stage when they pulled the power and turned on the house lights. The police took the guys offstage. I knew they would be accepted anywhere." Knight had predicted the powers of Grand Funk accurately: That year the band dismayed disgruntled critics when *On Time* shot to the top of the charts. In 1970 the band released three more albums in rapid-fire succession — *Grand Funk, Closer To Home,* and the *Live Album* — racking up sales of more than five million dollars. The National Association of Record Merchandisers voted them the "Best Selling New Group of 1970." The next year Grand Funk traveled 26,326 miles with eight thousand pounds of equipment in a grand tour of America, and its LP *Survival* was guaranteed of gold status before its release.

Another Michigan rocker, veteran Ted Nugent, rode the crest of American heavy metal, thoroughly disgusting critics and entertaining his screaming fans with a brand of Neanderthal rock. In 1975 after years of publicity stunts, first with the Amboy Dukes and then as a solo artist, "The Nuge" scored commercial success with a self-named album. That same year Aerosmith, formed in 1970 as a New Hampshire bar band, captured the attention of American metallers with their second album, *Get Your Wings*. In 1974 Blue Oyster Cult did the same with the LP *Secret Treaties*.

SOFT ROCK

Almost antithetical to heavy metal, an acoustic, soothing mutation of rock also achieved success in the 1970s. Packaged by a spate of laid-back singer-composers, it borrowed the style of early Dylan and depoliticized it, offering radio listeners tales of forlorn love and doomed relationships.

James Taylor became the prototype of the easy-going, down-home singer-songwriter. Rebounding from a self-imposed exile at McLean's mental hospital in Boston, Taylor traveled to London in 1968 and signed with the Beatles' Apple Records. Two years later, after the Beatles had disbanded and Apple had been immobilized by a mire of legal problems, Taylor recorded *Sweet Baby James* for Warner Brothers. His confessional "Fire and Rain," a song about his experiences at McLean's, his heroin addiction, and the suicide of a close friend, morbidly climbed the American singles chart. Taylor followed with the hits "Don't Let Me Be Lonely Tonight," "Long Ago, Far Away," "One Man Parade," "Mockingbird," and "You've Got a Friend."

Carly Simon, who married Taylor in 1972, first sang with her sister Lucy as a folkster duo, the Simon Sisters. By 1971 she had become a female counterpart of James Taylor with the release of her solo album *Carly Simon*. Her third LP, *No Secrets,* had rock gossip sheets buzzing about the possible subject of the song "You're So Vain." In a senseless debate that exemplified the worst of rock journalism, magazines such as *Rolling Stone* pinned the mortal sin of vanity on Warren Beatty, James Taylor, and even the hapless Mick Jagger, who backed Simon on the single.

Veteran songwriter Carol King (a.k.a. Carol Klein), who had written a number of hits for James Taylor, overshadowed Carly Simon and became the queen of the soft rockers. King had a history of success in the music industry before the outset of the 1970s. In 1958 she met and married lyricist Gerry Goffin. For seven years the couple churned out a string of hit singles: "Will You Still Love Me Tomorrow?" for the Shirelles; "Up on the Roof," "When My Little Girl Is Smiling," and "Some Kind of Wonderful" for the Drifters; "Take Good Care of My Baby," "Sharing You," and "How Many Tears" for Bobby Vee; "Don't Bring Me Down" for the Animals; "One Fine Day" for the Chiffons; Herman's Hermits' "I'm into Something Good"; and Gene Pitney's "Every Breath I Take." The songwriting duo even sent their babysitter, Little Eva, up the road to stardom with their composition "Locomotion." Before their divorce in 1965, the team had penned more hits than any other songwriters except John Lennon and Paul McCartney. After a series of tentative starts, in 1970 King finally released a solo album of her own material, *Carole King: Writer*. A year later, as the nation tried to forget about the Vietnam War, she soothed the country with a collection of ballads collectively named *Tapestry* and received a grammy award for "Best Album of the Year" for her effort. By 1979 King had sold over thirteen million copies of the disc and had become the most popular female soft rocker of the decade.

Some soft rock musicians gravitated around another female singer, Linda Ronstadt. Born in Tucson, Arizona, Ronstadt left home at the age of eighteen in search of stardom. The road first led to the group the Stone Poneys, and the hit "Different Drum." In 1968, when the band broke up, the singer went solo and released *Hand Sown, Home Grown*. But only in 1971, with a back-up band that included Glenn Frey, Don Henley, and Randy Meisner, did Ronstadt find commercial success. Her albums with the group easily sold over a million copies each. Frey, Meisner, and Henley eventually joined with Bernie Leadon and formed the Eagles, producing million-selling albums of their own. Their flowing, country-flavored mellowness, exemplified by such tunes as "Take It Easy," "Desperado," "Lyin' Eyes," and "The Best of My Love," encapsulated the mood of a generation that eschewed social concerns. Jackson Browne, a friend of Glenn Frey's, also became a favorite among fans of laid-back rock. In 1973 Browne's *For Everyman* album, which included his "Take It Easy," originally written for the Eagles, established his reputation in the soft-rock genre.

John Prine represented the best of the singer-songwriter genre. Born in Maywood, Illinois, Prine served a stint in the army and then worked in the post office before he turned to music professionally in 1969. A year after his professional debut, he played the Old Town in Chicago. At that club Prine was discovered by Kris Kristofferson and Steve Goodman, at the time both imaginative singer-songwriters themselves (listen especially to Kristofferson's "Me and Bobby McGee" and "Billy Dee"). John Prine sang country-flavored songs with biting, witty, and insightful lyrics about the effects of war on a returning Vietnam veteran ("Sam Stone"), the human repercussions of the sexual revolution ("Six O'Clock News"), the loneliness of old age ("Angel from Montgomery"), and unthinking patriotism ("Your Flag Decal Won't Get You into Heaven Anymore"). Commented Kristofferson: "Twenty-four

Photo by Bonnie Lippel; used by courtesy of
Peter Asher Management

Linda Ronstadt in action

years old and he writes like he's two hundred and twenty." By the end of the late-night performance, Kristofferson felt that watching Prine "must've been like stumbling onto Dylan when he first busted the Village scene." It was "one of those rare, great times when it all seems worth it." In 1971, with Kristofferson's help, Prine released his first album, following it with *Sweet Revenge* and *Diamonds in the Rough*. But despite his genius, which was recognized by such fellow artists as Bob Dylan, Prine never captured large-scale recognition.

Other singer-songwriters found a wider audience. British-born Cat Stevens (a.k.a. Steven Georgiou), starting his career in 1966 as a folksinger, wafted onto the American scene with two gold albums: *Tea for the Tillerman* (1971) and *Teaser and the Firecat* (1972). Neil Young, an eccentric Canadian who tasted success in the bands Buffalo Springfield and Crosby, Stills, Nash, and Young, attracted a following with the LP *After the Gold Rush* (1970). Critic Robert Hilburn of the Los Angeles *Times* captured the essence of the album when he wrote that "words like lovely, beautiful and romantic cannot often be applied to rock albums, but there haven't been many rock albums like Neil Young's '*After the Gold Rush*.' It is a delicate, fragile jewel. . . . Young's soft, disarming voice and the crisp haunting instrumentation are almost therapeutically gentle." The cryptic, warbly-voiced Young produced a series of other self-revelatory albums, which established him as a leader among the soft rockers.

Another import to America, Reginald Kenneth Dwight, known to millions as Elton John, teamed up with writer Bernie Taupin and conquered the United States and then the world. In 1971 they released the album *Tumbleweed Connection* and hit the stateside charts. In the next few years the prolific duo churned out fifteen albums, and by early 1976 they had sold over eighty million discs across the globe. Elton John's diamond-inlaid glasses, two-foot platform shoes, pink boas, sequined jumpsuits, and frantic stage antics, which included stomping on his piano Jerry Lee Lewis–style, became familiar sights in concert halls until oversaturation and personal disagreements between John and Taupin ended the success story.

The wild Elton John

ROCK FUSIONS

Whereas Elton John climbed to stardom by caricaturing himself, another group of musicians in the seventies tried to dignify rock by merging it with classical music or jazz. Emerson, Lake, and Palmer proved to be one of the most successful groups that combined classical music with rock. Formed in late 1969 during a chance meeting in San Francisco, Keith Emerson, Greg Lake, and Carl Palmer made their debut at the Isle of Wight Festival. Two years later they released their first album, calculatedly embellished with classical bombast. In the next year they delved even deeper into the pop classical field, cutting a live stage version of Moussorgsky's composition *Pictures at an Exhibition*. They continued to pump out product throughout the seventies: *Brain Salad Surgery* (1977); *Welcome Back, My Friends, to the Show That Never Ends* (1974); *Works* (1977); and *Love Beach* (1978).

Roy Wood, another Englishman (formerly of the group the Move) who wanted to explore the tenuous connection between rock and the classics, founded the Electric Light Orchestra in 1970. The band's first, self-titled LP, graced with cellos and violins, received favourable reviews. *ELO II*, issued in 1973 and including three former members of the London Symphony Orchestra, gave the band its first hit: a richly orchestrated version of Chuck Berry's "Roll Over, Beethoven." By the 1974 album *Eldorado*, ELO was assured of gold record status for its releases. Its subsequent LPs — *Face the Music* (1975), *Ole ELO* (1976), *A New World Record* (1976), *Out of the Blue* (1977), and *Discovery* (1979) — increasingly degenerated into saccharine pop, culminating in the soundtrack for the Olivia Newton-John extravaganza *Xanadu* (1980).

Other British groups took only a slightly more serious view of the marriage between rock and the classics. Yes, a band formed in 1968 during a meeting at a London businessmen's drinking club, La Chasse in Soho, struggled for acclaim until their 1972 *Fragile* album, which included the hit "Roundabout." The group produced a number of other LPs until a personality clash caused the departure of classically trained pianist Rick Wakeman.

Genesis, a band started by high-school chums Peter Gabriel, Tony Banks, Michael Rutherford, and Anthony Phillips, grafted a surrealistic, fairy-tale world on a largely classical base. Against an orchestral backdrop, they told weird stories of an eavesdropping lawnmower, giant hogweeds overrunning the earth, and a young, pertly dressed girl knocking a disembodied human head along the ground with a croquet mallet. On stage the bizarre Peter Gabriel assumed the personas of these characters through a wild array of props and settings. Shrugged Gabriel: "I just poodle about and put on silly costumes." In the escapist seventies the make-believe world created by Genesis seemed a perfect diversion.

The group King Crimson, fueled by the ideas of guitarist Robert Fripp, also entertained the masses with a blend of rock and classical sounds. In late 1969 critics raved over the debut album, *In the Court of the Crimson King*. Subsequent albums alternately enraged and pleased critics and fans, reflecting the unstable line-up of the band. By late 1972, of the original band members only Fripp remained, and the popularity of the group faded.

Other musicians attempted to wed rock with jazz in the "fusion" movement. Jazz great Miles Davis, who had been present at the inception of bop during the mid-forties, spearheaded the trend. In 1970 Davis blended a raw-edged, slightly dissonant sixties jazz with the electric sound of rock, emerging with *Bitches Brew*. Wrote Ralph Gleason in the liner notes on the album: "This music is new. This music is new music and it hits me like an electric shock and the word 'electric' is interesting because the music is to some degree electric music. . . . Electric music is the music of this culture and in the breaking away (not the breaking down) from previously assumed forms a new kind of music is emerging." The credits on the album read like a list of the who's who of the fusion movement: John McLaughlin on guitar, Joe Zawinul's electric piano on some cuts, Chick Corea's electric keyboard on others, and the soprano sax of Wayne Shorter. John McLaughlin, playing with the Graham Bond Organization in the early sixties and later with the Tony Williams Lifetime jazz outfit, went on to form the jazz-rock Mahavishnu Orchestra. Zawinul and Wayne Shorter continued the fusion experiment in Weather Report, and Chick Corea, who had been trained by his father, jazz musician Armando Corea, in 1972 brought together himself, Stanley Clarke, Joe Farrell, and Airto Moreira in Return to Forever. These musicians, along with such other artists as Phoebe Snow, the band Chicago, Blood, Sweat and Tears, the Soft Machine, and a number of mainstream jazz performers who hoped to make some money off the new style, defined and shaped the sound of the jazz-rock fusion.

Pink Floyd, a British psychedelic band in the sixties, changed course in the seventies and expanded upon fusion's flirtation with electronics. They first lent their computerlike wizardry to a series of movie soundtracks: *More* (1969), *The Valley* (or *Obscured by Clouds*) (1972), and *Zabriskie Point* (1970). Pink Floyd also composed the music for German and Dutch television specials about the American moon landing. In 1973 the band unveiled its masterpiece, *Dark Side of the Moon*, which took nine painstaking months to produce. The album soared to the top of the American charts and still registers on *Billboard's* Top 200 after eleven years. Later releases by Floyd — *Wish You Were Here* (1975), *Animals* (1977), and *The Wall* (1979) — continued to accentuate Wagnerian electronics overlaid with a cynical message of impending Orwellian disaster.

GLITTER ROCK

Glitter rock, probably the most representative form of seventies rock 'n' roll, brought together elements of the various musical styles of the decade: the bombast of classical rock, the wild stage antics of Elton John, and a parody of heavy metal, which pushed the strutting, macho swagger of metal music to its homosexual conclusion. The result was an excessively absurd rock theater designed for the space age.

David Bowie (a.k.a. David Jones) set the tone for glitter rock. Struggling for acceptance as a commercial artist, a saxophonist, a mime, and the leader of David Jones and the Lower East Side, in 1971 Bowie hired manager Tony DeFries, who snagged a contract for the singer with RCA. "The way I think about David," confided DeFries, "is as a building. . . . He has the potential, in my hands, anyway, to create the income to make a building on Sixth Avenue. . . . He is the beginning, potentially, of an empire syndrome." Bowie recorded the album *Hunky Dory,* which established an "airy-fairy" image for the self-professed bisexual singer. Daniel Halloway, writing for the *New Musical Express,* felt that the *Hunky Dory* persona provided a "surreal cartoon character brought to life for us all to enjoy." The next year Bowie expanded upon his new image: At London's Rainbow Theater on August 16, 1972, Bowie materialized from a cloud of dry ice adorned by a tight-fitting, glimmering jump suit, high-topped, sequined hunting boots, and orange-tinted hair. "His eyebrows," wrote Charles Shear Murray in the *New Musical Express,* "have vanished, replaced by finely sketched red lines. He's wearing red eyeshadow which makes him look faintly insect-like." Looking like the pilot of a UFO, Bowie called himself Ziggy Stardust and his band the Spiders from Mars. Said the self-made alien: "The only thing that shocks now is an extreme. . . . Unless you do that, nobody will pay attention to you. Not for long. You have to hit them on the head." "It's going to be a brave new world, and we either join it or we become living relics," added Bowie. The science fiction character Bowie had created transported seventies youths from social reality to a fantasy land, just as such movies as Star Wars did for millions of other Americans.

Bowie's style filtered down to other bands. Mott the Hoople (the name came from a novel by Willard Manus), driven by singer-pianist Ian Hunter, started out in 1969 as a folksy, country-western-flavored group and achieved only modest success. Just as they decided to disband in 1972, the outfit was given "All the Young Dudes" by David Bowie, and the band found themselves in nine-inch platform heels, heavy mascara, and foppish costumes. Hunter remembered, "We were considered instant fags. A lot of gays followed us around, especially in America." The band reinforced their image with sexually charged songs such as "Sucker" and "One of the Boys," riding the glitter-paved road to stardom.

The New York Dolls, led by guitarist Johnny Thunder and vocalist David Johansen, jumped into the Bowie-inspired glitter scene in 1973 with their first album. Although they thrashed out driving, proto-punk anthems such as "Personality Crisis," the Dolls nonetheless projected a glam/glitter image: The cover of their first album, done in gray and shocking pink with NEW YORK DOLLS written in lipstick, pictured the band members with permanents, heavy make-up, jewelry, and ruby lipstick. Johansen, a shoulder thrust forward, started wistfully into the mirror of his powder box. The other group members looked straight ahead, attired smartly in six-inch heeled boots, skin-tight leather or spandex pants, and provocative blouses.

Lou Reed, co-founder of the Velvet Underground, kept up with this local competition. In 1972 he cut *Transformer,* which on the back cover showed Reed dressed in drag and included his only commercial hit single, "Walk on the Wild Side." The lyrics of the song told the story of a man named Holly who, while hitchhiking his way across the U.S.A., plucked his eyebrows, shaved his legs, and took a walk on the wild side of transsexualism. The tune crawled to a valium-inspired beat.

Roxy Music, named after the popular chain of Roxy cinemas in England, was another in the long line of Bowie imitators. Started in 1970 by Brian Ferry — a singer who was once rejected by King Crimson — and punctuated by the eerily imaginative synthesizer of Brian Eno, Roxy Music released its first LP in 1972. Their stage presence, devised by futuristic clothes designer Anthony Price, aped Bowie's. Read the *Music Scene:* "Brian Eno has been seen traveling the Underground wearing heavily applied brown eye shadow, thick mascara, lipstick, black glitter beads, pearly nail varnish, and violent purple streaks in his blonde hair." The themes of some of Roxy's material pointed in the same decadent direction: On *For Your Pleasure* (1973) they included the song, "In Every Dream Home a Heartache," which told of the joys and sorrows involved in sex with an inflatable doll. Even though Eno departed in 1973 "to pursue a partially defined direction — probably involving further investigations into bioelectronics, snake guitar, the human voice, and lizard girls," the band continued to receive critical acclaim for *Stranded* (1974), *Country Life* (1975), and *Siren* (1975).

Others took Bowie's image to an even further extreme, becoming caricatures of a caricature. In 1965 members of a high school track team in Phoenix, Arizona, formed a band for a skit in the school assembly. They decided to continue after their debut and called themselves Alice Cooper. Singer Vince Furnier, the son of a local minister, eventually adopted the group's name as his own. The band's main influence, Cooper told a reporter from the *Berkeley Barb* in 1970, was television. "We didn't have a blues influence. The music that affected us was the saucy theme songs, like '77 Sunset Strip' and 'Bourbon Street Beat'. . . . Our conditioning has been television, our conditioning has been the space age, so that's the kind of music we're going to play. We're not going to play Delta blues, I couldn't care less about how many times his baby left him."

Cooper wedded television theatrics and sexual extremism to create a bizarre, but marketable fantasy. In 1971 Alice Cooper broke into the charts with the LP *Love It to Death,* the album cover showing Cooper's six-inch thumb thrusting through a three-inch-wide ring. On stage Cooper and his cohorts put on a degenerate show, throwing live chickens into the audience, axing off the heads of dolls, staging mock executions in fake electric chairs, and beating their fans over the head with six-foot-long inflated phalluses. Manager Shep Gordon encouraged the antics, reasoning that they "break the conditioning of the audience. People feel threatened by the sexual thing." Alice Cooper continued unabated on tours for the albums *Killer* (1971), *School's Out* (1972), and *Billion-Dollar Babies* (1973).

The band Kiss practiced similar antics, attempting to breathe life into comic book characters. The brainchild of New York schoolteacher Gene Simmons, the face-painted members of Kiss assaulted their audiences with rockets, police lights, snow machines, smoke bombs, and levitating drum kits. By 1975 the band had become one of America's hottest selling commodities. Across the Atlantic Ocean, Gary Glitter (born Paul Gadd), who had knocked unsuccessfully at the door of the music industry since 1965, and Alvin Stardust provided the most crass examples of British glitter. As a writer in *Time* observed in 1972, "with the revolt long since gone out of the music, what is left is really a new kind of vaudeville or sometimes a freak show."

THE BOSS

Bruce Springsteen, the New Jersey Boss, cut through the gloss of the seventies with a hard-edged mixture of R & B and the modern urban experience. The son of a bus driver, Springsteen felt drawn to music from an early age. "Music saved me. From the beginning, my guitar was something I could go to. If I hadn't found music, I don't know what I would have done."

In 1972 he met manager Mike Appel, who signed Springsteen with Columbia Records; his first LP, *Greetings from Asbury Park,* was labeled Dylanesque by the critics because of its street-wise, rapid-fire lyrics. The next year the Boss joined forces with the E Street Band — headlined by sax player Clarence Clemons, formerly one of James Brown's Famous Flames — and released *The Wild, the Innocent, and the E Street Shuffle.* In October 1975 amid an extensive Columbia publicity campaign in which Springsteen appeared on the covers of both *Time* and *Newsweek,* the Boss hit gold with *Born to Run.* Reported rock critic Ashley Collie in *Maclean's:* "Rock in the early 70s was going through a crisis: It was becoming a toothless old woman. The search was on to find someone to save the music and Springsteen, who in his Catholic schooldays had drawn Christ crucified on a guitar, was the perfect redeemer candidate, with his passion and innocence." At one point the pressures of sudden fame immobilized The Boss. "The hype just gets in the way. People have gone nuts. It's weird," he told *Newsweek* in 1975. But after the furor died down and after a lengthy legal suit against now ex-manager Appel, Springsteen produced more rocking albums, first *Darkness on the Edge of Town* (1978) and then *The River* (1980). In the

Photo by Aaron Rappaport; used by courtesy of Columbia Records

Bruce Springsteen: the New Jersey Boss

1970s, however, Bruce Springsteen represented one of the last bastions of R & B-based, gut wrenching rock and roll.

RIGHT WING ROCK

Most musicians, whether into heavy metal, soft rock, art rock, or glitter, took an apathetic if not hostile attitude toward social protest. Comparing the seventies to the sixties, lyricist Robert Lamm of the group Chicago asserted "the world in the past two years has done a 180 degree turn in terms of political expression. . . . These days nobody wants to hear songs that have a message." The members of Fleetwood Mac, a band that deserted hard-core blues for the pop balladry of the million-selling LP *Rumors* (1977), felt the same way about "message" music. "You see, we're not very intellectual about our music. We just write it, and if we like it, we play it," singer-pianist Christine McVie told a reporter. "We don't put any heavy things into why we do it, or what it's all about. Or anything like that." Added bassist John McVie: "There's no sort of big intense, underlying thing." Robin Gibb of the Bee Gees, a sixties pop group that latched onto the disco craze in the seventies, boasted that "we never used our music as a soapbox. That should be left to the politicians and poets." In 1975 the quotable Pete Townshend of The Who summed up the changed spirit: "The hard edges of rock are being evened out. The whole Woodstock generation that was interested in rock of the sixties — they're all growing up. As they mature, they get less angry and demand music with less built-in vehemence. It's not that there are fewer discontents with society. You find how to live with these things."

The few performers who articulated a political preference usually favored the right wing. Bowie, in many senses the symbol of seventies rock, believed "very strongly in fascism. . . . People have always responded with greater efficiency under a regimental leadership. . . . Television is the most successful fascist, needless to say. Rock stars are fascists, too. Adolf Hitler was one of the first rock stars."

Linda Ronstadt similarly stressed the need for "efficiency," and in 1978 hoped for a "real resurgence of patriotism in this country." Staging benefit concerts for left-liberals Tom Hayden, Jerry Brown, Gary Hart, and the antinuclear lobby only taught her "that I really didn't know what I was talking about. Who knows who should be President and if anybody should have a big interest in determining those things, shouldn't Standard Oil? I mean they have more to gain and more to lose. If something terrible happens to Standard Oil, a lot of people will be out of jobs. You can say what you want about big multi-nationals running the country and stuff, but the fact remains that we need that, we need their services, we need jobs from them and they are in a better position to decide what's going to be good for the economic climate of the country and for the rest of the world."

Likewise, the members of Rush, a Canadian band that came from the suburbs of Willowdale, Ontario, to conquer America in the seventies, expected salvation from the teachings of such right-wing writers as Ayn Rand. For drummer Neil Peart, the *Fountainhead* of Rand "was a confirmation of all the things I'd felt as a teenager. I had thought I was a socialist like everyone else seemed to — you know, why should anyone have more than anyone else? — but now I think socialism is entirely wrong by virtue of man himself. It cannot work. It is simply impossible to say all men are brothers or that all men are created equal — they are not. Your basic responsibility is to yourself." Added bassist Geddy Lee: "For us capitalism is a way of life. It's an economic system built on those who can, do, and succeed at it." Lee hoped to appeal to rockers "who, despite their love of loud, violent music, were themselves non-revolutionary, highly conservative and certainly self-centered."

MUSIC FOR MONEY

Most of the seventies superstars agreed that they produced their work for money, not art. For Alice Cooper, "the idea all along was to make $1 million. Otherwise the struggle wouldn't have been worth it. . . . I am the most American rock act. I have American ideals. I love money." Singer Harry Nilsson felt that "there is more to life than money. But money is the first plateau." Ricky Lee Jones, the jazzy, be-bop-influenced singer of the late seventies, charged that most of her fellow performers "do it just because it's big bucks, and that's why the state of the art of performing is so disgusting."

To make money, many musicians eagerly embraced the rock business establishment. Gene Simmons of Kiss equated a "successful rock and roll band" with "a well-oiled machine. It's a good business." "The fact of the matter is that popular music is one of the industries of this country," agreed Paul Simon, who launched a successful solo music and film career in the 1970s. "It's all completely tied up with capitalism. It's stupid to separate it. That's an illusory separation." And as Greg Geller, talent scout for Columbia, noted in the mid-1970s: "Now artists are more upfront about admitting that they are interested in selling some records. This is not an ivory tower age: there's some recognition that we're involved in commerce."

Some groups even willingly compromised their art for the sake of business. Art Garfunkel, despite his resolve to include only songs by Jimmy Webb on his *Watermark* album, bowed to company pressure and included "What a Wonderful World." "It ran against his concept of what the album should have been, but we sold far more than we would have without the single," boasted Greg Geller. Mick Jagger of the aging Rolling Stones, who had become a member of the slick jet-set during the seventies, sometimes wished "I wasn't me. I don't mean the real me — I'm quite happy with that but the person they all swear at. But every-time someone curses me, I think, 'Remember, remember, that's what makes me very rich.' " Likewise, James Taylor had always told himself, "I'm not going to make an album for commercial consumption, I'm going to make an album that I want to make: I'm willing to write this one off. I'd like to make an album like that. I probably won't."

For some, the record business paid off. Don McLean, who scored a hit with the song "American Pie," which described the decline of the sixties consciousness, was hardly the most commercially successful artist; yet he sold 4.5 million singles and 1.8 million albums of "American Pie" and netted around $1.1 million in royalties. Along with $460,000 in publishing and writing royalties and $200,000 in foreign sales, the singer-songwriter earned $1.6 million. After giving his manager the prescribed 10 percent, McLean took to the bank at least $1.2 million. Similarly, Carol King, getting about thirty-five cents for each of the 13 million copies sold of her *Tapestry* album, netted well over $4 million. Peter Frampton, a former Humble Pie guitarist who became one of the most publicized artists of the decade, grossed $67 million in

1978 on album sales and tours. For a night's work on the concert circuit, Neil Young walked away with $18,000. After paying his back-up crew $100,000, Young took home almost $2 million for a three-month tour in 1973.

Many seventies stars invested their earnings. Neil Young bought a thousand-acre ranch located north of San Francisco, a number of apartment buildings, and a shopping center. The Bee Gees, one of the biggest draws of the 1970s who vaulted to success after their appearance on the soundtrack to *Saturday Night Fever,* operate their own merchandising company, which sells — as Barry Gibb told it — "things like nice T-shirts. We deal in jewelry but only real gold plate. We're doing a little electronic piano with Mattel Toys that'll be available soon." They also market "a cute Andy Gibb doll." Alice Cooper financed such films as *Funny Lady* and *Shampoo* for tax shelters and invested in art, antiques, and tax-free municipal bonds. Despite his image as a primordial flamer, Ted Nugent owns a mink farm and trout operation. Says Bob Weed, the Nuge's financial manager, "all of this fits in with Ted's plan for acquiring land. Sure, we're involved in some oil and gas-lease tax shelters, but when I tell him about property, that's something he understands." All told, in 1973 *Forbes* estimated that at least fifty rock superstars earned and invested between two and six million dollars a year, each musician accumulating from three to seven times more than the highest paid executive in the United States.

THE RECORD INDUSTRY CLOSES RANKS

The record industry, consolidating into a few major companies, made it possible for rock stars to amass these astronomical sums of money. During the 1950s American business in general started to consolidate. By 1955 the fifty largest corporations controlled 27 percent of the national market and sold more than $86 billion worth of manufactured goods, a figure equal to more than one-fourth of the Gross National Product. The trend continued in the sixties, until by 1970 the market share of the six hundred largest companies increased to 75 percent, and the share held by the top two hundred corporations rose to over 60 percent. The 102 giants at the top of this pyramid, holding assets of $1 billion or more, controlled 48 percent of the market and made 53 percent of the profits.

The record industry followed this pattern. From an industry that included a number of viable independent companies during the 1950s, by 1973 the recording industry went to being almost completely controlled by six majors —CBS, Capitol, MCA, Polygram, RCA, and Warner Communications. The top four companies accounted for over 52 percent of all records and tapes sold, and the leading two — CBS and Warner-Elektra/Asylum-Atlantic — sold 38 percent of the total.

These companies, like other American conglomerates, had interests in other fields besides music. MCA owns Universal films, various television stations, Arlington and Mount Vernon cemeteries, a bank in Colorado, and the Spencer Gifts novelty chain. RCA, the twentieth largest corporation in the country, operates NBC television and radio; owns the Hertz Rent-A-Car company, Banquet Foods, the Cushman and Wakefield real estate firm, and Random House and Alfred Knopf publishers; and acts as a prime defense contractor.

These giant corporations built rock 'n' roll, which by 1975 accounted for 80 percent of all record sales, into a multi-billion-dollar enterprise. In 1950 record sales reached $189 million, and in 1955 they increased to $277 million. At the time, Columbia, RCA, Decca, Capitol, MGM, and Mercury led the field. But by 1973, in the United States alone the industry sold $2 billion in records and tapes and another $150 million in concert tickets. The total surpassed the combined gross revenues of Broadway ($36 million), professional sports ($540 million), and the movies ($1.3 billion), and was more than double the gross earnings of network television ($1 billion). By 1978 the record industry grossed about $4 billion. In the summer of that year alone, MCA made a profit of over $5.5 million, CBS cleared $48.5 million, and Warner netted $19.8 million.

Profits came in from around the world. In 1973 the companies sold $2 billion worth of records and tapes in the United States, a per capita expenditure of $9.70. That same year they sold over $555 million worth of records and tapes in Japan, $454 million in West Germany, $441 million in the Soviet Union, $384 million in the United Kingdom, which is controlled largely by the British Electrical Manufacturing Industries (EMI), and even $16 million in Poland. Per capita expenditures amounted to $7.57 in West Germany, $6.91 in the Netherlands, $7.64 in Sweden, and $5.14 in Japan.

To further penetrate the international market, Paramount Pictures, itself a subsidiary of Gulf and Western, bought a half-share of British EMI, which had world-wide sales of $965.8 million in 1978. In addition, EMI, Decca, and Phonogram set up recording studios in Nigeria. A Nigerian record factory, built for $15 million in 1978 by CBS, can press 25 million records a year with cheap Nigerian labor. As a writer in *Billboard* observed, "tradesters have long felt that Nigeria holds great potential for expansion in record and tape production and marketing, perhaps as the key area in the entire African continent."

Some executives, however, were not satisfied with their progress. Jerry Moss, chairman of A & M Records, wanted "to be double platinum, triple platinum, quadruple platinum. We're all in this platinum derby." Similarly, a spokesman for the multinational Commonwealth United Corporation reported "we have made marketing studies of the music industry and we see definite signs of unlimited growth potential in the field."

The underworld even became attracted to the profits of the recording industry. "I know that the — the Mafia, both the black Mafia and also the white Mafia, they are intimidating a lot of super rock stars," confessed one producer. "They — are threatening — if he's a musician, they are threatening to break his playing hand, and if he's a vocalist they are threatening to slit his throat. And they in turn — they are asking, and they're getting, 25 percent of the artists' fees in kickbacks." In 1979 the *Wall Street Journal* linked Mafia leader Anthony Spilotro and Daniel Seraphine, drummer for the band Chicago. Apparently, the Mafia also is involved in counterfeiting records by "bootlegging" (issuing unauthorized, usually live, discs) and "pirating" (reproducing authorized versions of albums and selling them without giving royalties to the artist or songwriters). According to one New Jersey tape pirate, "my people who I deal with . . . are . . . heavies in New York. I mean heavies. These are not guys like, uh, in Canton, Ohio. These are guys from Mulberry Street [the heart of Little Italy] beautiful people as long as you don't fuck them. If they think you're fucking them, they blow your head off, simple as that."

Such a business climate made it difficult for the existence of small independent companies. "It's tough being out there on your own," explained United Artist president Artie Mogull. "The record business has become big business and that requires big capital." As Neil Bogart of Casablanca Records put it: "The small labels can't compete financially in getting an act."

THE MAKING AND MARKETING OF A RECORD

The business of making a record begins with a contract. A record company usually offers an artist 10 to 15 percent of record sales as a royalty rate, and another $50,000 advance to make the album, which the performer must repay from subsequent royalties. Some established stars get considerably more: For example, Warner Brothers nabbed Paul Simon for an estimated $13 million, and CBS handed Paul McCartney a three-record contract, assuring him of $2 million for each LP and another $2 million for rights to some of the Beatles' material.

Once the artist cuts a master tape, the company manufactures the record. First, technicians make a two-track master tape from the twenty-four-track master recorded in the studio. Using a recording lathe, they cut a lacquer master from the tape and ship the lacquer to a pressing plant, where it is cleaned, sprayed with silver to make it electrically conductive, and plated with a solid nickel shell. Workers then remove the nickel plating, which results in a negative copy of the record, or a "metal master." This master is plated itself with nickel, which, when removed, yields a positive copy of the record known as the "metal mother." After checking for sound, this master is coated with nickel and becomes the "stamper," used to mold the polyvinyl chloride (PVC) into at least a thousand records that reach the consumer. Two stampers are fitted into a press, which is heated to 300 degrees, and a vinyl "biscuit" about 3 inches square and 2½ inches thick is placed between them. The press, exerting a pressure of about 150 tons per square inch, comes together and produces the LP, which is quickly cooled by water. The entire process, after the stampers have been prepared, takes about twenty-three seconds, and the complete procedure from the studio tape to the finished product costs roughly thirty-five cents per disc.

Artists then design the album cover. For some, the process is a creative effort. John Berg, who has produced over twelve hundred jackets for Columbia and Epic, takes a more businesslike approach: "Talk about 'art' is bullshit; it's advertising. I just want you to be able to find a record in the store. That's my biggest job." At times, the cost of the cover may exceed twenty thousand dollars, and it usually adds another fifteen cents to each album.

After finishing the product, executives begin to market it. Agencies hired by the companies, such as First Analytic Center, initially research possible markets for the LP. "We always have a war plan on every record," said Jerry Greenberg, president of Atlantic Records. Executives subsequently aim an intensive publicity campaign at a specific audience. Stu Ginsberg, head of publicity at RCA, tries "to create a snowball effect. So you arrange live tours in patterned locations so that the radio and press coverage will overlap. You want to come into a city with advance airplay, and you want to leave the city with press and more airplay. It spreads. New York stations spread to New Jersey, and so on." As RSO president Al Coury boasted, "sales like ours don't just happen. We make them happen! And I sell the sizzle." For help, Coury hired thirty-four promotional men, half of his total staff. Such promotion requires money, averaging ten cents per album sold. For example, RCA spent over $100,000 on David Bowie's first American concert tour. Others have relegated over $1 million for the promotion of a new album by a top-selling artist.

The selling of Sha Na Na, a seventies band of Columbia University students who specialized in fifties rock 'n' roll schlock, offers an example. "To build this group," explained Neil Bogart of Casablanca Records, "we created a music industry trend. We called it rock 'n' roll revival. With slogans, stickers, buttons, industry and consumer contests, and even black leather motorcycle jackets for our promotion staff, we brought back the fifties. We took an active part in securing bookings for Sha Na Na at rock palaces such as the Fillmore West. We transported the group from coast to coast, making sure they were seen by their audience and their potential record-buying public. We flew radio men, promotion men, and distributors into New York and San Francisco to see the group. . . . Before the album, they had appeared on the *Merv Griffin Show* and had been the subject of a feature in *Rolling Stone,* all of which led to their being invited to appear at Woodstock. In fact, by the time the Sha Na Na album was released, the Buddah office had taken on the aura of an Orange Julius on Saturday night in Brooklyn." Sha Na Na proved to Bogart that "talent may be compared to commercial products — the cigarette you smoke, the T.V. set you watch or the car you drive. You select that brand of product that you have been convinced is the one you should buy." Added Henry Anger, a senior vice-president for marketing at Polygram: "If pitching is 70 percent of baseball, promotion is 70 percent of the record business."

Radio figures prominently in the promotional efforts for an artist. Of the 181 important AM stations, 51 in twenty-four different cities are considered of prime importance and, according to marketing studies, account for 54 percent of overall record sales. If a song plays on WABC or KHJ, for example, it prompts an extra five thousand sales. FM radio, depoliticized in 1970 by arch-Republican FCC chairman Dean Burch, has the same effect on record sales. Having such importance, radio play is bought by many companies. Roger Karshner, former vice-president of sales at Capitol, found that "payola is still the industry's little bastard. No one will admit to him, but everybody pays child support, and the little devil keeps coming back for more — not openly, of course, but quietly in sneakers. The greedy little bloodsucker has gone underground."

Record companies also sell their product through promotional concerts, which take place around the time of an album's release. In every major city, such promoters as Howard Stein of New York, who grosses fifteen million dollars a year from his acts, work in tandem with the labels. They organize the specifics of a concert date for a set fee or a percentage of the gate.

The industry courts reviewers and writers as part of its promotional efforts. Rock columnist and author Richard Goldstein maintained his "illusions about the value-free purity of rock until the day in 1969 when my agent informed me that a large music publisher would pay me $25,000 for three presentations on the state of popular music. It was understood that I would favor this company's artists in my reviews." As a further incentive to reviewers, some companies have provided up to six copies of each new release worth more than $10,000 per year to major rock writers.

By the time a label has packaged and marketed an album, shipped it, and paid royalty fees to the artist and the publisher, an album costs roughly $1.55. To break even it must sell from 200,000 to 300,000 copies. If it sells less than 50,000 units, the artist will probably be dropped by the company. During the early and mid-seventies, executives released LPs by many new performers and hoped for the best. Goddard Leiberson, president of Columbia, called it "buckshotting — throwing everything against the wall to see what sticks." But as the American economic situation worsened in the mid-seventies, the labels became more careful about the artists they signed. In early 1979 Bob Krasnow, Warner's vice-president of talent, predicted, "You're going to be seeing fewer records with far more promotion behind them."

The artists who do make albums receive roughly sixty cents per disc sold. From their royalties they must repay the company for the $50,000 to $100,000 advance used for studio time, and must pay their manager the usual 10 percent fee. After everyone has been paid, most artists find themselves with little cash.

THE PRESSURES OF STARDOM

Even the commercially successful rock stars suffer from the pressures of the rock business. Many experience the lack of privacy that accompanies adulation by the masses. "Imagine sitting in a house like this, nice as it is, and not being able to go outside because of all these people coming past," complained Maurice Gibb of the Bee Gees. "They have a Universal-type tour bus that comes down the road every hour with loudspeakers."

A few performers begin to internalize their image. Initially David Bowie just acted out the part of the ultimate rock star, Ziggy Stardust. "Then everybody started to treat me as they treated Ziggy: as though I were the next Big Thing, as though I moved masses of people. I became convinced I was a messiah. Very scary . . . I realized I had become a total product of my concert character Ziggy." In rock and roll, agreed Todd Rundgren of Nazz and then Utopia, "your whole life becomes represented by what you do rather than what you are. To compensate for this you make a caricature of yourself . . . your life becomes a performance."

Pressures mount to a fever pitch during a tour. Touring, observed Dr. Eugene Landy, a Beverly Hills clinical psychologist who has counseled a number of rock stars, is "one of the worst things a person can do because it creates such pressure." It "stops you from having any kind of regularity or routine. There's nothing you can call a familiar place, a peaceful place." Moreover, lamented Don Henley of the Eagles and writer of "Life in the Fast Lane," "concerts can be real hard on you. You go out there night after night getting all this tremendous love from 20,000 people, and then 30 minutes later you're sitting in your hotel room alone watching the news on T.V." Offers of groupie sex after the show, added Dr. Landy, "can never be as exciting as standing out in front of all those people and getting an absolute response."

The grueling experience of touring sometimes ends in bodily harm. Tommy Johnston, former lead singer for the Doobie Brothers, a 1970s outfit that blended soft-rock with jazz influences, developed "stomach ulcers and was generally zinging out and couldn't handle the whole thing. We were doing between 150 and 200 dates a year at that point."

To alleviate the pain, many rock performers turn to drugs. Members of the heavy metal band Van Halen treat "any kind of physical or mental injury with alcohol — the kind you can swallow." Despite her resolve to the contrary, Linda Ronstadt has found that "there's always a night when I didn't get enough sleep so I don't run, and I'm afraid of eating so I do some cocaine, and then that's the end of it. Then it's uppers and coke for the rest of the tour." Don Henley felt that drugs offer "the only way some people can cope with the pressures. The ups and downs are extreme, and drugs help smooth them out." "Most people I know have some kind of problem with excess, either drinking too much or doing too much dope," agreed soft-rock singer Bonnie Raitt.

For the stars who manage to avoid drugs, loneliness remains a problem. As he stared out a window from his hotel room, Robin Zander of Cheap Trick, a pop-rock band from the Midwest, told a reporter: "That's the real world out there. I haven't been out there in three years, since the band started. I have no friends. Just the band, my manager, other people in the business. I don't trust anybody." Nicole Barclay of the all-female group Fanny said "that every business in the world is lonely, and that rock and roll is one of the professions that involves living and moving in a way that forces you to see that you're lonely," which is especially dangerous to performers, who search "for an ego boost because you don't feel you deserve it on a real-life level." Linda Ronstadt summed up life in the rock business: "It's incredibly lonely. Everybody I know is lonely. It has to be that way because of the life-style, all the traveling, the paranoia, the fact that your ass is on the line when you go on stage." Soon young rebellious rockers would strike out against a rock establishment that bred such isolation.

Punk Rock:
The Politics of Aggression

Punk rock, the socially conscious music of the late seventies, challenged and threatened big business rock, which had dominated the music scene for almost a decade. In an economically troubled England, tough, radical punk rock reared its spiked head. Punkers screamed for change: They wanted to change the economy, change a racist mentality, and even change the static social system, which made the rich richer and left the poor with a smaller share of the economic pie. Crying for equality, they joined hands with the dreadlocked Rastafarians, who swayed to reggae, the radical music of an economically enslaved Jamaica. Across the Atlantic a more arty, but nonetheless political, punk rock raised its fist especially in the avant-garde capital of the world, New York City. Like its British counterpart, New York punk confronted head-on the slick commercial rock establishment.

THE PUNK ATTACK IS MOUNTED

Punk rock, growing out of a deteriorating British economy, represented the most dramatic and full-scale attack upon corporate rock. In 1974 the inflation rate in England stood at about 24 percent. A year later it had climbed three more points. Simultaneously, between 1974 and 1977 the unemployment rate shot up 120 percent and increased by more than 200 percent among the young.

In such a depressed economic climate, many British youths no longer found it possible to identify with plump rock stars, who lounged by their pools in the California sun and sipped margaritas. Said Johnny Rotten, lead singer of the Sex Pistols, the group that would shock Britain in 1977: "The millionaire groups were singing about love and their own hang-ups. That's stupid. You don't sing about love to people on the dole. We're totally against apathy of any kind. We have got to fight the entire super band system. Groups like The Who and the Stones are revolting. They have nothing to offer the kids anymore. All they're good for is making money." Joe Strummer of The Clash — a band that in 1977 crashed onto the airwaves with such punk anthems as "I'm So Bored of the U.S.A." and "All the Young Punks" — complained about the "wank rock groups like Boston and Aerosmith. What fucking shit." Generation X, a band fronted by the statuesque Billy Idol, parodied The Who's "My Generation" with their "Your Generation," which ridiculed The Who's rendition as outdated and meaningless. Sham 69, a four-man punk band, similarly warned of a new era with their "Whose Generation." As rock critic Dave Marsh noticed at the time, punks "rejected the idea and the worship of a rock aristocracy."

When they turned their backs on the rock elite, angry British youths dispelled the myth of the heroic, virtuoso performer. As "a teenager," Joe Strummer told *Musician* magazine, "I felt that musicians were a world apart — a secret society that I could never join. So I didn't bother to try until I was almost too old. I just hope it doesn't seem so impossible like it did for me watching Eric Clapton at Wembly and thinking, *I could never do that.*" "When I first started making records," agreed Brian Eno, who first played synthesizer for Roxy Music and then led punks to a more arty synthesis, "there was this whole accent in rock and roll on heroic instrumentalists who could play quickly, skillfully and technically. I thought then, and still think, that isn't what music is about."

Hundreds of British teens, thirsting for some means to vent their anger and frustration, felt the same as Eno and used music as an outlet: Steve Jones of the Sex Pistols learned guitar after he joined the group and by 1977 drowned out critics with his propulsive work on the Pistols' LP; Siouxsie Sioux, an avid fan of the Pistols, decided to use her own talents and formed Siouxsie and the Banshees; and Polystyrene (a.k.a. Marion Elliot) of X-Ray Spex, a young British black, followed Siouxsie's

The infamous Johnny Rotten

lead and delivered cutting, piercing vocals on *Germ Free Adolescents*. As Sex Pistol manager Malcolm McLaren pointed out, it was not the timbre of the voice nor the intricacy of the guitar-work but the sheer energy that defined punk.

These punkers — "British working-class children, who have no memory of swinging London and cannot find jobs" in the words of *Time* — began to wrest rock from wealthy, aging soloists, who had played to thousands in huge stadiums. They shoved it into the hands of the poor teens who streamed into small clubs on weekends and challenged the audience by shouting and spitting at them, blurring the distinction between artist and spectator.

Courtesy of The Daily *of the University of Washington*

Siouxsie Sioux of the Banshees

THE SEX PISTOLS

The Sex Pistols led the punk legion. They were a notorious band of Londoners — Johnny Rotten sneering and spitting out the vocals, Sid Vicious, the self-destructive bass player who replaced Glen Matlock in 1977 because Matlock "was into the Beatles;" drummer Paul Cook, and guitarist Steve Jones. Formed in late 1975 by ex–New York Dolls manager Malcolm McLaren, the Pistols (first called the Swankers) began to play club dates the next year. "When the Pistols first started," remembered Johnny Rotten, "we found it impossible to get gigs. The business bends over backwards to help the big bands. If you're not established you've got no chance. But by hook or by crook, we forced gigs onto people." In September 1976 the band headlined a two-day punk festival at London's 100 Club. A month later the Pistols signed with EMI and released their first single, "Anarchy in the U.K.," which shocked listeners with its message: "We want to destroy/ Don't know what I want but I know how to get it/ I want to be an anarchist — anti-christ/ I is the enemy/ I is anarchy." Said Rotten: "There'll always be something to fight — apathy's the main thing. The Pistols are presenting one alternative to the apathy and if you don't like it, that's just too bad. Anarchy is self-rule and that's better than anything else." Assailed by adverse public opinion and recalcitrant employees who refused to press the record, EMI cut the Pistols from its roster in January 1977. An official EMI memo blasted the Pistols for their "disgraceful . . . aggressive behavior."

A & M Records and then Virgin took on the band. Virgin marketed a second single, "God Save the Queen," which coincided with Queen Elizabeth's Silver Jubilee and which was banned immediately: "God save the queen, a fascist regime/ It made you a moron, a potential H-bomb/ God save the queen she ain't no human being/ There's no future in England's dream." Said McLaren: "It's not a version of the national anthem but the boys' personal tribute to the Queen."

The Sex Pistols: kings of punk

Next, the gutsy Virgin Records released "Pretty Vacant." The song began with a thumping, driving bass line. Pounding drums and then a slashing guitar joined the bass. Finally the painfully jagged voice of Johnny Rotten coughed up lyrics that captured the anger and frustration of poor British youths: "There's no point in askin' you'll get no reply/ I just remembered, I don't decide/ I got no reason, it's all too much/ You'll always find me, out to lunch — we're out of lunch/ We're so pretty, oh so pretty . . . we're vacant/ We're so pretty, oh so pretty . . . vacant/ And now, we don't care." In December 1977 the Sex Pistols released the punk opus, *Never Mind the Bollocks*. It topped the British charts despite the ban many radio stations placed on it.

ROCK AGAINST RACISM

Racism was the target of other punk bands. Some punkers formed Rock Against Racism after an August 14, 1976, concert in Birmingham, where a drunken Eric Clapton lectured concertgoers about Britain "becoming a black colony within ten years." "Musicians were coming out with the 'Blame the Blacks bit,' " remembered one organizer. "Bowie and Clapton were the last straws — how dare they praise Hitler or want to repatriate the race that had created the music they profitably recycled." Consequently a number of punk bands fought "back against the creeping power of racist ideas in popular culture" and attacked the right-wing, neo-Nazi National Front. By April 1977 Rock Against Racism had organized into fifty-six chapters and drew over eighty thousand adherents to a concert headlined by The Clash, who lifted the throng to its feet with such left-wing anthems as "White Riot," "London's Burning," and "Career Opportunities."

In September of that same year another Rock Against Racism crowd wildly cheered Elvis Costello (a.k.a. Declan McManus), who delivered such messages as "Welcome to the Working Week" and "Less Than Zero," the last a vitriolic assault on right-wing leader Oswald Mosely "with the Swastika tattoo," who called for the repatriation of British blacks. Costello later penned "Oliver's Army," a song about life in the British military: "There was a checkpoint Charlie, he didn't crack a smile/ But it's no laughing party, when you've been on the murder mile/ Only takes one itchy trigger/ One more widow, one less white nigger." He also composed "Green Shirt," "Two Little Hitlers," and "What's So Funny (About Peace, Love and Understanding)."

In June 1978 fifty thousand turned out to see The Clash, Tom Robinson, X-Ray Spex, and Sham 69. Tom Robinson shouted at the crowd that National Front members, although they "look just like you and me," must be combated "at school and at work. . . . If music can erase even a tiny fraction of the prejudice and intolerance in this world, then it's worth trying." "Through my lyrics," added Morgan Webster of Sham 69, "I want to show the Front that they're fucking assholes." "We're against fascism and racism. I figure that goes without saying,"

Elvis Costello

agreed Joe Strummer of The Clash. By the end of 1978 over 250,000 youths had rocked against fascism and racism in more than thirty-five concerts held across England.

Tom Robinson put forward another demand for social change: gay rights. "Being gay myself," he told some San Francisco journalists, "I'm concerned with gay liberation. But I see that as part of an overall and much, much larger picture. You can't demand freedom for gay people without freedom for people of all color skins. No way! It isn't possible. If we can keep a few kids from joining the National Front, or keep a kid from being beaten up, we've achieved something."

Polystyrene of X-Ray Spex sang out for women's rights. In her 1977 "Oh Bondage" she screamed "Oh Bondage, up yours" to the adage that little girls should be seen but not heard.

THE JAMAICAN CONNECTION:
REGGAE AND SKA

British punks, dedicated to racial and social equality, championed reggae. Reggae grew out of the Jamaican Rastifarian religion, which emerged as early as the 1930s, when rotund American Marcus Garvey urged Jamaican blacks to return to the Ethiopian kingdom of Haile Selassie, the Lion of Judah. Garvey's back-to-Africa message appealed to many Jamaicans who were exploited by the British colonial system. Even after political independence in 1962, Jamaica remained a poor economic colony of Great Britain: Over 35 percent of the labor force was unemployed, most of them living in the slums of West Kingston. Trapped in this poverty-stricken situation, many Jamaicans cultivated Rastafarianism into a coherent set of beliefs: Selassie became the prophet Prince of God, or Jah, and after his fall he became the martyred King; the Ethiopian colors — orange, green, and red — were adopted as the Rasta standard; Jamaicans began to sport a plaited hairstyle known as dreadlocks; and in the late 1960s reggae, which combined African and indigenous Jamaican rhythms, replaced the westernized calypso to become the music of the countercultural religion. Peter Tosh, one of the fathers of reggae, explained, "Reggae, the word, means 'king's music,' and I play the King's music. The King put many princes on earth, and the music is given to those who praise Him. You have to be spiritually inclined to deal with this kind of talent."

Reggae originated in the slums of the Jamaican capital. "When I came to Kingston at about 16 years of age," Tosh remembered, "I soon realized that nine out of ten singers found themselves in poverty in Trenchtown, the ghetto. It was me, Bob Marley, Bunny Livingstone, Joe Higgs, the Maytals — we'd sit around every night and just sing. At that time, me and Joe Higgs were the only ones who could play the guitar. Finally Joe Higgs helped to get us into the studio with Sir Coxsone Dodd producing, and that was the start of recording for me and Bob and Bunny." In 1964 Tosh and his friends called themselves the Wailers and hit the Jamaican charts with the ska-influenced "Simmer Down." Two years later another Wailer ska song, "Rude Boy," which immortalized the outlaws of Kingston's shantytown, reached the number-one spot in the former British colony.

Around 1970 the Wailers abandoned the more traditional Jamaican ska for a new music that was rooted in Rastafarianism, and became known as reggae. They delivered such songs as "African Herbsman" and "Rasta Revolution." In 1973 they released the reggae LPs *Catch a Fire* and *Burnin':* the second included "I Shot the Sheriff," a song ironically covered by Eric Clapton. Two years later the Wailers cut *Natty Dread,* a testament to the Rastafarian culture.

The Wailers, along with other reggae groups such as Toots and the Maytals, Burning Spear, Black Uhuru, and Steel Pulse, lambasted the racism and the capitalism that Britain had imposed upon them. Burning Spear (a.k.a. Winston Rodney) used the Rastafarian dialect to express his belief the everyone should "be equal or i-qual and get an equal share. An' everyman entitled to dem share an' should get dem share. . . . The work is to bring the whole world together. See. That is naturality. Non-violence, less pollution, more togetherness, more industry, less institution like prisons; more schools, more hospitals. These things come through the music. And the music is those things and those things is the music." Jamaican producer Lee Perry told a reporter that reggae "denounces the very heart of the system on which much of the capitalist world is built." Not just voicing rhetoric, many reggae bands such as Bob Marley and the Wailers actively backed the government of socialist prime minister Michael Manley. At one 1976 rally for the Prime Minister, Marley barely escaped an assassination attempt. Such actions dovetailed with the leftist protests of white British punks, and reggae bands such as Steel Pulse, Aswad, and Matumbi became mainstays on the bills of Rock Against Racism concerts.

Some British youths took ska — the light, happy Jamaican music that predated reggae — and fused it with the radical message and the energy of punk. "We were the first band which wanted to combine punk and reggae because we liked them both," recalled Jerry Dammers of the racially integrated Specials, one of the most influential of the new ska groups, which included the Selecter, Madness, Bad Manners, and the Bodysnatchers. "Both were rebel music," said fellow Special member Horace Panter. Guitarist Dave Wakeling of the English Beat, another

Photo by Cam Garrett

Steel Pulse: Reggae Against Racism

HORACE - Bass   NEVILLE - Vocals   RODDY - Guitar   BRAD - Drums   TERRY - Vocals   LYNVAL - Guitar   JERRY - Organ

The Specials: two-tone originals

English ska group from Birmingham, rediscovered ska because "it said what a terrible world this was — with a smile on its face." The Specials' anthem, "Concrete Jungle," exemplified Wakeling's definition of the new music. The song bopped to an upbeat tempo, telling listeners: "I'm going out tonight/ I don't know if I'll be alright/ Everyone wants to hurt me/ Baby danger in the city/ I have to carry a knife/ Because people threaten my life/ I can't dress just the way I want/ Get chased by the National Front/ Concrete jungle, animals are after me."

THE INDEPENDENT LABELS

Independent labels sprang up to distribute this politicized music. In 1976 Rough Trade Records began pressing discs. In the words of staffer Allan Sturdy, the label hoped to "provide an alternative to the music establishment so that a record could be available that otherwise wouldn't." It first recorded the astounding debut LP of the politically minded Ulster band Stiff Little Fingers, which wrote such diatribes as "Alternative Ulster," "Suspect Device," "Law and Order," "Rough Trade," and the sarcastic, sobering "White Noise," which detailed white Britain's racism toward blacks, Pakistanis, and the Irish. The new independent based its operations on cooperation since, as Rough Trade's Howie Klein commented, most "record companies are part of an anti-social movement in Western society, part of the industrial complex that enslaves people." They split profits fifty/fifty between the company and the artist, keeping the prices as low as possible and funneling business profits back into the company. Also, the twenty-five staffers at Rough Trade democratically made decisions about material, rejecting songs that were sexist or racist. "I wouldn't sign a band that was racist or sexist or fascist or anything like that," Klein told a reporter.

The ethic of Rough Trade spread: Factory Records in Manchester; Edinburgh's Fast Product; Red Rhino in New York; Graduate Records in Dudley; and the ska label, Two-Tone. Although a few independents such as I.R.S., Virgin, and Stiff became small versions of the majors, many followed the example of the humanistic Rough Trade. A spate of independent newspapers and magazines such as *Damage, Slash, New York Rocker, Vacation, Hot Press, Sounds,* and *Another Room* publicized the independent releases.

Some punk bands, after starting with the independents, signed with major labels for better distribution of their records. Tom Robinson, facing the contradiction between his leftist politics and the money-making goals of his label, asserted that one has "to use the capitalist media to reach the people. And I do feel that pop music is the way to reach people. Ideally, I'd like to be played on AM stations rather than FM stations, rather than the rarified atmosphere. I'd rather be played in taxis, in factories, for housewives working at home." Joe Strummer tried "to do something new, we're trying to be the greatest group in the world, and that also means the biggest. At the same time, we're trying to be radical — I mean, we never want to be *really* respectable — keep punk alive." Added Mick Jones of The Clash: "We realized that if we were a little more subtle, if we branched out a little, we might reach a few more people. We finally saw we had been reaching the same people over and over. This way if more kids started hearing the record, maybe they'd start humming the songs, they'll read the lyrics and learn something from them."

RIGHT-WING REACTION

Right-wing groups made The Clash's resolve difficult. In 1977 the *British Patriot,* the magazine of the National Front, warned its readers that The Clash was "the most left-wing of the contemporary groups." To diffuse their influence, it instructed National Fronters to keep "an eye out for posters that advertise Clash concerts so that they may be removed from walls and boardings and reconsigned to the gutter where they will reach the most appropriate clientele." During their first tour of Great Britain, The Clash met resistance. Police repeatedly stopped their tour bus for little or no excuse, and the band members were arrested and fined for such dire offenses as forgetting to return hotel keys. In the United States, Epic Record executives at first refused to issue the group's debut LP, *The Clash* (EMI April 1977), branding it "too crude" for American consumption. They put out the album two years later in an altered form.

Other punk bands also met opposition. In July 1978 the National Front burned down two auditoriums used for Rock Against Racism shows. A year later British police stormed into the Southall Musicians Cooperative — the home of white and black punkers and reggae musicians — and wantonly smashed instruments and sound equipment. Benefit concerts for the Cooperative, organized by The Clash and Pete Townshend of The Who, generated enough money to replace the damaged goods. Yet throughout the late seventies, the new Teddy Boys and the skinheads — fans of hard rock bands such as Humble Pie, Status Quo, and Judas Priest — attacked punks in gangland fashion. Townshend called the skinheads and the Teddies "fascist. They despise everybody who isn't like them. It's a kind of toy fascism, fed by organized fascism; fed by Martin Webster and the National Front." In 1979 these right-wing teens, organizing into the Young National Front, launched a Rock Against Communism movement to counterbalance Rock Against Racism. They also formed rock groups such as Ventz, Column 44, and Tragic Minds for the sole purpose of disseminating propaganda such as "Master Race," "White Power," and "Kill the Reds."

A barrage of criticism against punk came from a bewildered establishment, reminiscent of the outcries against the Elvis Presley of 1956 and the early Beatles. Much of the venom was directed at the kings of punk: the Sex Pistols. On April 10, 1976, *Melody Maker* told its readers that the Pistols "do as much for music as World War II did for the cause of peace." Conservative MP Robert Adley called the group "a bunch of ill-mannered louts, who seem to cause offense wherever they go." One vicar of the Anglican church, his face muscles tightened and his head raised high, planted himself outside a Sex Pistols concert at Welsh Hall and warned concert goers: "Keep out of there! They're the Devil's Children." When the single "Anarchy in the U.K." came to Hayes record factory, women packers refused to handle the disc. In 1977 the BBC banned Pistols songs from the air; almost every local council in Britain censured them; publications refused to print ads for the band in the music press; royalists armed with knives and iron pipes attacked Johnny Rotten and Paul Cook after the release of "God Save the Queen"; and American companies rejected distribution deals for the Pistols' LP *Never Mind the Bullocks*. Despite this concerted effort, the Pistols, and British punk, survived.

AMERICAN PUNK

American punk bands, centered in the New York City club CBGB's, predated the British movement and played a more art-inspired brand of punk.

Patti Smith, one of the many women who entered the ranks of rock through punk, became a leading figure in American punk. She "had it real tough financially when I was young. . . . I wasn't horrified by Altamont, it seemed natural to me. Every school dance I went to, somebody was stabbed." The daughter of a Pitman, New Jersey, factory worker, Smith herself worked in a factory and later sang about her experience in "Pissing in a River." After she unexpectedly got pregnant and had the child, Smith moved to New York City "with five dollars and a can of spray for my stitches." Once in town, she wrote and publicly read a William Burroughs-Arthur Rimbaud style of poetry. Eventually she put her words to music, first singing with Blue Oyster Cult, then with ex-Doors keyboardist Ray Manzarek, and finally with her own band, which included rock critic/guitarist Lenny Kaye. Her 1975 solo debut, *Horses,* included the ironic "Gloria (In Excelsis Deo)", which expertly interwove rebellion against religion with Van Morrison's sixties rock classic, "Gloria." It led critics to proclaim Smith a punk Dylan. Idolizing "all the great Sixties guys" who "had sort of a political consciousness," Patti was "determined to make us kids, us fuck-ups, us ones who could never get a degree in college, whatever, have a family, or do regular stuff, prove that there's a place for us."

Other New York avant-gardists also strove for an equalitarian goal. In 1977 the Talking Heads, four students from the Rhode Island School of Art, burst forth from CBGB's with a self-named album and a razor-sharp single, "Psycho-Killer," which included lyrics in French. Asked about his view of the music, leader David Byrne said "if anything, rock and roll should fit the proletarian view of art, which is partly what made punk so powerful." The Dead Boys, a Cleveland band comprised of ex-steelworker-turned-singer Stiv Bators, lead guitarist Cheetah Chrome, and drummer Johnny Blitz, blasted inequality in "Third Generation Nation," in which they lashed out against corporate rock.

Two friends, Richard Hell (a.k.a. Meyers) and Tom Verlaine (a.k.a. Miller), traveled from Delaware to New York City to do the same. Verlaine, who named himself after the French symbolist poet, formed the band Television, which released two albums of arty, deft social criticism. Hell, who journeyed to the City to "become a real sophisticated writer," first played with Television, then with ex-New York Dolls guitarist Johnny Thunders in the Heartbreakers, and finally formed the Voidoids. In 1976 the spiked-haired, ripped T-shirt Hell (his fashion would inspire the Sex Pistols and the rest of British punk) delivered the New York punk anthem "Blank Generation," a bitter, snarling testament of rebellion without a cause. As an antidote to such aimlessness, Hell proposed a community of trust in such songs as "Betrayal Takes Two." Explained Hell: "It's not that I espoused Nihilism. What I did was

Courtesy of Hilly Kristal and Sire Records

The Dead Boys: *Young, Loud, and Snotty*

describe the way I felt, and hope that by frankly talking this way when everybody else was talking about 'love and peace blah blah blah' I could legitimize and somehow make it possible to be proud of *not* being there, *not* being passive. What seemed real exciting then [was] *everybody* coming around to this kind of attitude."

REACTION AND RIDICULE

Segments of established society ridiculed the punk movement. To Linda Ronstadt, "punk is so constipated it should be called hemmorhoid rock." Anthony Burgess, the author of the futuristic *Clockwork Orange,* told the readers of *Psychology Today* "all that punk singers can bring to the presentations of their songs is the gesture of sexual obscenity or of impotent rage. There is a lot of caged simian gibber. . . . British youth, like American and French and Upper Slobovian youth, needs a good kick in the pants and a bit of solid education." Keith Richard of the Rolling Stones feared that "once rock and roll gets mixed up in No Nukes and Rock Against Racism . . . it's not rock and roll." Commercial radio in America virtually boycotted punk: John Winnamon, vice-president and general manager of KLOS-FM in Los Angeles, told a Congressional committee that punk rock "borders on revolution." And during a punk concert in the Los Angeles Elk Lodge, a police squadron, unprovoked, burst in on six hundred spectators and abruptly ended the performance.

The American business community, however, dealt with the most lethal blow to punk. Initially, punks created a fashion directly related to their politics: They adopted the art form of such agitational-propaganda (agit-prop) Russians as Malevich, Tatlin, and Rodchenko, and as Anthony Burgess noticed, "they wear with snarling pride the marks of the downtrodden. Hair is cropped because long hair holds lice. Clothes are not patched, since patching denotes skill and a seedy desire for respectability; their gaping holes are held together with safety pins." But in 1977

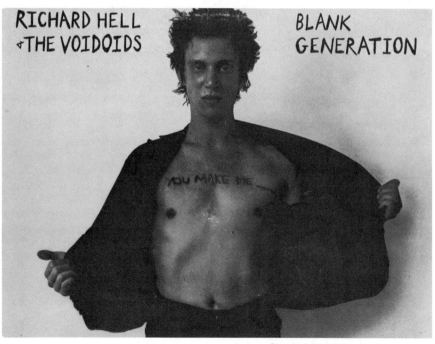

Photo by Roberta Bayley; used by courtesy of Richard Hell and Sire Records

Richard Hell: king of New York punk and originator of punk fashion

Newsweek observed, "both Saks on Fifth Avenue and Bonwit Teller carry gold safety pins at prices up to $100, and noted British designer Zandra Rhodes recently created a collection of gowns for Bloomingdale's that incorporate stylized rips and glitter-studded safety pins — at $345 to $1,150 a gown." By June 1980 *Mademoiselle* offered its readers the choice between "punk or prep" in a four-page spread. "The future of punk is in jeopardy," *Newsweek* told its readers, "the Establishment is ripping off the painfully established punk identity." Richard Hell lamented, "punk was intended to be a whole kind of consciousness. But then *it* got corrupted into being simply a style or fad."

CORPORATE ROCK RIDES THE NEW WAVE

The American recording industry further deflated punk by creating the "new wave" phenomenon. A catch-all term for any band whose members sported skinny black ties, wraparound sunglasses, and short, spiked hair, "new wave" depoliticized punk. As the *Wall Street Journal* informed its readers, "the music has been given a new name to fit its establishment image: Punk has been redubbed 'New Wave.' Groups once considered on the rebellious fringes of rock are now status quo. After two number-one singles Debbie Harry of Blondie has been transformed from a Bowery bar trash queen to a *People* magazine cover girl. . . . Punk's worst fears seem to have been realized; New Wave is just another commercial fad." Deborah Harry subsequently became a model for Murjani jeans and appeared as a host on *The Muppets Show* and *Solid Gold,* the slick, hour-long flashdance commercial for pop music. "We're definitely not an underground group anymore. The only place for us to go where people think we're crazy is to hang out with Chuck Mangione," Clem Burke of Blondie confided to a reporter in June 1981.

A spate of other groups flooded the new wave market, borrowing the energy of punk but ignoring punk politics: From Boston came the Cars, a witty bar band that manufactured snappy pop melodies such as "My Best Friend's Girl" and the often-reworked "[Let the] Good Times Roll." The unlikely town of Athens, Georgia, produced the satiric, tongue-in-cheek B-52s, who stole Yoko Ono's wild vocal inflections to deliver such ditties as "Rock Lobster," "Planet Claire," and the modern love song "Lava." The Pretenders, fronted by Patti Smith sound-alike Chrissie Hynde, rocked the new wave. Even Patti Smith herself abandoned punk for self-indulgent stardom in her last album, aptly titled *Wave.* The Ramones, a raucous but loveable band from New York City, rode the new wave from the dingy confines of CBGB's to movie stardom in *Rock 'n' Roll High School.* A frantic, buzz-saw guitar attack mixed with zany lyrics ("Now I Wanna Sniff Some Glue," "I Don't Wanna Go Down to the Basement," and "I Wanna Be Your Boyfriend") proved to be their formula for commercial success.

British pop stars also rose out of the new wave. Joe Jackson sang

Joey Ramone: a CBGBs original

his way to the top of the charts with "Look Sharp" and "I'm the Man." Other English pop sounds included the humorous pop of the Buzzcocks; the smooth, rolling tunes of XTC, who favored buttondown shirts amid the punk heyday; and the more frenetic, though sugar-coated, rock of the Jam, who stridently supported the Queen when the Pistols' "God Save the Queen" hit the airwaves. Said Paul Weller, guitarist for the Jam: "We're into changing the music scene, but nothing's gonna be changed politically. . . . I don't think you can really break down the establishment."

By 1979 even some soft rockers adopted a punk image: Linda Ronstadt appeared with spiked hair on the pink and black album cover of *Mad Love;* Billy Joel, the piano man, stood poised in front of a glass house, dressed in a black leather jacket and armed with a rock on the cover of *Glass Houses;* and Cher, the folksinger turned disco queen, suddenly surprised the rock public by appearing garbed in full punk regalia as the lead singer of the short-lived Black Rose. In 1979 Sandy Pearlman, a producer for the early Clash, lamented, "no one's really very scared of punk, especially the record companies. They've sublimated all the revolutionary tendencies this art is based on."

THE DISINTEGRATION OF PUNK

Besides being co-opted by the record companies, punk fell apart at the seams for a number of other reasons. Some alienated American youths took the punk form and pushed it to the right end of the political spectrum. Devo, a band from Akron, Ohio, lambasted the "devolution of society — the fat man in the double-knit suit sitting watching television and becoming pear-shaped. The submissive form in the contoured chair." Yet the machine-like Devo disavowed rebellion. Said Jerry Casale of the group: "Cooperating with a large corporate body like Warner Brothers, that's the only way to survive. It's syncing up with the real situation. We live in a corporate society. You inject your information into the program. Rebellion is obsolete, an outmoded way to live." After their 1978 debut album, *Are We Not Men,* Devo began to crank out a series of slick pop hits, and their satire of technological society became a self-parody.

Some Boston bands put forward an even more explicit message. Unnatural Axe's song "Youth Corps" contained the verse: "We're apolitical, ahistorical/ We don't care about the past/ We're moving for sure/ An Aryan culture takeover/ Lightin' fast." In the Boston club The Rat, related one local black, "this white person came up and grabbed me, and started beating me against the wall, screaming 'white supremacy, white supremacy, don't forget what skin you're in, boy.'" Other American punks began to wear Nazi armbands and Iron Crosses.

At the other extreme, some left-wing bands concluded that punk failed to properly reflect their perspective. The Raincoats, an all-female English band, felt that "the basic theme in rock and roll is what goes on between men and women. Rock and roll is based on black music. And it's based *in* the exclusion of women and the ghettoization of blacks. Which is why we want to put a bit of distance between what we do and the rock and roll tradition." Other female groups such as the primitive-sounding Slits, and sexually integrated bands such as Delta Five, Cleveland's Pere Ubu, A Certain Ratio of Manchester, and the Mekons of Leeds, similarly abandoned a sneering punk for a minimalist, electronic form

Photo by Cam Garrett

Devo

that captured the jittery tension of their industrial environments. As Cabaret Voltaire, a Sheffield group that took its name from a Dadaist sect in Zurich, contended, "we've taken the standard rock or beat music and stripped it bare."

Still others felt that punk constricted them musically. Brian Eno "tried to maintain an enthusiasm for punk, but there just isn't much happening there in the way of ideas. Finally, I realized, Goddamn! there's a whole *world* of interesting music out there. Why bother about this little scene right here? So what if punk dies off." Eno, along with David Byrne and the other Talking Heads, began to experiment with a fusion of African beats, rap, and electronic music — some called it "techno-ethnic." Byrne lectured reporters that the days of "Psycho Killer" had come to a close: He did not feel "any connection to rock and roll." Elvis Costello abandoned the anger of *Armed Forces* (1978) for American country music in *Almost Blue* (1981) and the laid-back ballads of *Imperial Bedroom* (1982) and *Punch the Clock* (1983), the last even including the mellow trumpet of Chet Baker. In late 1979 Tom Robinson confessed to *Melody Maker* that "after two and a half years, [punk] has become a bit tame and predictable. It's time to move on and try something fresh." He opted for the electronic pop of Sector 27. Amid a 1980

European tour, a disgusted Joe Strummer complained to the *New Musical Express* that "punk rock has just hit Europe in a big way, but it's totally worthless. It's nothing but a complete 1976 revival . . . just another fashion. It's become everything it wasn't supposed to be. I was emotionally shattered . . . completely disheartened to see what's happened to the seeds of what we planted. If those pricks and kids like them are the fruits of our labors, then they're much worse than those people they were meant to replace." Slowly, The Clash deserted their boisterous "White Riot" sound for a more subtle blend of reggae, stripped-down dub and the fast-talking politically minded rap music of *Sandinista* (1980) and *Combat Rock* (1982).

Even Johnny Rotten, the king of punk, who had worn a crown of spiked hair, deserted punk rock. He felt that the Sex Pistols had extended the rock form to its outer limits: "The Pistols finished rock and roll. That was the last rock and roll band. It's all over now. . . . Rock and roll is shit. It's dismal. Grand-dad danced to it." In late 1978 after

Photo by Cam Garrett

The Cure: punk settles into a depression

the Sex Pistols had disbanded following a tumultuous American tour and the overdose death of bassist Sid Vicious, Johnny Rotten (now John Lydon) formed Public Image Limited (PiL) with guitarist Keith Levene and bassist Jah Wobble. Like other groups such as Killing Joke, the Cure, and Joy Division, PiL wove an intricate, dissonant fabric of half-melodies and industrial noise that forced listeners to jitter and clench their teeth from tension. Lydon explained to *Trouser Press*, "I've grown very far away from human beings. I like being detached; I don't even like shaking hands. I don't like sweat. I think everyone is ugly. Faces disgust me and feet really make me reek. I think the human body's about one of the most ugly things ever created." Rather than people, the ex-Pistol found cameraderie with "machines. Lots of buttons on record players. Knobs and gadgets, electrical equipment of any kind." The wild exhuberant violence of the Sex Pistols, and the rest of punk rock, had dissolved into a disturbing depression.

10

The 1980s: The Age of Revivalism and the Future of Rock

"Consider all the different bands and different types of music in the charts," Paul Weller of the Jam pointed out in mid-1981. "You've got the Stray Cats, Spandau Ballet, and it's all different styles. Not all of it is blatantly commercial. If punk's done nothing else it's changed that, so any sort of music can get somewhere." Added David Ball of the disco-synthesizer band Soft Cell: "Synthesizer bands now have got a lot to thank punk bands of '77 for. The punk thing gave anybody a chance to get up and do it."

The many bands that appeared in the wake of British punk harked back to the rock and roll past. Whereas punkers reinfused rock with a passion and a social consciousness, rockers in the early eighties favored reworkings of time-tested styles — heavy metal, Bowiesque synthesizers, psychedelia, soul, rockabilly, and R & B — that had been wrenched from their social and historical contexts. Rock became a succession of styles devoid of content, fads manufactured for those too young to remember the originals. In a rerun of the seventies, Bruce Springsteen broke through the sterile, self-indulgent structure of corporate rock and delivered a stinging testimonial on life in America, *Born in the U.S.A.*

Springsteen and others like him used the past to create new strains of rock: They brought rock 'n' roll into the eighties and held out a hope for the future of rock.

WEST COAST PUNK

In the early eighties shadows of the past survived. The spiked head of punk surfaced in California, particularly in the smog-filled, fairy-land-gone-sour Los Angeles. There, bands such as X, the Circle Jerks, Black Flag, Fear, Bad Religion, the Descendants, and the Germs turned British punk inside out. These West Coast punks stole the hyperactive roar of British punk but forsook protest for a terminal depression. Henry Rollins, the latest in a long line of vocalists for Black Flag, blurted out to *Trouser Press,* "there are no songs telling you to do anything [on *Damaged* (1981)]. There are no political songs that speak out on some topic. I'm not into songs about the fucking six o'clock news." Instead, Rollins opted for such morose commentaries as "Depression," "Dead Inside," and "Life of Pain." Explained the shouter: "Pain is my girlfriend; that's how I see it. I feel pain every day of my life. When you see me perform, it's that pain you're seeing, coming out. I put all my emotions, all my feelings, and my body on the line. People hurt me, I hurt myself — mentally, physically." X, a band fronted by vocalist Exene Cervenka and guitarist Billy Zoom, pleased the L. A. hardcore with similarly depressive tales such as "Nausea" and "Sex and Dying in High Society." Whereas British punks demanded change, the L. A. hardcore vociferously contended that the system had degenerated beyond repair. As much as anything else, the overdose suicide of Darby Crash, lead singer for the Germs, exemplified the self-destructive, black frustration that defined American hardcore punk.

If political at all, many L. A. punks adopted the right-wing stance of a President whom they apparently disavowed. Mostly middle-class suburbanites, they sported Nazi armbands, shaved their heads military-style, and sometimes "trashed" hungry bums for entertainment. Roger Rogerson of the Circle Jerks prodded fellow band members to "join the fucking party or get out of here! You guys always bitch at me for wearing Nazi armbands. Well, it's white people's country, and if you don't like it, you can go back to your fucking country and eat your fucking dog!" Derf Scratch of Fear quickly became disillusioned with such rantings. Somehow raising the ire of a few L. A. punkers when he strode across the dance floor after a set, Scratch ended up in Canoga Park Hospital for four days with seven broken bones in his face and a drainage cup taped to his neck. Said Derf: "They're all these rich kids and they're spoiled and have all kinds of money from their parents. They got into the punk scene and the only way they can prove to themselves and their friends that they're punks is to beat somebody up. Because they can't really say, 'Yeah, I'm punk, I don't have any morals, and fuck the middle class,' because that's right where they came from."

Henry Rollins of Black Flag

The Dead Kennedys kept the left wing of punk alive. Directed by Jello Biafra, who once ran for mayor of San Francisco, the DKs demanded social reform in such classics as "Holiday in Cambodia," "Let's Lynch the Landlord," the anti–Jerry Brown "California Uber Alles," and "Moral Majority." They ridiculed fellow punkers for their right-wing posture in "Nazi Punks Fuck Off":

> Ten guys jump one, what a man
> You fight each other, the police state wins
> Stab your backs when you trash our halls

The 1980s: The Age of Revivalism and the Future of Rock   **197**

Slam dancer in flight

> Trash a bank if you got real balls
> You still think swastikas look cool
> The real Nazis run your schools
> They're coaches, businessmen and cops
> In a real fourth reich you'll be the first to go

The Dead Kennedy's own label, Alternative Tentacles, gave aspiring punks like D.O.A., a political thrash band from Vancouver, British Columbia, a chance to commit themselves to vinyl. The message of the Kennedys, however, largely went unheard. By the eighties, punk rock generally had degenerated into the macho, slam-dancing violence of frustrated, middle-class adolescents.

THE NEW WAVE REVISITED

The "new wave" drowned out the clatter of the L. A. hardcore in a sea of vibrant, colorful images and musical cotton candy. A seemingly endless stream of bands grabbed the limelight before each of them in turn faded into oblivion, eclipsed by another one-hit wonder. Their swelling ranks included R.E.M. from Athens, Georgia; the bubbly Cyndi Lauper; the Missing Persons, distinguished by the squeaky-voiced Dale Bozzio; and the Motels, fronted by the sultry-sounding Martha Davis. From Australia trooped the snappy Big Country, Men at Work, and INXS. Great

Jello Biafra of the Dead Kennedys

Britian provided a revamped, posturing Billy Idol, who had left Generation X for Kiss manager Bill Aucoin and pop stardom; the serious Tears for Fears; and groups masterminded by ex–Sex Pistols svengali Malcolm McLaren, including Bow Wow Wow, marked by the cherubic, fifteen-year-old shouter Annabella Lwin and Adam Ant, who abandoned punk in 1978 for pirate outfits and tales of the American frontier *(Kings of the Wild Frontier,* 1980).

Madonna elbowed her way to the top of the pops during late 1984 and early 1985. Born of Italian-American parents in Detroit in 1960, Madonna Louise Ciccone overcame personal adversity through a blatant, calculated use of her feminine mystique. With the help of a succession of boyfriends, she engineered a record contract with Sire and a co-starring role in the movie *Desperately Seeking Susan.* The singer-dancer-actress then climbed the charts by casting herself as an irresistible, sexually aggressive, bitchy Barbie Doll: The cover of her second album, entitled *Like a Virgin,* pictured her in a flimsy, lace bodice, cinched by a belt that carried the inscription "Boy Toy"; in one scene of her film debut, Madonna sat on top of a jukebox, legs spread, and cooed to a suitor, "Got a quarter, wanna play?"; and her mid-1985 tour of twenty-seven cities merited such headlines as "she's sleazy, trashy,

Courtesy of The Daily of the University of Washington

Annabella Lwin of Bow Wow Wow

cheap and completely out of your price range." "From the time that I was very young I just knew that being a girl and being charming in a feminine sort of way could get me a lot of things," reasoned Madonna. "And I milked it for everything I could." Her flirt-as-hero tactic worked well. "Like a Virgin" hit the number-one slot in *Billboard* and *Desperately Seeking Susan* played to favorable reviews and packed houses.

One group reached the rarified heights of pop superstardom. The Police, an outfit consisting of Sting (a.k.a. Gordon Sumners) on vocals, drummer Stewart Copeland, and Andy Summers on guitar, started out during the punk explosion of 1977 and released a buzzsaw-guitar single, "Fall Out." But Sting, as he told *Musician,* "slowly but surely, subversively brought my own sense of melody into [our music], largely by the use of reggae." The Police collectively dyed their hair blonde and assaulted the pop world with the album *Outlandos d'Amour* (1978). They steadily gained popularity, and two years later *Zenyatta Mondatta* and the single "De Do Do Do" turned into platinum. The Police followed with *Ghost in the Machine* (1981) and their most commercially successful LP, *Synchronicity* (1983). Stewart Copeland outlined the group's formula for continued success: "Playing pop music is very hard to do and we just happen to be good at it. In this instance, the people who are good at it also happen to be quite able musicians, but being technically

The pop power of The Police

proficient is really secondary. . . . Very important to a large majority of our following is the fact that we're three photogenic guys." He further explained that "we go for melodies and the best melodies are the ones that are most easily understood. We don't have anything on the records that sounds difficult to play; if it sounds difficult, we'll get rid of it."

MTV

MTV, the nonstop commercial for pop, propelled many chartbusters like the Police to prominence. The brainchild of Robert Pittman, a former radio program director, MTV aimed its message at the under-twenty-five-year-old crowd. Pittman reasoned to *Time* magazine that these "material-oriented" teens "use music to define their identity the way people in middle age use cars and homes." He also recognized the growing importance of video among youth: In 1981, young Americans had dropped 20 billion quarters into the 100,000 Pac-Man machines across the country. Trying to appeal to the twin teen attractions, Pittman started a music-video channel for Warner Communications.

Pittman stalked "the TV babies" with videoized music, recycling the sixties ad campaign, "I want my Maypo!" into "I want my MTV." He first broadcast MTV in August 1981 to three hundred cable outlets and a possible 2.5 million homes. By the end of 1985 MTV hit two thousand cable outlets and over 26 million households. More than 13 million viewers, mostly between the ages of thirteen and twenty-four, watched MTV every week. According to industry analyst Mark Riely, the channel grossed more than $20 million in the first two-and-a-half years of its existence. In 1984 the revenues jumped to $73 million a year.

MTV provided a needed marketing tool to an industry that had peaked in 1978 when it had shipped 726 million records and tapes to world-wide retail outlets. Simon Fields, a director of London Limelight

Photo by Mike Owen; used by courtesy of
Capitol Records

Duran Duran

Productions, which has produced more than three hundred rock videos, cautioned, "we have to remember we are making a sales tool. These are little commercials. It is our job to make an artist look good." Elvis Costello put it more sarcastically: A rock video "is just an advertisement without a stupid talkover."

These "little commercials" proved very effective in some cases. Norman Samnick, senior vice-president of Warner Communications, boasted that "Duran Duran owes its life to MTV." Duran Duran's synthesizer player, Nick Rhodes, conceded that "MTV was instrumental in breaking us in America."

THE BLITZ

The Blitz or New Romantic movement, which included Duran Duran, provided MTV with fashion-conscious fodder. First surfacing at the Blitz Club in Covent Garden, London, during the late seventies, it consisted of working-class youths disillusioned with punk. New Romantics formed such bands as Duran Duran, Classix Nouveaux, Depeche Mode, Gary Numan and the Tubeway Army, Spandau Ballet, and Visage — the last an amalgam of members from Magazine and Ultravox held together by Blitz's king, Steve Strange. These working-class British teens wanted to forget about their lower-class lives by dressing well and creating a party atmosphere. "Most kids who actually live there are *sick* of the streets," Gary Kemp, the leader of Spandau Ballet, told an interviewer. "What they do want to do is look their best when they open the front door. . . . They want to be in a club with great lights, and look really good and pick up girls." Kemp had "never been into a rock scene; it's very middle class. But discos are always parties because you have to make your own visual entertainment. Spandau Ballet was created out of a scene that was very fashion-conscious, very club-oriented. The attitude behind it has always been there; mods, skinheads and the soul kids — just kids who want to dress smart and enjoy themselves. My dad was a Teddy boy and my older cousin was a mod. It's hereditary, I guess."

Fashion even became more important than the music. Admitted Gary Kemp: "The music is irrelevant. The most important thing in a club is the people, not the music they listen to. *You* become the most important person. *You* become the visual aspect of the evening, rather than the band." Rejecting the conscious self-denial of punk, British teens such as Kemp spliced whitened disco-funk to the mod rage for fashion to create a short-lived Blitz.

The New Romantics, though quickly losing popularity, lived on in a series of synthesizer–drum machine outfits that played computerized music for the computer age. Their ranks included Orchestral Manoeuvers in the Dark (OMD); Soft Cell; Thomas Dolby, a session man for the likes of Foreigner and Joan Armatrading before climbing the charts with "She Blinded Me with Science"; the wacky Thompson Twins; and

Gary Numan and synthesizer

Yazoo. This techno-pop supplied a steady but unimaginative and passionless beat to rock music. The style, admitted Scott Ryser of the synthesizer band the Units generally did not "have much depth to it. I like it for dancing, but it's hard to take seriously."

HEAVY METAL OF THE EIGHTIES

Some youths demanded more driving music than techno-pop and latched on to a rock style that had never completely disappeared — Heavy Metal. Legions of teenage boys marched to the crashing chords of veteran metal bands that had tenaciously persisted into the eighties, groups such as Deep Purple, AC/DC, Judas Priest, the Scorpions, and Van Halen. Ozzy Osbourne, the force behind the original Black Sabbath, resurfaced with the Blizzard of Ozz and proved his mettle by biting off the heads of a bat and a live dove.

New heavy metallers burst on the scene, all venting the pent-up, dark aggression of the young in an age of increasing unemployment. Some affected a glam-glitter, transsexual image (Motley Crue, Twisted Sister). Others strapped on spiked wristbands and leather armor and released albums with excalibur-inspired artwork on the covers, taking listeners to an idealized, heroic age of medieval knights and damsels in distress (Saxon, Accept, Krokus, Dokken). Others just played raunchy, roaring R & B-based rock and roll (Motorhead, Girlschool, Iron Maiden).

Metallers of the eighties paid homage to their roots. "The first time I heard a Led Zeppelin record I knew that that's what I wanted to do until I died," recalled Marc "The Voice" Storace, lead singer for Krokus. Joe "Throat" Elliot, the lead vocalist for Def Leppard, had similar sources of inspiration: "We hate the term 'heavy metal'," he told a reporter. "What it is, is hard rock. It's been around since the sixties, and will be around until the year 2000 and beyond. . . . In 1971 there were only three bands that mattered. Led Zeppelin, Black Sabbath, and Deep Purple. As years went on, hard rock did feel a certain loss of popularity with record audiences. But around 1979 or '80, it came back again. Suddenly, there was us, Iron Maiden and Saxon doing really well."

A LITTLE BIT OF SOUL

Some groups delved even further back into rock history for inspiration. Annie Lennox, the redheaded lead singer of the Eurythmics, identified her "vocal style very much with black soul music. Not with blues, but with 60s soul. It really struck a chord in me, and I can't get away from that." Boy George, the androgynous impetus behind Culture Club, "hated punk" and substituted, in his words, an "imitation soul." In 1984 Prince Rogers Nelson, or just Prince, attracted national attention with *Purple Rain,* a top-selling album and a million-dollar movie. Prince, who had released five albums before *Rain,* combined the flamboyant costumes of Jimi Hendrix with the wild-haired, effeminate, pencil-thin-mustached look of Little Richard to deliver a soulful message of carnal salvation to his disciples. A few other bands such as ABC and Dexy's Midnight Runners (especially listen to the Runners' reworking of Van Morrison's "Jackie Wilson Said") jumped on the soul bandwagon.

Motown returned to the forefront with Michael Jackson. In 1969 a ten-year-old Michael had danced his way from a rough neighborhood in Gary, Indiana, to national prominence as the leader of the Jackson Five. He aped James Brown's frenzy and Smokey Robinson's romantic pleadings, for a hit with "I Want You Back." "We're labeling it soul bubble-

The Eurythmics: soul survivors

gum," smiled Motown President Berry Gordy. "It's a style that appeals
to the younger teens." Other chartbusters followed: "The Love You
Save," "I'll Be There," "Never Can Say Goodbye," "Maybe Tomorrow,"
"Corner of the Sky," "Sugar Daddy," and "Lookin' Through the Windows." By the end of the seventies, Michael Jackson had helped his
musical family sell over ninety million records. In 1976 Michael left the
Motown stable for Epic Records; three years later he released a solo
venture, *Off the Wall,* which sold over five million copies.

The eighties unveiled a new and even more successful Michael
Jackson: The singer underwent cosmetic surgery, which according to
one biographer gave his face "a slicker, almost European visage." In
December 1982 he cut *Thriller,* which built upon his smooth Motown
sound and contained such pop blockbusters as "Beat It" and "Thriller."
The LP, promoted by a $1.2 million MTV video of the title song, appealed

to everyone from rock fans to easy listeners and mercurially shot up the charts. At last count it had sold over thirty-five million units, far outdistancing the former best-selling album of all time, the soundtrack to *Saturday Night Fever*.

To capitalize upon the hit LP, Epic created a Michael Jackson industry: posters, buttons, "Thriller" painter caps, duffel bags, bubblegum cards, key chains, a single sequined glove (Michael's trademark), and a cuddly Michael Jackson doll. Three competing biographies of the new music idol sold over one million copies each. Even an hour-long documentary about the making of the video *Thriller* sold nearly one million units. By 1984 Michael Jackson, a Jehovah Witness who never swore, drank, smoked, or even uttered the word "funky" (he used "jelly" instead), had amassed a $75 million fortune, and was singled out by President Ronald Reagan as a model for American youth. He had become a symbol of the conservative commercialism of eighties rock.

NEO-PSYCHEDELIA

Some eighties groups harked back to a noncommercial age and submerged themselves in a dense neo-psychedelia that echoed the Doors and the Velvet Underground. In the late 1970s, as British punk made its last stand, a university dropout from Glasgow started Postcard Records, launching the psychedelic revival. He recorded such groups as Aztec Camera, Joseph K, and Orange Juice. The Doors-Velvet sound spread: The Violent Femmes, a Milwaukee group, won over hip college students across America with their mixture of folk and psychedelia; and the Smiths from Manchester made inroads into the rock market with their post-Velvet pop. Other notable adherents to the revived paisley standard included the Psychedelic Furs, the Electric-Prunes-sounding Green on Red, the Dream Syndicate, and Salvation Army (later called Three O'Clock).

ROCKABILLY REVIVAL

A few rockers wanted a raunchier sound than psychedelia and reclaimed rockabilly. The revival started in Great Britain, when Shakin' Stevens (a.k.a. Michael Barratt) recombined American country and rhythm and blues. He first earned a gold single with an old Rosemary Clooney tune, "This Ole House," and then gained international success with "Marie, Marie." Of his good fortune, Stevens claimed, "I suppose I have to thank punk . . . for getting people back to basics and paving the way for rock and roll again." A spate of "cat" groups followed Shakin's blue suede shoes — the Stray Cats, the Polecats, the Rockats, and the Bluecats. The Shakin' Pyramids from Scotland also played to a boppin' 'billy beat. These rockabillies resurrected pointed shoes, pompadour hair styles, tight black pants, and a music with a primal beat.

The Violent Femmes: folk-rockers in the eighties

In the States, Robert Gordon began to recondition old rockabilly gems such as Carl Perkins's "Boppin' the Blues" and Eddie Cochran's "Summertime Blues." The Cramps, a strange mixture of rockabilly, punk, and the occult, banged through renditions of such classics as the Trashmen's "The Bird." The name of the group, pointed out vocalist Lux Interior, "isn't just a joke, it also refers to the tension, the cramps that all these true rockabillies had in the 50s — what they went through to make that music and scene happen was just as revolutionary as the blue-haired punks of 1976. They firmly believed that they were possessed, had the devil inside of them."

American talent scouts even unearthed an authentic rockabilly star, Joe Ely. Growing up in Lubbock, Texas, the home of Buddy Holly, Ely got his start in music with the First Baptist Church choir. He then began listening to country radio: "I guess my roots are sort of a combination of Bob Wills and Lefty Frizzell, as well as the rise of rockabilly." Soon he began to offer his own brand of rockabilly. By the mid-eighties, hundreds bopped to the swinging sound of rockabillies like Ely.

The Cramps: mixing rockabilly and the occult

R & B FOR THE EIGHTIES

Some artists looked back even further into the rock past for roots. George Thorogood, a wizard of the Elmore James–style guitar, recorded supercharged versions of such R & B standards as James's "Madison Blues" and "Can't Stop Lovin'," Bo Diddley's "Ride on Josephine," "It Wasn't Me" by Chuck Berry, and John Lee Hooker's "One Bourbon, One Scotch, One Beer" and "New Boogie Chillen." In the 1982 *Bad to the Bone,* Thorogood and the Delaware Destroyers added some R & B originals including the mean-sounding "Bad to the Bone," "Miss Luann," and the frenetic "Back to Wentzville."

The Blasters from Los Angeles followed the path that Thorogood had blazed, releasing four albums of R & B and rockabilly-flavored rock and roll. Said the Blasters' guitarist Dave Alvin: "There are guys who tell me they stopped listening to music when Elvis went into the Army, and now they'll listen again because of people like us, Joe Ely, George Thorogood. And it's not nostalgia — it's the realization of a deferred dream. They've been waiting for it to come back, to make sense to them again." "We are the connection to Chuck Berry and Gene Vincent, Little Richard going crazy," asserted Alvin.

Others carried fifties R & B into the eighties. Graham Parker, a former gas station attendant, in 1976 had released two seminal R & B-drenched LPs, *Howlin' Wind* and *Heat Treatment.* He continued his R & B style into the eighties with his masterpiece, *Squeezing Out Sparks.*

George Thorogood: the rebirth of Elmore James

Nine Below Zero, taking their name from a Sonny Boy Williamson song, joined the rhythm and blues legion with a 1981 debut album. The Iron City Houserockers, the Nighthawks, and the Fabulous Thunderbirds also adapted the gritty, boisterous sound of R & B to the computer age.

Frank "Son" Seals provided perhaps the most innovative R & B of the eighties. The son of Jim Seals who ran the Dipsy Doodle nightspot in Osceola, Arkansas, Son grew up with the Delta blues. "Blues is the first thing I ever heard," he told writer Robert Palmer. "When I was a kid, it seemed kind of like a dream. Blues was all we had on the jukebox — Muddy Waters, Jimmie Rogers, Elmore James. Guys like [guitarist]

Photo by Brad Bramson; used by courtesy of
Vision Management and Warner Bros.

The Blasters: R & B and rockabilly roots

Robert Nighthawk, Joe Hill Louis and later Albert King would play in
the Dipsy Doodle on weekends." Seals, merging his Delta influences
with more modern ideas, settled in Chicago. He now delivers a biting,
updated, slightly funky version of Chicago rhythm and blues.

BRUCE SPRINGSTEEN
AND THE FUTURE OF ROCK

Amid the various revivals, Bruce Springsteen combined the rock and
roll heritage with concerns of the eighties to create a new path for rock.
In 1980 he ushered in the decade with a double album, *The River,* which
continued his Born-to-Run preoccupation with girls and cars ("Cadillac
Ranch," "I'm a Rocker," and "Crush on You"). But in the title song he
hinted at a new direction to his music, relating the tale of a beaten-down
factory worker who lost both his love and his job because of a collapsing
economy. The New Jersey Boss expanded on his newly discovered
realism in his next album, *Nebraska* (1982): It was an acoustic LP
distinguished by straightforward lyrics that chronicled the troubles and
loneliness experienced by present-day blue-collar Americans. As Bruce
told *Musician,* the album was "kind of about a spiritual crisis, in which

Photo by Steve Kagan; used by courtesy of
Alligator Productions

Son Seals plays R & B for the eighties

man is left lost. It's like he has nothing left to tie him to society anymore. He's isolated from the government. Isolated from his job. Isolated from his family. And, in something like 'Highway Patrolman' isolated from his friends."

Two years later Springsteen fused his social concerns with the infectious rock 'n' roll of the E Street Band to create his masterpiece, *Born in the U.S.A.* The danceable music combined the sounds of Chuck Berry, Bo Diddley, Elvis, Buddy Holly, and Bob Dylan into a refreshing, explosive mixture. Moreover, The Boss had left his cars-and-girls, us-against-the-world naiveté behind. "I think 'Born in the U.S.A.' kind of casts a suspicious eye on a lot of things," he mused. "That's the idea. These are not the same people [as in 'Born to Run'] anymore and it's not the same situation. . . . It's certainly not as innocent anymore."

On the LP Springsteen applied his primal rock and roll to the blue-collar problems of the eighties: He sang of the wrenching depression of a lumber worker who lost his job and his wife when hard times hit ("Downbound Train"). In the brooding "My Hometown,' Bruce bleakly detailed the changes sweeping a town in the depressed heartlands of industrial Middle America: "Now main street's whitewashed windows and vacant stores: Seems like there ain't nobody wants to come down there no more/ They're closing down the textile mill across the railroad tracks/ Foreman says these jobs are going boys and they ain't coming back/ to your hometown." Springsteen gave his most powerful testament in the title cut: Like a dying animal, he wailed lyrics about the plight of a lower-class Vietnam veteran ten years after the war. Cried Bruce: "Down in the shadow of the penitentiary/ Out by the gas fires of the refinery/ I'm ten years burning down the road/ Nowhere to run ain't got nowhere to go/ Born in the U.S.A./ I was born in the U.S.A." President Reagan, who evidently had not listened to the lyrics of the song, complimented Springsteen on his patriotism. Quipped then Democratic presidential candidate Walter Mondale, "Bruce was born to run, not born yesterday."

Despite an unadorned realism, *Born in the U.S.A.* offered hope through music. In "No Surrender" The Boss sang, "now young faces grow old/ and hearts of fire grow cold/ we swore blood brothers against the wind/ I'm ready to grow young again/ and hear your sister's voice calling us home/ across the open yards/ well maybe we could cut someplace of our own/ with these drums and these guitars/ blood brothers in the stormy night with a vow to defend no retreat no surrender." In the mid-1980s Springsteen represented a stark realism tinged with hope.

The Boss backed his socially relevant words with action. He consistently refused offers of corporate sponsorship: "We get approached by corporations. It's not something that struck me as the thing that I wanted to do. Independence is nice. That's why I started this." Without hoopla, he donated money to unemployed steelworkers, striking copper miners, and food banks.

Other rock and rollers also began to address socially relevant issues. U-2 from Ireland lashed out against the senseless war in their country. Midnight Oil, whose lead singer Peter Garrett almost won a seat in the Australian Senate, called for nuclear disarmament. Steven Van Zandt, formerly of the E Street Band, produced an anti-apartheid album. Such rock stars as Springsteen and Bob Dylan joined forces and staged the "We Are the World" benefit for the starving masses in Ethiopia.

A few months later Bill Graham, the rock impresario of the psychedelic era, helped Bob Geldorf of the Boomtown Rats put together the star-studded "Live Aid," another benefit for Ethiopian famine victims. "What Live Aid did was to make artists aware of their awesome power to create positive things," commented a hopeful Graham. The promoter, who had lost a sister and a mother in Nazi concentration camps, also organized a rally against President Reagan's visit to the German military cemetery in Bitburg, West Germany: Two days after the demonstration, arsonists firebombed and destroyed Graham's office in San Francisco. Still other rockers battled government wives who headed the ultra-conservative Parents' Music Resource Center (PMRC), which sought the censorship of rock records.

By the mid-eighties Springsteen and other like-minded performers had infused rock with a renewed purpose. Only the youth of America and Great Britain can decide if this discontent over social injustice, such a constant theme in rock history, will be sustained and will again sweep the ranks of rock and roll.

Selective Bibliography

This bibliography consists of the material that I found most useful in the preparation of this book. It does not intend to be a comprehensive survey of the thousands of books and articles on rock and roll in the past thirty years, but rather offers the reader a concise guide to the books, articles, and interviews that I consider the most important in understanding rock as social history. The many quotes and statistics used in this book have been taken from these books and articles. I have not used footnotes in order to save space and make the text more readable.

GENERAL

BELZ, CARL. *The Story of Rock.* New York: Harper and Row, 1971.

DACHS, DAVID. *Anything Goes: The World of Popular Music.* Indianapolis: Bobbs-Merrill, 1964.

DEMOTT, BENJAMIN. "Rock as Salvation." In *Pop Culture in America,* ed. David Manning White. Chicago: Quadrangle, 1970.

EISEN, JONATHAN, ed. *The Age of Rock.* New York: Vintage, 1969.

———, ed. *The Age of Rock*. Vol. 2. New York: Vintage, 1970.

FONG-TORRES, BEN, ed. *The Rolling Stone Rock and Roll Reader*. New York: Bantam, 1974.

———, ed. *What's That Sound*. New York: Anchor, 1976.

FRITH, SIMON. *Sound Effects: Youth, Leisure and the Politics of Rock*. New York: Pantheon, 1982.

GILLETT, CHARLIE. *The Sound of the City*. New York: Dell, 1970.

HIBBARD, DON, and PATRICIA KALEIALOHA. *The Role of Rock*. Englewood Cliffs, N.J.: Prentice-Hall, 1983.

LOGAN, NICK, and BOB WOFFINDEN. *The Illustrated Encyclopedia of Rock*. New York: Harmony, 1977.

LYDON, MICHAEL. *Rock Folk*. New York: Dial, 1971.

MARSH, DAVE, and JOHN SWENSON, eds. *The Rolling Stone Record Guide*. New York: Random House, 1979.

MILLER, JIM, ed. *The Rolling Stone Illustrated History of Rock and Roll*. New York: Random House, 1976.

NITE, NORM. *Rock On*. New York: Popular, 1974.

PARELES, JON, and PATRICIA ROMANOWSKI, eds. *The Rolling Stone Encyclopedia of Rock and Roll*. New York: Summit, 1983.

Rolling Stone, editors of, ed. *The Rolling Stone Interviews*. New York: Paperback, 1971.

———. *The Rolling Stone Interviews*. Vol. 2. New York: Warner, 1973.

———. *Rolling Stone Rock Almanac*. New York: Macmillan, 1983.

ROXON, LILLIAN. *Rock Encyclopedia*. New York: Grosset & Dunlap, 1969.

SHAW, ARNOLD. *The Rock Revolution*. London: Collier, 1969.

STAMBLER, IRWIN. *Encyclopedia of Pop, Rock and Soul*. New York: St. Martin's, 1977.

CHAPTER 1: THE BLUES, ROCK 'N' ROLL, AND RACISM

COHAN, LOU. "Bo Diddley: The Man with the Beat." *Thunder Road* (June 1980), 26–29.

DEZUTTER, HANK. "Willie Dixon." *TWA Ambassador* (July 1980), 39–41.

GILLETT, CHARLIE. *Making Tracks*. London: Sunrise/Dutton, 1974.

GURALNICK, PETER. *Feel Like Going Home*. London: Dutton, 1971.

———. *Lost Highways*. New York: Vintage, 1982.

"Howlin' Wolf Interview." *Living Blues* (Spring 1970), 13–17.

"Intermission with Fats." *Living Blues* (November/December 1977), 16–19.

KEIL, CHARLES. *Urban Blues*. Chicago: University of Chicago Press, 1966.

LARNER, JEREMY. "What Do They Get from Rock and Roll?" *Atlantic Monthly* (August 1964), 44–49.

OLIVER, PAUL. *Blues Fell This Morning: The Meaning of the Blues*. New York: Horizon, 1960.

———. *Conversation with the Blues*. New York: Horizon, 1965.

O'NEAL, JAMES, and AMY O'NEAL. "Eddie Boyd Interview." *Living Blues* (November/December 1977), 11–15.

———. "Jimmie Rogers Interview." *Living Blues* (Autumn 1973), 11–20.

———. "Jimmy Reed Interview." *Living Blues* (May/June 1975), 16–37.

———. "John Lee Hooker Interview." *Living Blues* (Autumn 1979), 14–22.

PALMER, ROBERT. *Deep Blues*. New York: Penguin, 1982.

———. "Muddy Waters: The Delta Son Never Sets." *Rolling Stone,* October 5, 1978, pp. 53–56.

PENN, ROBERTA. "Bo Diddley." *The Rocket* (September 1983), 19.

SAWYER, CHARLES. *The Arrival of B. B. King*. New York: Doubleday, 1980.

SHAW, ARNOLD. *Honkers and Shouters*. New York: Collier, 1978.

———. *The Rockin' 50s*. New York: Hawthorn, 1974.

SIDERS, HARVEY. "Talking with a King: B.B. King." *Downbeat,* March 30, 1972, pp. 14–15.

STEARNS, MARSHALL. *The Story of Jazz*. New York: Mentor, 1958.

STUCKEY, FRED. "Chuck Berry: Exclusive." *Guitar Player* (February 1971), 20–23.

"Turkish Tycoons: The Erteguns." *Time,* July 28, 1967, p. 43.

WHITE, CHARLES. *The Life and Times of Little Richard*. New York: Harmony, 1984.

CHAPTER 2: ELVIS AND ROCKABILLY

"Beware Elvis Presley." *America,* June 23, 1956. p. 295.

CONDON, E. "What Is an Elvis Presley." *Cosmopolitan* (December 1956), 54–61.

"A Craze Called Elvis." *Coronet* (September 1956), 153–57.

"Elvis: A Different Kind of Idol." *Life,* August 27, 1956, pp. 101–9.

"Elvis Presley: He Can't Be but He Is." *Look,* August 7, 1956, pp. 82–85.

ESCOTT, COLIN, and MARTIN HAWKINS. *Sun Records*. New York: Quick Fox, 1975.

GOLDROSEN, JOHN. *Buddy Holly*. New York: Putnam, 1979.

"Great Elvis Presley Industry." *Look,* November 13, 1956, pp. 98–100.

HAGARTY, BRITT. *The Day the World Turned Blue: A Biography of Gene Vincent*. Vancouver: Talonbooks, 1983.

HILBURN, ROBERT. "Invincible Jerry Lee Lewis Says, 'The Killer Ain't Through Yet.'" Reprinted in the *Seattle Times,* November 29, 1981, p. E14.

HOPKINS, JERRY. *Elvis: A Biography*. New York: Warner, 1971.

House of Representatives. *Congressional Record,* 86th Congress, First Session, March 3, 1959, vol. 105, part 3, p. 3203.

"Howling Hillbilly Success." *Life,* April 30, 1956, p. 64.

"Lonely and All Shook Up." *Time,* May 27, 1957, p. 101.

MABLEY, JACK. "Radio and Video." *Downbeat,* August 8, 1956.

PALMER, ROBERT. "Billy Burnette Rekindles the Family Magic." *Rolling Stone,* November 27, 1980, pp. 16–17.

———. *Jerry Lee Lewis Rocks*. New York: Delilah, 1981.

"Presley Spells Profit." *Newsweek,* February 18, 1957, p. 84.
"Rock 'n' Roll Battle: Boone vs. Presley." *Colliers,* October 26, 1957, p. 101.

CHAPTER 3: DICK CLARK, PHILADELPHIA SCHLOCK, AND PAYOLA

CLARK, DICK. *Rock, Rolls and Remembers.* New York: Popular, 1978.
———. *To Goof or Not to Goof.* New York: Fawcett, 1963.
Hearings Before the Subcommittee on Communications of the Committee on Interstate and Foreign Commerce: Amendment to the Communications Act of 1934. United States Senate, 85th Congress, Second Session.
LEUCHTENBURG, WILLIAM. *A Troubled Feast: American Society since 1945.* Boston: Little, Brown, 1973.

CHAPTER 4: BOB DYLAN AND THE NEW FRONTIER

"Angry Young Folk Singer." *Life,* April 10, 1964, pp. 109–16.
CARMAN, WALT. "The Children of Bobby Dylan." *Life,* November 5, 1965, pp. 43–50.
CHAPLIN, RALPH. *I. W. W. Songs* (32nd ed.). Chicago: Ralph Chaplin, 1968.
"The Folk and the Rock." *Newsweek,* September 20, 1965, pp. 88–90.
GLEASON, RALPH. "The Times They Are A-Changing." *Ramparts* (April 1965), 36–48.
HENTOFF, NAT. "Profiles." *New Yorker,* October 24, 1964, pp. 64–90.
"I Am My Words." *Newsweek,* November 4, 1963, pp. 94–95.
"Just Playin' Folks." *Saturday Evening Post,"* May 30, 1964, pp. 24–29.
"Let Us Now Praise Little Men." *Time,* May 31, 1963, p. 40.
RODNITZKY, JEROME. *Minstrels of the Dawn.* Chicago: Nelson-Hall, 1976.
SCADUTO, ANTHONY. *Bob Dylan.* New York: New American Library, 1979.

CHAPTER 5: THE MODS VS. THE ROCKERS AND THE BRITISH INVASION OF AMERICA

"Air Pollution." *Newsweek,* August 16, 1965, p. 76.
"Beatlemania." *Newsweek,* November 18, 1963, p. 104.
Billboard, January 25, 1964.
———, February 15, 1964.
BROWN, MICK. "A Conversation with George Harrison." *Rolling Stone,* April 19, 1979, pp. 71–75.
"Building the Beatle Image." *Saturday Evening Post,* March 21, 1964, p. 36.
BURDON, ERIC. "An Animal Views America." *Ebony* (December 1966), 160–70.

CHARONE, BARBARA. *Keith Richard: Life as a Rolling Stone.* New York: Doubleday, 1982.

COTT, JONATHAN. "Mick Jagger: The King Bee Talks about Rock's Longest Running Soap Opera." *Rolling Stone,* June 29, 1978, p. 45.

Daily Express, May 19, 1964, p. 1.

Daily Mirror, May 18, 1964.

DALTON, DAVID. *The Rolling Stones.* New York: Knopf, 1981.

DAVIES, HUNTER. *The Beatles.* New York: McGraw-Hill, 1968.

GAMBACCINI, PAUL. "A Conversation with Paul McCartney." *Rolling Stone,* July 12, 1979, pp. 39–46.

"George, Paul, Ringo and John: The Beatles in the U.S." *Newsweek,* February 24, 1964, pp. 54–57.

"Interview with John Lennon and Yoko Ono." *Playboy* (January, 1981), 75–106.

"Letters to the Editor." *Newsweek,* September 13, 1965.

London Times, March 9, 1964.

———, March 30, 1964.

———, March 31, 1964.

———, April 1, 1964.

———, April 4, 1964.

———, May 28, 1964.

MARSH, DAVE. *Before I Get Old: The Story of the Who.* New York: St. Martin's, 1983.

"Mick Jagger and the Future of Rock." *Newsweek,* January 4, 1971, pp. 44–48.

MURPHY, MARTY. "I Took Paul and Ringo to the Space Needle." *Seattle Times,* February 12, 1984, pp. F1–4.

"New Madness: R & B Quartet Called the Beatles." *Time,* November 15, 1963, p. 64.

New York Times, February 17, 1964, p. 20.

"Pop's Bad Boys." *Newsweek,* November 29, 1965, p. 94.

"The Real John Lennon." *Newsweek,* September 29, 1980, pp. 76–77.

"Rolling Again." *Newsweek,* November 17, 1969, p. 137.

SANCHEZ, TONY. *Up and Down with the Rolling Stones.* New York: Morrow, 1979.

SCADUTO, TONY. *Mick Jagger: Everybody's Lucifer.* New York: Berkeley, 1974.

SCHAFFNER, NICHOLAS. *The British Invasion.* New York: McGraw-Hill, 1983.

Washington Post, February 12, 1964.

WENNER, JANN. *Lennon Remembers: The Rolling Stone Interviews.* San Francisco: Rolling Stone Press, 1971.

CHAPTER 6: ACID ROCK

BOCKRIS, VICTOR, and GERALD MALANGA. *Up-Tight: The Velvet Underground Story.* New York: Omnibus, 1983.

FONG-TORRES, BEN. "Love Is Just a Song We Sing." *Rolling Stone,* February 26, 1976, pp. 58–87.

GLEASON, RALPH. *The Jefferson Airplane and the San Francisco Sound.* New York: Ballantine, 1969.

GUSTAITIS, RASA. *Turning On.* New York: New American Library, 1969.

HANSEN, JAY. *The Other Guide to San Francisco.* San Francisco: Chronicle, 1980.

"The Hippies." *Time,* July 7, 1967, pp. 18–22.

"Jerry Garcia: In Search of the X-Factor." *Musician* (October 1981), 64–73.

JOHNSON, JON E. "Janis/Big Brother Disc." *Pulse* (April 1985), 23.

"Kicking Out the Jams." *Newsweek,* May 19, 1969, p. 117.

KUNEN, JAMES SIMON. *The Strawberry Statement.* New York: Avon, 1970.

"Open Up, Tune In, Turn On: The Airplane." *Time,* June 23, 1967, p. 53.

PERRY CHARLES. "From Eternity to Hell." *Rolling Stone.* February 26, 1976, pp. 38–55.

"The Rock Family." *Life,* September 24, 1971, pp. 46–53.

SINCLAIR, JOHN. *Guitar Army.* New York: Douglas, 1972.

"Star Plunged from Heights to Depths: Skip Spence." *Seattle Times,* November 1, 1981, p. F12.

SWARTLEY, ARIEL. "Lou Reed Reconsidered." *Mother Jones* (June 1985), 16–19.

"Swimming to the Moon: Jim Morrison." *Time,* November 24, 1967, p. 106.

"This Way to the Egress: The Doors." *Newsweek,* November 6, 1967, p. 101.

"Timothy Leary Interview." *Playboy* (September 1966), 93–112.

WOLFE, BURTON. *The Hippies.* New York: New American Library, 1968.

ZAPPA, FRANK. "The Oracle Has It." *Life,* June 28, 1968, pp. 82–92.

"Zapping with Zappa." *Newsweek,* June 3, 1968, p. 91.

CHAPTER 7: THE VIOLENT YEARS: THE WHITE BLUES AND THE SOUL EXPLOSION

"After the Riots." *Newsweek,* August 21, 1967, pp. 18–19.

"An American Tragedy: 1967." *Newsweek,* August 7, 1967, pp. 18–34.

"At War with War." *Time,* May 18, 1970, pp. 6–14.

"Cities." *Time,* August 4, 1967, pp. 13–18.

"The Cities: What Next?" *Time,* August 11, 1968, pp. 11–12.

"Class of '69: The Violent Years." *Newsweek,* June 23, 1969, p. 63.

CLEAVER, ELDRIDGE. *Soul on Ice.* New York: Delta, 1968.

"A Dignified Protest." *Time,* March 29, 1968, p. 56.

ELLISON, MARY. *The Black Experience: American Blacks since 1865.* New York: Harper, 1974.

FLEXNER, STUART BERG. *I Hear America Talking.* New York: Van Nostrand, 1976.

GARLAND, PHYL. "Eclipsed Singer Gains New Heights as Leading Female Recording Artist." *Ebony* (October 1967), 47–52.

GEORGE, NELSON. *Where Did Our Love Go? The Rise and Fall of the Motown Sound*. New York: St. Martin's, 1985.

HENDERSON, DAVID. *Jimi Hendrix: Voodoo Child of the Aquarian Age*. New York: Doubleday, 1978.

HIRSHEY, GERRI. *Nowhere to Run: The Story of Soul Music*. New York: Times Books, 1984.

JONES, LEROI. *Blues People*. New York: Morrow, 1963.

"Lady Soul: Singing Like It Is." *Time,* June 28, 1968, pp. 62–66.

"Lean, Clean and Bluesy: John Fogerty." *Time,* June 27, 1969, p. 58.

LLORENS, DAVID. "Wilson Pickett." *Ebony* (October 1968), 130–35.

"Pop Singers: James Brown." *Time,* April 1, 1966, p. 75.

"The Races: Hot and Cool." *Newsweek,* April 22, 1968, pp. 24–26.

"Rampage and Restraint." *Time,* April 19, 1968, pp. 15–17.

"The Rebellion of the Campus." *Newsweek,* May 18, 1970, pp. 28–33.

"Rebirth of the Blues." *Newsweek,* May 26, 1969, pp. 82–85.

"Recorddom's Berry Gordy." *Ebony* (February 1966), 31–39.

ROSENMAN, JOEL, JOHN ROBERTS, and ROBERT PILPEL. *Young Men with Unlimited Capital*. New York: Harcourt Brace Jovanovich, 1974.

SHAW, ARNOLD. *The World of Soul*. New York: Coronet, 1971.

"Singers: Aretha Franklin." *Time,* January 5, 1968, p. 48.

"Singing Is Better Than Any Dope." *Newsweek,* October 19, 1970, p. 125.

"Take Everything You Need Baby." *Newsweek,* April 15, 1968, pp. 31–34.

"Voice of Experience: Jimi Hendrix." *Newsweek,* October 9, 1967, pp. 90–92.

WELCH, CHRIS. *Hendrix*. New York: Flash, 1973.

CHAPTER 8: CORPORATE ROCK

ALVAREZ, TINA. "Group Experiences Heartbreaks with Success." *Arizona Daily Wildcat,* January 24, 1980, p. E1.

ATKINSON, TERRY. "Van Halen's Big Book." *Rolling Stone,* June 14, 1979, p. 14.

"Backstreet Phantom of Rock." *Time,* October 27, 1975, pp. 48–58.

BARCLAY, DOLORES. "The Beat Has Mellowed." *Easton Express* (Pennsylvania), May 16, 1979.

BERNSTEIN, PETER. "Growth Rocks the Record Industry." *Fortune,* April 23, 1979, pp. 59–68.

CHAPPLE, STEVE, and REEBEE GAROFALO. *Rock 'n' Roll Is Here to Pay: The History and Politics of the Music Industry*. Chicago: Nelson-Hall, 1977.

COLLIE, ASHLEY. "Springsteen: Here Comes the Knight." *MacLeans,* December 18, 1978, p. 5.

CROWE, CAMERON. "David Bowie Interview." *Playbody* (September 1976), 57–72.

————. "Joni Mitchell Interview." *Rolling Stone,* July 26, 1979, pp. 47–53.

DAVIS, CLIVE, and JAMES WILLWERTH. *Clive: Inside the Record Business*. New York: Ballantine, 1976.

FELDER, ROB. "Black Sabbath." *Rolling Stone,* October 19, 1978, p. 28.

GILMORE, MIKAL. "Stan Cornyn." *Rolling Stone,* November 30, 1978, p. 40.

GREENBERG, PETER S. "Rock and Big Bucks." *Playboy* (January 1981), 201–70.

GREENE, BOB. *Billion Dollar Baby.* New York: New American Library, 1974.

GRIFFIN, BRIAN. "AC/DC Classic Big Rock." *Pulse* (August 1985), 34.

HENSKE, JAMES. "Mud on the Tracks." *Rolling Stone,* September 7, 1978, pp. 42–44.

HERBST, PETER. "Linda Ronstadt Interview." *Rolling Stone,* October 19, 1978, pp. 57–59.

———. "James Taylor Interview." *Rolling Stone,* September 6, 1979, pp. 38–43.

HILBURN, ROBERT. "Rockin' in Death's Fast Lane." Reprinted in the *Easton Express* (Pennsylvania), March 2, 1979, p. E18.

HOLDEN, STEPHEN. "Ricky Lee Jones in the Cool World." *Rolling Stone,* May 31, 1979, p. 13.

HOROWITZ, IS. "$15 Million Nigerian Press Plant." *Billboard,* December 2, 1978, p. 1.

ISLER, SCOTT. "Gregg Geller." *Rolling Stone,* February 22, 1979, pp. 28–29.

———. "John Berg Covers the Hits." *Rolling Stone,* January 25, 1979, p. 34.

"James Taylor: One Man's Family of Rock." *Time,* March 1, 1971, pp. 49–50.

KIRKEBY, MARC. "Counterfeiting." *Rolling Stone,* April 17, 1980, pp. 20–21.

LODER, KURT. "The Record Industry Tightens Its Belt." *Rolling Stone,* September 20, 1979, pp. 28–29.

MACGREGOR, ROY. "Meet Rush." *MacLeans,* January 23, 1978, p. 24.

McLAINE, DAISANN. "Cheap Trick Finds Heaven." *Rolling Stone,* June 14, 1979, p. 52.

"The Making of a Rock Star: Bruce Springsteen." *Newsweek,* October 27, 1975, pp. 57–63.

"The Man Who Sells the Sizzle: Al Coury." *Time,* December 25, 1978, pp. 48–49.

MARSH, DAVE. *Born to Run: The Bruce Springsteen Story.* New York: Dell, 1979.

———. "The Profits Go Up." *Rolling Stone,* December 14, 1978, p. 45.

"New Day at Black Rock." *Time,* December 31, 1973, p. 48.

ORLOFF, KATHERINE. *Rock 'n' Roll Woman.* Los Angeles: Nash, 1974.

"Pete Townshend." *Seventeen* (August 1975), 214.

"Pop Records: Moguls, Money and Monsters." *Time,* February 12, 1973, pp. 61–63.

"The Return of Slowhand." *Time,* July 15, 1974, p. 81.

"Return to Good-Times Rock." *Time,* June 2, 1975, p. 59.

"Rock and Roll's Leading Lady: Joni Mitchell." *Time,* December 16, 1974, pp. 63–66.

"The Rockers Are Rolling in It." *Forbes,* April 15, 1973, pp. 28–39.

"Rose Petals and Revolution." *Time,* November 28, 1969, p. 90.

SHANNON, DAVID. *Twentieth Century America.* Vol. 3 (2nd ed.). Chicago: Rand-McNally, 1969.

SPITZ, ROBERT STEVEN. *The Making of Superstars.* New York: Doubleday, 1978.

STOKES, GEOFFREY. *Star Making Machinery: The Odyssey of an Album.* Chicago: Bobbs-Merrill, 1976.

VALLELY, JEAN. "Linda Ronstadt Interview." *Playboy* (April 1980), 85–116.

"Vaudeville Rock." *Time,* October 30, 1972, p. 81.

Wall Street Journal, January 29, 1979, p. 1.

WALLACE, ROBERT. "Independents Struggle for Survival." *Rolling Stone,* June 14, 1979, pp. 34–36.

———. "Warner Brothers May Issue Fewer Albums." *Rolling Stone,* March 8, 1979, p. 10.

CHAPTER 9: PUNK ROCK: THE POLITICS OF AGGRESSION

"Anthems of the Blank Generation." *Time,* July 11, 1977, pp. 46–47.

BURGESS, ANTHONY, and JOHN LOMBARDI. "Plastic Punks." *Psychology Today* (November 1977), 120–26.

CIOE, CRISPIN, and RAFI ZABOR. "The New Reggae." *Musician* (November 1981), 48–50.

"The Clash." *Musician* (May 1981), 45–72.

"Commando Squad Attacks Musicians' Coop." *In These Times,* June 13–19, p. 20, 1979.

DANCIS, BRUCE. "Artistic Control and Records Too." *In These Times,* June 4–17, 1980, pp. 20–21.

———. "Into the 80s with Synthesizer and Spud Rock." *In These Times,* November 15–21, 1978, p. 27.

———. "Reggae Today." *In These Times,* October 25–31, 1978, p. 23.

———. "Tom Robinson Talks to ITT." *In These Times.* May 16–22, 1979, p. 24.

DAVIS, STEPHEN. *Bob Marley.* New York: Doubleday, 1985.

FLIPPO, CHET. "Nothing Lasts Forever: The Stones." *Rolling Stone,* August 21, 1980, pp. 38–42.

GILMORE, MIKAL. "The Clash: Anger on the Left." *Rolling Stone,* March 8, 1979, p. 22.

———, and SPOTTSWOOD ERVING. "Brian Eno." *Musician* (April 1981), 50–52.

———. "The Talking Heads." *Rolling Stone,* November 29, 1979, pp. 23–24.

GOLDBERG, MICHAEL. "Tom Robinson's Straight Talk on Being Gay." *In These Times,* July 19–25, 1978, p. 23.

HALASA, MALV. "The English Beat Can't Stop Dancing," *Rolling Stone,* November 13, 1980, pp. 24–25.

HAMSHER, JANE. "Stiv Bator and the Dead Boys." *Damage* (July 1980), 12.

HEBDIGE, DICK. *Subculture and the Meaning of Style.* New York: Methuen, 1979.

HEY, JOHN D. *Britain in Context.* Blackwell: Oxford, 1979.

HOPKINS, TOM. "Dada's Boys." *McLeans,* June 13, 1977, p. 42.

ISLER, SCOTT. "Blondie." *Trouser Press* (June 1981), 19–23.

———. "Fear and Loathing on the West Coast." *Trouser Press* (June 1980), 20–23.

MCCORMICK, MOIRA. "Richard Hell." *Trouser Press* (November 1982), 14.

MARCUS, GREIL. "Pete Townshend Interview." *Rolling Stone,* June 26, 1980, pp. 34–39.

———. "Wake Up!" *Rolling Stone,* July 24, 1980, pp. 38–43.

MARSH, DAVE. "It Takes a Lot to Laugh: The Punks." *Rolling Stone,* September 21, 1978, p. 21.

PECK, ABE. "Devo: Mutants from Akron." *Rolling Stone,* January 25, 1979, p. 27.

"Performance Rights in Sound Recordings." *Subcommittee on Courts, Civil Liberties and the Administration of Justice of the Committee on the Judiciary.* U. S. House of Representatives, 95th Congress, 2nd Session, June 1978.

"Prep or Punk." *Mademoiselle* (June 1980), 182–84.

"Rock Bottom: Punk Fashions." *Newsweek,* June 20, 1977, pp. 80–81.

Rock on Right." *Billboard,* August 22, 1981, p. 53.

"The Ska Above, the Beat Below." *Time,* April 7, 1980, p. 75.

SPRINGER, COLE. "Yes! Devo." *Trouser Press* (January 1979), 14–18.

STEVENSON, RAY. *Sex Pistols File.* London: Omnibus, 1980.

VIBBERT, SPENCER. "Punk, Boston Style." *Boston Globe Magazine,* March 2, 1980, pp. 8–40.

Wall Street Journal, May 30, 1980.

YOUNG, CHARLES M. "Visions of Patti." *Rolling Stone,* July 27, 1978, pp. 51–54.

ZABOR, RAFI. "John Lydon's PiL." *Musician* (November 1984), 42–48.

ZUCKERMAN, ED. "The Rise of Rock Against Racism." *Rolling Stone,* December 14, 1978, pp. 40–41.

CHAPTER 10: THE 1980s: THE AGE OF REVIVALISM AND THE FUTURE OF ROCK

BITHER, DAVID. "Joe Ely." *New York Rocker* (September 1981), 34.

"The Blasters." *Bam,* May 21, 1982, pp. 19–20.

CONSIDINE, J.D. "The Police." *Musician* (December 1981), 59–65.

"Elvis Costello." *L. A. Weekly,* September 16–22, 1983, p. 41.

"The Eurythmics." *Trouser Press* (October 1983), 13.

FLIPPO, CHET. "Bruce Springsteen." *Musician* (November 1984), 56–59.

"His Highness of Haze: Prince." *Time,* August 6, 1984.

HOCHSWENDER, WOODY. "Slam Dancing." *Rolling Stone,* May 14, 1981, pp. 29–32.

JONES, PETER. "Shakin' Stevens Sound Sweeps Europe." *Billboard,* October 10, 1981, p. 43.

LEA, RANKING JEFFREY. "Circle Jerks." *New York Rocker* (September 1981), 24–26.

"Madonna: Hollywood Sizzle." *People,* May 13, 1985, pp. 40–45.

LODER, KURT. "Dress Right." *Rolling Stone,* June 23, 1981, pp. 14–19.

MCLINDEN. AIMLESS. "More Cheap, More Gimmicks: The Cramps." *Damage* (July 1980), 16.

"MTV Video." *Time,* December 26, 1983, pp. 62–64.

"The Peter Pan of Pop: Michael Jackson." *Newsweek,* January 10, 1983, pp. 52–54.

PORTER, MARTIN, and STEVEN SCHWARTZ. "Madonna." *Seattle Times,* April 7, 1985, p. L1.

POSTEL, ERIC. "Heavy Metal Thunder." *Pulse* (September 1983), 1–10.

SALEWICZ, CHRIS. "Kemp: A Revolt into Style." *The Face* (October 1982), 25–26.

SILVER, LANI. "Fire Still Burns for Bill Graham." *Mother Jones* (January 1986), 8–9.

SOMMER, TOM. "Adam Ant." *Trouser Press* (July 1981), 13.

———. "Black Flag." *Trouser Press* (June 1983), 23–24.

SWAN, CHRISTOPHER. "Rock Video Quakes." Reprinted in *Seattle Times,* June 2, 1985, p. E1.

SWEETING, ADAM. "Paul Weller on Tape." *Trouser Press* (June 1981), 35–38.

TOMASHOFF, CRAIG. "Joe Ely's Rockabilly." *Washington Daily,* May 15, 1981, p. 11.

"The Tour, the Money and the Magic." *Newsweek,* July 16, 1984, pp. 64–70.

WELLER, ANDY. "The Brave New World of 'Old Wave' Music." *Washington Daily,* May 4, 1984, p. 21.

YOUNG, CHARLES M. "Metal." *Musician* (September 1984), 42–60.

YOUNG, JON. "Joe Ely." *Trouser Press* (September 1981), 15.

———. "Keys to the Future." *Trouser Press* (May 1982), 22–35.

ZAPPA, FRANK. Z Pack.

ZUCCHINO, DAVID. "Big Brother Meets Twisted Sister." *Rolling Stone,* September 20, 1985, pp. 9–66.

Selective Discography

This discography includes the albums that I consider to be the best and the most representative of the artists mentioned in this book. In most cases, I have favored LPs that are still in print. For those pivotal albums that are no longer in print, consult Jerry Osborne, *The Original Record Collector's Price Guide: Record Albums,* 4th edition (Phoenix: O'Sullivan Woodside & Co., 1982), for a price list. All records listed are domestic issues unless otherwise noted. Also, the reader should be aware that the liner notes on many of these records provide a wealth of information for the study of the social history of rock and roll.

CHAPTER 1: THE BLUES, ROCK 'N' ROLL, AND RACISM

Baker, Laverne, *Her Greatest Recordings* Atco SD-33-372

Ballard, Hank, and the Midnighters, *Hank Ballard and the Midnighters* King K-5003X

Berry, Chuck, *Chuck Berry's Golden Decade* Chess 2CH-1514

———, *Chuck Berry's Golden Decade vol. 2* Chess 2CH-60023
———, *Chuck Berry's Golden Decade vol. 3* Chess 2CH-60028
Bland, Bobby Blue, *The Best of Bobby Bland* ABC/Duke DLPS-84
Crudup, Arthur "Big Boy," *Crudup's Mood* Delmark DS-621
Diddley, Bo, *Bo Diddley's 16 All Time Greatest Hits* Checker LP-2989
Dixon, Willie, *I Am the Blues* Columbia CS-9987
Domino, Fats, *Million Sellers by Fats* Liberty LM-1027
Drifters, *16 Greatest Hits* Trip TOP-16-6
Fulson, Lowell, *Lowell Fulson* Kent 5020
Hooker, John Lee, *Greatest Hits of John Lee Hooker* United 7769
Houston, Joe, *Rock and Roll with Joe Houston and His Rockers* Tops L-1518
Howlin' Wolf, *Big City Blues* United 7717
———, *Evil* Chess 1540
———, *Original Folk Blues* United 7747
James, Elmore, *History of Elmore James* Trip 8007-2
———, *The Resurrection of Elmore James* United 7787
James, Etta, *Etta James Sings* United US-7712
Johnson, Robert, *Robert Johnson: King of the Delta Blues Singers vols. 1 and 2*
   Columbia CL 1654, CL 30034
King, B. B., *B. B. King Live* United US 7771
———, *B. B. King on Stage* United 7736
———, *The Great B. B. King* United US 7728
———, *The Jungle* United US 7742
———, *Rock Me Baby* United US 7733
Little Richard, *The Fabulous Little Richard* Specialty SP-2104
———, *Here's Little Richard* Specialty SP-2100
———, *Little Richard* Specialty SP-2103
Little Walter, *Boss Blues Harmonica* Chess 2CH-60014
McPhatter, Clyde, *Clyde McPhatter's Greatest Hits* Mercury SR-60783
Otis, Johnny, *Great Rhythm and Blues Oldies vol. 13* Blues Spectrum BS-113
Patton, Charley, *Charley Patton: Founder of the Delta Blues* Yazoo L-1020
Ravens, *The Ravens* Hit Parade HHPS-007
Reed, Jimmy, *The Best of Jimmy Reed* VeeJay SR-1039
Sykes, Roosevelt, *Urban Blues* Fantasy F-24717
Tampa Red, *Bottleneck Guitar* Yazoo 1039
Turner, Big Joe, *Turn on the Blues* United 7759
Various Artists, *Dedication vol. 2* Silhouette 10007 (Alan Freed Show)
———, *Gabe's Dirty Blues* Gusto GTS-110
———, *Rock'n'Roll Radio Show Starring Alan Freed* Radiola MR-1087
———, *Roots of Rock* Fairway RR-4200
———, *Wizards from the Southside* Chess 8203
Walker, T-Bone, *Blues Classics* BluesWay BLS-606
Waters, Muddy, *Down on Stovall's Plantation* Testament T-2210
———, *McKinley Morganfield a.k.a. Muddy Waters* Chess 2CH-6006
White, Bukka, *Blues Masters vol. 4* Blue Horizon BM-4604

Williamson, Sonny Boy, *Bummer Road* Chess 1536

Witherspoon, Jimmy, *The Best of Jimmy Witherspoon* BluesWay BLS-6051

CHAPTER 2: ELVIS AND ROCKABILLY

Burgess, Sonny, *Legendary Sun Performers: Sonny Burgess* Charley CR 30136 (Import)

Burnette, Johnny, and the Rock and Roll Trio, *Johnny Burnette and the Rock 'n' Roll Trio* Solid Smoke SS-8001

Cash, Johnny, *The Sun Story vol. 1* Sunnyvale 9330-901

Cochran, Eddie, *The Eddie Cochran Singles Album* United Artists UAK 30244 (Import)

Everly Brothers, *The Everly Brothers' Greatest Hits* Barnaby 2BR-6606

Gordon, Rosco, *Legendary Sun Performers: Rosco Gordon* Charley CR30133 (Import)

Haley, Bill, and the Comets, *Bill Haley's Greatest Hits* MCA 2-4010

Holly, Buddy, *Twenty Golden Greats* MCA 3040

Lewis, Jerry Lee, *Jerry Lee Lewis from the Vaults of Sun* Power Pak 247

———, *Jerry Lee Lewis' Original Golden Hits vol. 1* Sun 102

———, *Jerry Lee Lewis' Original Golden Hits vol. 2* Sun 103

———, *Jerry Lee Lewis' Original Golden Hits vol. 3* Sun 128

Orbison, Roy, *Roy Orbison: The Original Rock Sound* Sun 113

Perkins, Carl, *Greatest Hits* Columbia LE 100117

Presley, Elvis, *Elvis Presley* RCA LSP-1254(e)

———, *Elvis* RCA LSP-1382(e)

———, *A Date with Elvis* RCA LSP-2011(e)

———, *For LP Fans Only* RCA LSP-1990(e)

———, *Sun Sessions* RCA APMI-1675

Vincent, Gene, *Gene Vincent and His Blue Caps* Capitol N-16209

CHAPTER 3: DICK CLARK, PHILADELPHIA SCHLOCK, AND PAYOLA

Anka, Paul, *Paul Anka His Best* United Artists UA-LA922-H

Checker, Chubby, *Chubby Checker's Greatest Hits* Abkco 4219

Darin, Bobby, *The Bobby Darin Story* Atco 131

Dion and the Belmonts, *60 Greatest of Dion and and the Belmonts* Laurie SLP-6000

Nelson, Ricky, *Legendary Masters Series* United Artists UAS-9960

———, *Ricky* Liberty LM-1004

Valens, Richie, *History of Richie Valens* Rhino RNBC 2798

CHAPTER 4: BOB DYLAN
AND THE NEW FRONTIER

Baez, Joan, *In Concert, Part 1* Vanguard 2122
———, *In Concert, Part 2* Vanguard 2123
Beach Boys, *Best of the Beach Boys* Capitol DT-2545
Byrds, *Mr. Tamborine Man* Columbia CS-9172
Donovan, *Donovan's Greatest Hits* Epic 26836
Dylan, Bob, *Another Side of Bob Dylan* Columbia PC-8993
———, *Bob Dylan* Columbia PC-8579
———, *The Freewheelin' Bob Dylan* Columbia PC-8786
———, *The Times They Are A-Changin'* Columbia PC-8905
Jan and Dean, *Legendary Masters Series* United Artists 9961
Lovin' Spoonful, *The Best of the Lovin' Spoonful* Kama Sutra 2608-2
Ochs, Phil, *All the News That's Fit to Sing* Elektra 7269
———, *I Ain't Marchin' Anymore* Elektra 7287
Paxton, Tom, *Ain't That News* Elektra 7290
Simon and Garfunkel, *Simon and Garfunkel's Greatest Hits* Columbia PC-31350
Van Ronk, Dave, *Dave Van Ronk* Fantasy 24710

CHAPTER 5: THE MODS VS. THE
ROCKERS AND THE BRITISH INVASION
OF AMERICA

Animals, *Best of the Animals* Abkco 4426
Beatles, *Beatles' Second Album* Capitol ST-2080
———, *Early Beatles* Capitol ST-2309
———, *Introducing the Beatles* VeeJay 1062
———, *Meet the Beatles!* Capitol ST-2047
———, *Something New* Capitol ST-2108
Dave Clark Five, *Dave Clark Five's Greatest Hits* Epic BN-26185
Fontana, Wayne, and the Mindbenders, *Game of Love* Fontana SRF-67542
Freddie and the Dreamers, *Best of Freddie and the Dreamers* Capitol SM-11896
Gerry and the Pacemakers, *Best of Gerry and the Pacemakers* Capitol SM-11898
Herman's Hermits, *Best of Herman's Hermits* MGM SE-4315
Hollies, *The Hollies Greatest Hits* Epic KE-32061
Kinks, *The Kinks Greatest Hits* Reprise RS-6217
Kramer, Billy J., and the Dakotas, *Billy J. Kramer and the Dakotas* Capitol SM-11897
Mann, Manfred, *Best of Manfred Mann* Capitol N-16073
Rolling Stones, *December's Children* London PS-451

————, *Hot Rocks, 1964–1971* London 2PS-60617

————, *Out of Our Heads* London PS-429

————, *The Rolling Stones* London PS-375

————, *The Rolling Stones Now!* London PS-420

————, *12 × 5* London PS-402

Small Faces, *Ogden's Nut Gone Flake* Abkco 4225

Them, *Them Featuring Van Morrison* Parrot BP-71053-54

Who, *Tommy* MCA 2-10005

————, *The Who Sings My Generation* MCA 2-4068

Yardbirds, *The Yardbird's Greatest Hits* Epic PE-34491

CHAPTER 6: ACID ROCK

Doors, *The Doors* Elektra 74007

————, *L. A. Woman* Elektra 75021

————, *Morrison Hotel* Elektra 75007

————, *Strange Days* Elektra 74014

Fugs, *The Fugs* ESP 1028

————, *It Crawled into My Hand, Honest* Reprise RS-6305

————, *Virgin Fugs* ESP 1038

Grateful Dead, *Best of Skeletons in the Closet* Warner 2764

Jefferson Airplane, *Jefferson Airplane Takes Off* RCA AFL1-3584

————, *Surrealistic Pillow* RCA AFL1-3766

————, *Volunteers* RCA AFL1-4459

MC5, *Kick out the Jams* Elektra EKS-74042

Moby Grape, *Moby Grape* Columbia CS-9498

Mothers of Invention, *Freak Out* Verve V6-5005-2

Quicksilver Messenger Service, *Happy Trails* Capitol ST-120

Velvet Underground, *The Velvet Underground* MGM SE-4617

————, *White Light/White Heat* Verve V6-5046

CHAPTER 7: THE VIOLENT YEARS: THE WHITE BLUES AND THE SOUL EXPLOSION

Blue Cheer, *Vincebus Eruptum* Phillips PL-9001

Blues Magoos, *Psychedelic Lollipop* Mercury SR-61096

Brown, James, *Soul Classics vol. 1* Polydor 5401

————, *Soul Classics vol. 2* Polydor 5402

Canned Heat, *The Best of Canned Heat* Scepter CTN-18017

Charles, Ray, *Greatest Hits of Ray Charles* Atlantic SD-7101

Cream, *Disraeli Gears* RSO RS-1-3010

————, *Fresh Cream* RSO RS-1-3009

Creedence Clearwater Revival, *Bayou Country* Fantasy F-8402

————, *Creedence Clearwater Revival* Fantasy F-8382

———, *Green River* Fantasy F-8393
———, *Willy and the Poor Boys* Fantasy F-8397
Electric Flag, *The Best of Electric Flag* Columbia C-30422
Four Tops, *Anthology — The Four Tops* Motown MS-809
Franklin, Aretha, *Aretha Arrives* Atlantic SD-8150
———, *Aretha Now* Atlantic SD-8186
———, *I Never Loved a Man (The Way I Love You)* Atlantic SD-8139
———, *Lady Soul* Atlantic SD-8176
Gaye, Marvin, *Anthology — Marvin Gaye* Motown M9-791A3
Hendrix, Jimi, *Are You Experienced?* Reprise RS-6261
———, *Axis Bold as Love* Reprise RS-6281
———, *Electric Ladyland* Reprise 2RS-6307
———, *Hendrix in the West* Reprise MS-2049
———, and Otis Redding, *Historic Performances Recorded at the Monterey International Pop Festival* Reprise MS-2029
Joplin, Janis, *Big Brother and the Holding Company* Columbia C-30631
———, *Cheap Thrills* Columbia KCS-9700
King, Albert, *Travelin' to California* King KS-1060
Martha and the Vandellas, *Anthology — Martha and the Vandellas* Motown 778
Miller, Steve, *Anthology* Capitol SVBB-11114
Pickett, Wilson, *The Best of Wilson Pickett* Atlantic SD-8151
Redding, Otis, *Best of Otis Redding* Atco SD-2-801
Robinson, Smokey, and the Miracles, *Anthology — Smokey Robinson and the Miracles* Motown 793
Ryder, Mitch, *Mitch Ryder and the Detroit Wheels Greatest Hits* Virgo SV-12001
Sam and Dave, *The Best of Sam and Dave* Atlantic SD-8218
Sledge, Percy, *Best of Percy Sledge* Atlantic SD-8210
Supremes, *Diana Ross and the Supremes Greatest Hits* Motown M8-237V
Temptations, *Anthology — The Temptations* Motown 782
Ten Years After, *SSSSH — Ten Years After* Deram DES-18029
———, *Ten Years After* Deram DES-18009
Various, *Woodstock* Cotillion SD3-500
———, *Woodstock 2* Cotillion SD2-400
Winter, Johnny, *Johnny Winter* Columbia CS-9826
———, *Serious Business* Alligator AL4742

CHAPTER 8: CORPORATE ROCK

AC/DC, *Highway to Hell* Atlantic, 19244
Alice Cooper, *Alice Cooper's Greatest Hits* Warner BSK-3107
Black Sabbath, *Paranoid* Warner BSK-3104
Bowie, David, *The Rise and Fall of Ziggy Stardust and the Spiders from Mars* RCA AYL1-3843
Chicago, *Chicago* Columbia GQ-33258

Davis, Miles, *Bitches Brew* Columbia PG-26
Deep Purple, *Machine Head* Warner BSK-3100
Eagles, *Their Greatest Hits 1971–1975* Asylum 6E-105
Electric Light Orchestra, *ELO's Greatest Hits* Columbia FZ-36310
Emerson, Lake and Palmer, *Best of Emerson, Lake and Palmer* SD-19283
Genesis, *The Best of Genesis* Buddah BDS-5659-2
Grand Funk Railroad, *Grand Funk* Capitol SN-16177
John, Elton, *Elton John's Greatest Hits* MCA 5224
Jones, Ricky Lee, *Ricky Lee Jones* Warner BSK-3296
King, Carol, *Tapestry* Ode 77009
King Crimson, *In the Court of the Crimson King* Atlantic SD-19115
Kiss, *Kiss: The Originals* Casablanca NBLP-7032
Kristofferson, Kris, *Me and Bobby McGee* Monument Z230817
Led Zeppelin, *Led Zeppelin* Atlantic SD-19126
———, *Led Zeppelin II* Atlantic SD-19127
———, *Led Zeppelin III* Atlantic SD-19128
Mott the Hoople, *All the Young Dudes* Columbia PC-31750
New York Dolls, *New York Dolls* Mercury SRM-1-675
Nugent, Ted, *Ted Nugent* Epic PE-33692
Petty, Tom, and the Heartbreakers, *Tom Petty and the Heartbreakers* Shelter 52006
Pink Floyd, *Dark Side of the Moon* Harvest SMAS-11163
———, *The Wall* Columbia PC2-36183
Prine, John, *John Prine* Atlantic SD8296
Reed, Lou, *Walk on the Wild Side (The Best of Lou Reed)* RCA APL1-2001
Ronstadt, Linda, *Greatest Hits* Asylum 6E-106
Roxy Music, *For Your Pleasure* Atco SD-36-134
Simon, Carly, *Best of Carly Simon* Elektra 6E-109
Springsteen, Bruce, *Born to Run* Columbia PC-33795
———, *Greetings from Asbury Park* Columbia JC-31903
Status Quo, *Piledriver* A & M SP-4381
Stevens, Cat, *Tea for the Tillerman* A & M QU-54280
Taylor, James, *James Taylor's Greatest Hits* Warner 2561
Various, *Saturday Night Fever* RSO RS-2-4001
Yes, *Classic Yes* Atlantic SD-19320
Young, Neil, *Decade* Reprise RS-2257

CHAPTER 9: PUNK ROCK:
THE POLITICS OF AGGRESSION

B-52s, *The B-52s* Warner BSK-3355
Blondie, *Parallel Lines* Chrysalis CHR-1192
Burning Spear, *Marcus Garvey* Island 9377
Cars, *The Cars* Elektra 6-135

Clash, *The Clash* Epic JE-36060

——, *Give 'Em Enough Rope* Epic NE-35543

Costello, Elvis, *Almost Blue* Columbia FC-37562

——, *Armed Forces* Columbia JC-35709

——, *My Aim Is True* Columbia JC-35037

——, *This Years Model* Columbia JC-35331

Dead Boys, *Young, Loud and Snotty* Sire SR-6038

Devo, *Q: Are We Not Men (A: We Are Devo)* Warner BSK-3239

English Beat, *I Just Can't Stop It* Sire SKR-6091

Generation X, *Generation X* Chrysalis CHR-1169

Hell, Richard, and the Voidoids, *Blank Generation* Sire 6037

Jackson, Joe, *Look Sharp* A & M 1025

Jam, *All Mod Cons* Polydor PD1-6188

Marley, Bob, and the Wailers, *Burnin'* Island 9256

——, *Catch a Fire* Island 9241

——, *Natty Dread* Island 9281

Pretenders, *The Pretenders* Sire 3563

Public Image Limited (PiL), *Flowers of Romance* Warner BSK-3536

Ramones, *The Ramones* Sire SRK-6020

Robinson, Tom, *Power in the Darkness* Harvest STB-11778

Selector, *Too Much Pressure* Chrysalis 1274

Sex Pistols, *Never Mind the Bollocks Here's the Sex Pistols* Warner K-3147

Sham 69, *Tell Us the Truth* Sire K-6060

Siouxsie and the Banshees, *The Scream* Polydor PD-1-6207

Smith, Patti, *Easter* Arista AS-4171

——, *Horses* Arista AL-4066

Specials, *The Specials* Chrysalis 1265

Steel Pulse, *Reggae Fever* Island MLPS-9613

Stiff Little Fingers, *Inflammable Material* Rough Trade 1

Talking Heads, *Talking Heads 77* Sire 6036

Television, *Marquee Moon* Elektra 7E-1098

Toots and the Maytals, *Funky Kingston* Island 9330

Various, *Dance Craze: The Best of British Ska . . . Live!* Chrysalis 1299

——, *Rock Against Racism's Greatest Hits* Rock Against Racism 1LP (Import)

X-Ray Spex, *Germ Free Adolescents* EMI INS 3023 (Import)

CHAPTER 10: THE 1980s: THE AGE OF REVIVALISM AND THE FUTURE OF ROCK

Ant, Adam, *Kings of the Wild Frontier* Epic NJE 37033

Black Flag, *Damaged* SST 9502

Blasters, *The Blasters* Warner BSK-3680

Cramps, *Gravest Hits* IRS SP-501

Culture Club, *Colour by Numbers* Virgin 9E-39107
Dead Kennedys, *Fresh Fruit for Rotting Vegetables* IRS SP-70014
Def Leppard, *Pyromania* Mercury 422-810308
Dexy's Midnight Runners, *Searching for the Soul of Rebels* EIA SN-16288
Duran Duran, *Duran Duran* Capitol ST-12158
Ely, Joe, *Musta Gotta Alotta* Southcoast MCA 5183
Eurythmics, *Sweet Dreams (Are Made of This)* RCA AFL1-4681
Fear, *The Record* Slash 1-23933
Germs, *GI* Slash 1-23932
Gordon, Robert, *Robert Gordon* Private Stock 2030
Green On Red, *Gravity Talks* Slash 1-23964
Iron City Houserockers, *Love's So Tough* MCA 3099
Jackson, Michael, *Thriller* Epic QE-38112
Mink DeVille, *Mink DeVille* Capitol ST-11631
Motorhead, *Ace of Spades* Mercury SRM-1-4011
Numan, Gary, *Replicas* Atco SD-38-117
Parker, Graham, *Heat Treatment* Mercury 1117
———, *Howlin' Wind* Mercury 1095
Police, *Outlandos d' Amour* A & M SP-4753
———, *Synchronicity* A & M SP-3735
Prince, *Purple Rain* Warner K-3366
Psychedelic Furs, *The Psychedelic Furs* CBS 36791
Quiet Riot, *Metal Health* PSH FZ-38443
Saxon, *The Power and the Glory* CRR BRZ-38719
Scorpions, *Blackout* Mercury SRM-1-40309
Seals, Son, *Midnight Son* Alligator AL 4078
Shakin' Pyramids, *Skin 'Em Up* Virgin 203-628 (Import)
Shakin' Stevens, *Get Shakin'* Epic FE-37415
Soft Cell, *Non-Stop Erotic Cabaret* Sire SRK-3647
Spandau Ballet, *Journeys to Glory* CYS FV-41331
Springsteen, Bruce, *Born in the U.S.A.* Columbia QC-38653
———, *The River* Columbia PC2-36854
Stray Cats, *Stray Cats* Stray 1 (Import)
Thorogood, George, *Bad to the Bone* EMI ST-17076
———, *George Thorogood and the Destroyers* Rounder 3013
Various, *Decline and Fall of Western Civilization* Slash 1-23934
Violent Femmes, *Violent Femmes* Slash 1-23845
Visage, *Visage* Polydor 1-6304
X, *Los Angeles* Slash 104

Index

Sonny and Cher, 76, 191
Spandau Ballet, 203
Specials, 182–83
Specialty Records, 16
Speckled Red, 5
Spence, Skip, 125
Springsteen, Bruce, 163–64, 195–96,
    211–14
Starr, Ringo, 83, 87, 92, 93
Status Quo, 154
Stevens, Cat, 157
Stevens, Shakin', 207
Stewart, Rod, 151, 152, 154
Stiff Little Fingers, 184
Strange, Steve, 203
Student protests, 67, 130–32, 147–50
Sun Records, 34–41
Supremes, 144, 145
Sykes, Roosevelt, 5

T

Talking Heads, 186, 192
Taylor, James, 155, 166
Teenagers, 15
Television, 186
Temptations, 144–45
Ten Years After, 134
Them, 99
Thorogood, George, 13, 209
Tosh, Peter, 181
Townshend, Pete, 82, 83, 84, 86, 165,
    185
Turner, Ike, 11, 35

U

U-2, 213

Uriah Heep, 154

V

Valens, Ritchie, 52
Van Halen, 172
Van Zandt, Steve, 213
Vee Jay Records, 13–14
Velvet Underground, 111
Vincent, Gene, 42–43, 52–53
Violent Femmes, 207, 208

W

Wailers, 181
Waters, Muddy, 6–8, 18, 100, 101,
    154
Weather Report, 160
Who, 84–87
Williamson, Sonny Boy II, 10–11, 13,
    134
Winter, Johnny, 137–38
Wolf, Howlin', 8–9, 35, 153, 154
Woodstock festival, 147–48
Wyman, Bill, 102

X

X, 196
X-Ray Spex, 175–76, 179, 180

Y

Yardbirds, 98
Yes, 159
Young, Neil, 157–58, 167